Where Misfits Fit

Where Misfits Fit

Counterculture and Influence in the Ozarks

Thomas Michael Kersen

University Press of Mississippi / Jackson

The University Press of Mississippi is the scholarly publishing agency of the Mississippi Institutions of Higher Learning: Alcorn State University, Delta State University, Jackson State University, Mississippi State University, Mississippi University for Women, Mississippi Valley State University, University of Mississippi, and University of Southern Mississippi.

www.upress.state.ms.us

The University Press of Mississippi is a member of the Association of University Presses.

First printing 2021
∞

Library of Congress Control Number available
Hardback ISBN 978-1-4968-3542-0
Trade paperback ISBN 978-1-4968-3543-7
Epub single ISBN 978-1-4968-3444-4
Epub institutional ISBN 978-1-4968-3545-1
PDF single ISBN 978-1-4968-3546-8
PDF institutional ISBN 978-1-4968-3547-5

British Library Cataloging-in-Publication Data available

Contents

Acknowledgments

The Ozark Symposium has been the springboard from which much of what is in this book began. I will always be grateful that Brooks Blevins was the first to invite me to come and hear the various presenters. After that first visit, I was hooked and have faithfully attended every year. Thus, my admiration and gratitude to Craig Albin, Philip Howerton, Leigh Adams, Jason McCollum, and others who planned and held the Ozark Symposium. I want to thank the McCollums for their support over the years. A very special thank you for Jared Phillips for his critique, insights, and kind words about my manuscript.

The chapter on Ozark identity was one of my first presentations at the Ozark Symposium in West Plains, Missouri. In the years since then, I was encouraged by a number of the people at the symposium to publish the piece in *Elder Mountain*, the Ozark Symposium's journal. With the help of Candis Pizzetta, whom I asked to come on board as cowriter, we got the article published. She is the very definition of a renaissance woman and has been very helpful with her advice and just listening to me as I began this book.

I want to thank M. Thomas Inge for insights on the Lil' Abner chapter and Brian Irby on the UFO chapter. Thanks for all the founding members who offered their time for interviews on the Dan Blocker Singers chapter: Randy Brockman, Ed Eudy, and Dan Hazel. I was very lucky to have met Jacqueline Froelich, who works as a public radio reporter in Arkansas. Her story on the Purple People answered some key questions I had. Moreover, her reporting really led me to reevaluate my assumptions about that group.

Early on, I learned how hard it is to get permission to use pictures for the various chapters. Ralph Drew at *Los Angeles Times* was very professional and quick in responding to my queries about using one of their photographs of the Dan Blocker Singers. I was overwhelmed with the generosity of photographer, Jim Mayfield, who let me use images he took of Black Oak Arkansas and the Ozark Mountain Daredevils. Another wonderful photographer and all-around Renaissance man, Arrow Ross, sent me a number of beautiful pictures to choose from for the Hot Mulch chapter. The talented Billy Higgins let me use some of his pictures of Mulberry families in the back-to-land chapter. I am also thankful to the Fellowship for Intentional Communities for permission to use two beautiful line drawings they published by the late Ronn Foss in *Communities*. Finding Ken Steinhoff's amazing pictures of Buck Nelson's 1966 Spaceship Conference in the Missouri Ozarks was an amazing piece of luck. I appreciate his generosity and humor.

In writing the chapter about the Hot Mulch Band and back-to-land movement in Missouri, I had the pleasure of meeting several wonderful people. A number of people met with me in Springfield to share their memories and thoughts. Louise Wienckowski and husband shared their home and offered an amazing spread for all of us. Thank you! Jon is truly one of the most talented musicians I ever met. David Haenke's deep understanding of the Ozarks and its culture are without peer, and his passion about environmentalism is an indication of what a treasure he is for the region. Denise Henderson Vaughn has an encyclopedic knowledge of the many aspects of the back-to-land life in the Missouri Ozarks. She truly is a scholar of the region and kept me straight on the facts. Likewise, Nancy Spaeder provided much information about Seven Springs. One of the most interesting people I have ever met is Ron Hughes. He and the other Mulchers are among the most caring people and generous—willing to share their time, many coming from long distances to visit with me in Springfield. They also spent time emailing or talking with me on the phone. Thanks to Jeff Dunshee and Patty Van Weelden for their email comments. Last, like others who knew her, I am amazed by the multitalented Cat Yronwode, and I am very thankful for the time she spent with me talking about the Missouri Ozarks back in the 1960s and 1970s and so much more.

Although I didn't interview members of either Black Oak Arkansas or Ozark Mountain Daredevils, I am thankful for their entertaining songs with thoughtful lyrics. After this project, my appreciation for both bands has grown enormously.

I worked closely with two families in writing the Arkansas back-to-land chapter. I am thankful to Karen Driver sharing about the early days for the Driver family. Doug and Cathy Strubel also shared their early years. I have always admired Karen, Doug, and Cathy for their vision and courage. Donald Sharp was a key teacher of mine. He and his wife, Bobbie LeBlanc Sharp, have become great friends over the years. Since high school, I have regarded Dana Maria Phillips as one of the most thoughtful people I ever met. Her insights and review of the chapter are really appreciated. I want to thank my father, Michael Kersen, and late mother, Debra Dodge, for filling in the gaps about my own family situation. Kim Kersen was a great help too. Thanks to my brother, Blake, and his wife for their support and letting me stay with them when I visited for research. The same to Mike and Audrey Gund. My sisters, Vicci and Bridget, and their families have always been there for me.

The Jackson Discussion Group is led by Carol Anderson, Anthony Mawson, and others. The group meets every month in Jackson, Mississippi, to discuss all sorts of topics. I was given an opportunity to talk about some of the things in the book. Members were also very supportive of my efforts. Dierdre Payne is an extraordinary friend and poet for the discussion group. I want to thank member Fred Wiggins in particular for looking at the manuscript. Moreover, Jodie and Paul Gore are among my closest friends, and I am humbled by how much they helped me with this project and other things.

I am grateful for my friendship with Steven Yates. One of the reasons I look forward to going to the Ozark Symposium every year is to spend some time with Steven. His optimistic spirit makes him a joy to be around—as are all the interesting conversations we have on music and the Ozarks.

I could not have asked for a better editorial team than Katie Keene, Mary Heath, and Camille Hale. They all are very friendly and flexible. Besides the editors, book cover designer Jennifer Mixon, Shane Gong, Jordan Nettles, and any other staff who worked on my book truly are an asset to the University Press of Mississippi. I thank the press for the opportunity to work with them.

The task of writing would have been immeasurably more difficult without the support of Criminal Justice and Sociology Department chair Etta Morgan. The same goes for the former dean of liberal arts Mario Azevedo, and the current dean, Candis Pizzetta, both of whom have always been there for me. Thanks also for history professor Mark Bernhardt for listening to my worries and shop-talking writing and related issues. Along with Etta, other colleagues, students, and others in the Jackson State University community have been wonderful.

One of my closest friends is Larry Bates. He and his wife have helped me in many ways over the years. The same is true for Richard Hudiburg. Without them I would not be where I am. The same goes for all the fine folks at Unitarian Universalist Church of the Shoals such as Toni and Kenneth Brooks, my home church of the Unitarian Universalist Church of Jackson, Klare Lane and other members of Our Home Universalist Unitarian Church in Ellisville, Mississippi.

Thank you to Mckenzie Kersen, my daughter. You make me proud, and I love you. My wife, Lisa Gund Kersen, has always been there for me. She has sacrificed much for me to write this book, and she is my number one booster. I dedicate this book to her.

Where Misfits Fit

The Ozarks

When my family and I moved to the Arkansas Ozarks in the late 1970s as part of the back-to-the-land movement, we had no idea what was in store for us. Everything and everyone were so different. I certainly had no idea what a tick was or whether people in Arkansas were referred to as Arkansawyers or Arkansans. Before leaving for the Ozarks, I didn't even have a sense of what the South was except what little we learned about the region in school.

After years of minimizing my communal experience, I have come to realize that the Ozarks and the people who live there are something unique and worth studying. Some time has passed since I was a teenager, but I have found myself reflecting on those years in the hills. Part of that return to my past has manifested itself in a yearly gathering at the Ozark Symposium in West Plains, Missouri, that brings together artists, musicians, scholars, and others devoted to sharing the Ozark culture. I have been fortunate enough to participate in the symposium for a number of years, and much of this book is based on topics I have presented at those meetings.

All regions and places are unique in their own way, but the Ozarks has an enduring place in American culture, in that they offer the ability to explore American life through the lens of one of the last remaining cultural frontiers in American society. Perhaps because the Ozarks were relatively isolated from mainstream American society, or at least on the margins of it, their identity and culture are liminal and often counter to mainstream culture. Whatever the case, looking at the Ozarks is more than a regional study because it offers the student insights into changing ideas about what it means to be an American and, more specifically, a special type of southerner.

In contemporary times, many scholars are devoted to studying the Ozarks, such as J. Blake Perkins, Brian Campbell, Josh Lockyear, and Jared Phillips. Perkins focuses his work on interregional conflict between the common Ozarkian, who tended to be progressive politically, and the local elites, who were more interested in bettering themselves. Campbell and Lockyear offer a detailed history of the various groups and organizations that emerged in the Ozarks in the 1970s and 1980s, which focused on sustainability, communalism, and other progressive ideals. Phillips ably describes the interesting amalgam of both hippy back-to-the-landers and native Ozarkers—something he terms "Hipbillies." It is Phillips's argument that old-time natives were able to find, in the back-to-the-landers, a way to perpetuate traditional cultural practices. Brooks Blevins has contributed greatly to providing a rich historical account of the region that weaves in many sociocultural threads. One major theme in Blevins's work is that the Ozarks are really made up of two pieces, one piece real and lived, and the other based on myth and stereotypes. Thus, more scholars are focusing on the Ozarks, giving the region a breadth and depth of attention it deserves.

In 1930, sociology professor Walter Cralle of Southwest Missouri State University, gave a talk entitled "Is there an Ozarker?"[1] He argued that the region was too large and diverse to paint with a small brush. However, he did list some elements of Ozark culture he thought should be preserved in some fashion, the first of which was its distinctive language. Next, like other mountain cultures, the Ozarks has a great deal of superstition and folklore. Last, pastimes such as square dancing and traditional music are being "driven back into the hills, and [are] seldom found even in small communities, but usually only in more remote rural regions."[2] He argued that the nonmaterial culture (e.g., ideas, customs, etc.) should be appreciated as much as the material culture (e.g., furniture, crafts). Ozark observers since then have fretted about the loss of traditional culture as modernity has made inroads into the Ozarks.

Geographically, the Ozarks make up an area located in the northern part of Arkansas and the southern to middle part of Missouri. Following geographer Milton Rafferty, the Arkansas Ozarks are bordered in the south by the River Valley region.[3] In fact, the Ozark foothills begin in many of the northern parts of the River Valley counties of Arkansas. The Ozarks make up a sizable part of Missouri, where they are bordered in the southeast by Cape Girardeau and in the northeast by St. Louis. The Missouri Ozarks extends up

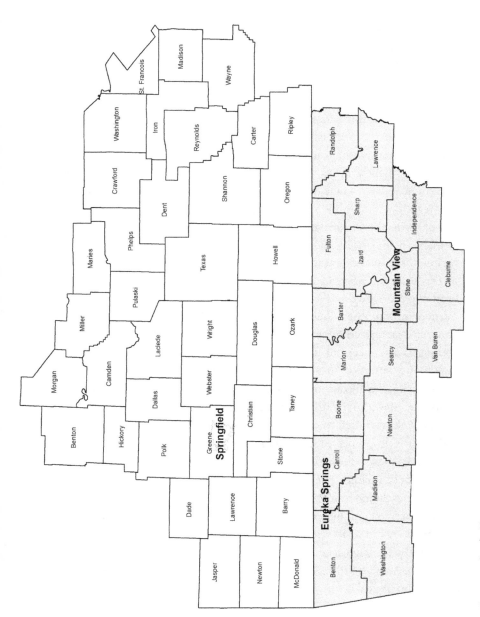

Figure 1.1 Ozarks Map.

through the central plateau and to the Missouri River, and they end when they meet Kansas City in the west. There even is a small part of the Ozarks in eastern Kansas and Oklahoma.

Because of the Ozark Mountains' ruggedness and their people's isolation, it was one of the last frontiers in the country. Historian Frederick Jackson Turner was one of the first scholars to study the frontier as a transformative space. His ideas are contested highly in academic circles, but I find his notions about mountains and culture interesting. He noted that over the course of American history, "From the time the mountains rose between the pioneer and the seaboard, a new order of Americanism arose."[4] The pioneers of the nineteenth century, and more recently the back-to-the-landers, left the comfort of civilization to strike out for somewhere new. They moved to the edge of mainstream society and were often marginalized. Once settled in the new region, these settlers found that they created something new and different.[5]

Frederick Jackson Turner argued that the frontier was an in-between or liminal place between the coasts and the mountains. Anthropologist Victor Turner, among others, helped conceptualize liminality as a rite of passage phase characterized by ambiguity or a stage between a beginning and an ending.[6] The concept of liminality has been extended beyond rites of passage to any situation in which there is an "in-between" space, such as the space between civilization and wilderness. The concept has even been used to analyze power in the urban landscape. Such was the case when sociologist Sharon Zukin studied the space between business and public areas in cities and the way power played into the mix.[7] In the case of my research, I consider the Ozarks itself a liminal place; it is a "betwixt and between" region at the crossroads of various types of cultural heritages, and one in which isolation and independence spurred a diverging culture.

This "betwixt and between" state of the Ozarks often puts the region and its inhabitants in a situation of challenging normative structure of society at all levels. The region abounds with blurred boundaries such as southern/nonsouthern, past/future, and individualistic/communalistic. It also attracts people who live on the margins of society, sometimes known as tricksters, or "edgemen" as Turner called them.[8] Last, when looking at the Ozarks, one is confronted with the question of whether the region "live[s] with and in the nation as a whole" and how the nation regards the region.[9]

The liminal nature of the Ozarks fosters eccentricity and creativity. The Ozarks has also captured the imagination of people outside the region and motivated them to engage in alternative or countercultural activities. The region has lured all types of edgemen and women: folks that were part of counterculture groups, communards, cultists, and UFO enthusiasts. In addition to fringe groups, reporters, Hollywood personalities, and other key figures in popular culture have found the mythopoetic aspects of the region exciting to explore and exploit. Al Capp used Lil' Abner's Dogpatch, a mythic Ozarks, to explore social problems. Even real towns, such as Eureka Springs, have a long history as places many people believe possess a mystical energy vortex. To a greater extent than in other regions, some Americans sought an idealized version of the Ozarks to found communes and follow back-to-the-land practices.

Moving past previous research that discusses the Ozarks as a unique region, I argue that the Ozarks is a liminal region, or a "thin place." They are a place that defies conventional categorization and often attracts creative, often marginal people. The Ozarks are where the sacred and paranormal worlds are close by. Such places, like the town of Eureka Springs, foster inclusiveness and creativity. This live-and-let-live attitude was attractive to communal folk who wanted to make their lives and the world a better place. It is also a region that appealed to the religious devout, LGBT individuals, alternative economic practitioners, and others as somewhere they could live more freely and openly than was the case in most other regions.

As it turns out, people can have "thin" personalities too, according to psychiatrist and author Ernest Hartman.[10] Thin-boundary folks are more likely to experience nightmares but are also noted for greater creativity and flexibility in work, life, and love. They are more likely to consider themselves less as members of any particular group. In relationships, they become a part of their mate, even taking on their mannerisms in some cases. They are also more likely to express some paranormal belief or experience. In many ways, they are like Victor Turner's liminars. Like tricksters, Hartman noted that a thin-boundary person "will often be seen as a bit unreliable—a critic, a rebel, 'not a team player.'" In the following chapters, a number of thin-boundary characters will emerge.[11]

Another facet of what makes the Ozarks liminal is that the region is filled with anomalies, contradictions, and paradoxes.[12] For reasons that are not entirely clear, the region is filled with paranormal phenomena or is conducive to such activity. UFOs, humming, spirits, and other events are heavily reported in the region. Some residents of Eureka Springs say all the paranormal activities are the result of unique qualities of the Ozark Mountains or its springs.

One example that taps into the contradictory nature of the Ozarks is that it is both inclusive and exclusive. On the one hand, there has been a long history of welcoming immigrants into the region, while on the other, the region's treatment of African Americans and other minority groups has sullied its history. Although the Ozarks are famous for welcoming back-to-the-landers, the region has also attracted cults and militias based on an exclusive racial identity. Much of what is covered in this book has racial/ ethnic threads woven throughout.

A major paradox found in the Ozarks centers on the way modernity affects individuals, communities, and the region as a whole. Modernity was one of the foremost topics on which founding sociologists focused in the nineteenth and early twentieth centuries. German sociologist Max Weber believed that modernity would lead to a more bureaucratic, rational world in which individual aspirations would replace those of communities.[13] The work of Weber and others offered some way of explaining the sense of disconnection that led people to leave urban life's amenities and comforts for a more austere, but often more community-oriented life in the Ozarks. Modernity changes the way we regard ourselves and what it means to be an American, whether southerner or otherwise. Modernity was not an insignificant worry for leaders and scholars of the region as they believed that the modern world and its values were usurping traditions, folklore, and other facets of Ozark life that so many people find enchanting. Television, movies, and other types of popular culture have a part in spreading modernity, which often is contrasted with rural life for comedic effect, such as when urbanites move to the country, as in *Green Acres*, or country folks settle in the city, as in *The Beverly Hillbillies*.

Ever-changing values and the rise of technology and mass culture have influenced what we think about community. More isolated communities, as well as communities of the past, were tight-knit and centered on family and close friends who tended to interact in personal, face-to-face encounters. Many people were drawn to the Ozarks to be a part of such communities. On the other hand, modern life has forced people to share more of their lives with people outside their family and friends. Often, modern life becomes too predictable, pecuniary, and bureaucratic. To borrow a term from anthropologist Victor Turner, modernity is too structural.[14] Thus, all sorts of groups and people marginalized by mainstream society left the cities for the Ozarks and other rural areas of America because they found modern life hollow and unsatisfying. They set out to find a more authentic life filled with closer connections with family and friends, something akin to Josiah Royce's beloved community, but what Turner called communitas. Societies and cultures are held together to norms, traditions, laws, and other structural binds. Communitas, on the other hand, is "spontaneous, immediate, and concrete." It is what seekers to the region wished to create in a variety of ways.[15]

In the pages to follow, I use my sociological imagination as a scaffolding for the narrative about the Ozarks, modernity, and popular culture. Part of the sociological imagination depends on exploring the cultural and historical contexts that have shaped the lives of a number of different groups that have called the Ozarks home. To meet the challenge of such a narrative, I agree with Flannery O'Connor, who wrote, "There is a certain embarrassment about being a storyteller in these times when stories are considered not quite as satisfying as statements and statements not quite as satisfying as statistics; but in the long run, a people is known, not by its statements or its statistics, but by the stories it tells."[16] In some ways, numbers and equations offer a sense of authority and completeness of a more rationalized, structured world. In graduate school, my studies in demography presented the story as a concise equation of births, deaths, and migration that seemed to work well—and they do to some extent. The same is also true of other quantitative research. However, this book is not just about facts, observations, and statistics, but is more about exploring complex and more qualitative concepts such as *communitas* and liminality through sources such as folklore, legends, oral histories, and other cultural artifacts.

Time is important in both structural and liminal terms. In many cases, important biographical facts spread over one's life become linear and compressed. Modern life is hard to understand without reference to a matter-of-fact regard to time such as clocks, schedules, and calendars. On the other hand, Ozark author Ken Carey wrote of the liminal side of time that "powerful experiences of being wholly attentive to the present moment have a curious link with one another that can sometimes make events a decade apart seem separated by no more than a few moments."[17] My teenage years, living as a back-to-the-lander, seem like yesterday. However, our memories are patchy and, in some cases, reinforced to follow scripts to fill in doubtful areas. Thus, using diverse sources corrects some of these issues.

Much of the popular culture that has influenced my life deeply was that of the 1960s and 1970s. More than my perceptions about this particular period in American history, much of the literature that looks at modern American culture treats the 1960s as a major turning point. Music critic and former *Rolling Stones* editor Anthony Decurtis suggested that the "lessons" of the 1960s were

> the belief that we are not simply individuals but part of a larger culture that requires our most earnest efforts and ideas; the conviction that the worlds within and outside ourselves are subject to transformation, that our actions can shape the future, that what we choose to do matters deeply; the insistence that America has a place for our best selves, and to the degree that it doesn't, it must be changed; the notion that music can help formulate a vision toward which we can aspire.[18]

Most of these "lessons" focus on change and change agents; often, people I refer to as liminars. They work on the margins, have thin boundaries, and are creative. The stories told in this book highlight these people and events that shaped Ozarkian culture, and in some instances, the way Ozarkian culture helped shape American culture.

For example, what led people to make the important decision to leave a city and move to an isolated area such as the Ozarks? Alternatively, what would inspire a person to create a new identity and faith that others will follow? Using interviews, newspapers, official documents, and other sources, these stories offer a range of meanings and inflection points.[19]

I used various sources researching this book. For example, I interviewed people, conducted field research, analyzed survey data other researchers gathered, and reviewed various documents, such as newspaper articles, government reports, and other materials. Such a mixed-method approach brought me closer to what I think is the story for each chapter and allowed me to focus more on deeper descriptions that helped me describe the various social processes that undergird each of the stories.[20] A mixed-method, interpretive approach makes me a participant who is more "connected" with the subject matter because I can identify more information about topics, associations, and processes.[21] Comparing case studies, as Howard Becker noted: "if you find it, whatever it is, in one place, you'll find some version of. It in other places like it too. Maybe not going by the same name, or dealing with exactly the same problem, but similar enough to let you know where to look, what to look for to understand the case you're investigating, and what new things might be worth looking for in the old case, which you thought you knew all about."[22] Each of the nine chapters focuses on a particular facet of the Ozarks. Often, two or more cases are compared and contrasted to generate new insights and questions. According to Howard Becker, a researcher uses one case to explain another through analogy. For example, my back-to-the-land experiences allow me to create analogies when I encounter other alternative lifestyles, thereby gaining a recognition of the similarity that one case has in understanding another.[23]

A final note on methods and my role as a researcher: much of my experience in life has been as an outsider in various communities, and my peripatetic life has meant I often find that as a thin-boundary person, I have a foot in more than one culture. One of my favorite early sociologists, Georg Simmel, discussed such a person as I am as "the stranger" who traverses a number of communities ably because he or she isn't beholden to any particular one. Thus, the outsider may see things that others in the community do not. Simmel wrote: "Because he is not bound by roots to the particular constituents and partisan dispositions of the group, he confronts all of these with a distinctly "objective" attitude, an attitude that does not signify mere detachment and nonparticipation, but is a distinct structure composed of remoteness and nearness, indifference and involvement."[24]

Such a person, sociologist Robert Park noted, "is on the margin of two cultures and two societies."[25] That liminal place is a valuable place for a sociologist to occupy.

One aspect of culture in the Ozarks on which I will focus is identity, real or imagined. In chapter 2, "Exploring Regional Identity in Arkansas: Salience of the Ozark Term," I am guided by sociologist John Shelton Reed's inquiry about the South. He asserted that a southern regional identity was found in "the part of the country where people think they are Southerners." Approximately 85 percent of Arkansans identify themselves as southerners based on polls conducted in the 1990s to early 2000s. However, southern identity in the Ozarks is a bit more nuanced than Reed and other scholars recognized. Following Miller and other scholars instead, I accept the notion that the Ozarks form an alternative cultural tradition in the South.[26]

For Arkansas and Missouri, the term "Ozark" is better than Reed's "Dixie," which he used as a measure of southernness. I argue that the Ozarks more accurately capture the liminal nature of the region's inhabitants. However, the term "Ozark" is much more common throughout the state than are "Dixie," "Rebel," or other similar terms. Thus, rather than becoming less southern and more Americanized, Arkansans are identifying increasingly more with Ozark culture. This didn't just happen. For example, consider this piece from *The Mountain View Echo* in 1909:

> A man don't have to be born in the Ozark Mountains to be a good Ozarker, but he must be born again after he adopts the country. When he gets to the point where he thinks nothing equals the Ozark country, that its mountains are the highest and most beautiful, its valleys the deepest and richest, Ozark water the purist and clearest, Ozark fruit the best in the world[,] the Ozark women the healthiest and prettiest that grace God's footstool—then he is an Ozarker in deed and in truth and entitled to membership in the First Families of the Ozarks.[27]

After reviewing various newspapers in Missouri and Arkansas, my sense of the region is that an "Ozark Culture" emerged when people began to identify themselves and others in relation to the Ozarks, for example, by naming athletic teams and clubs after the region. Much of this occurred in the late nineteenth century, but it really became common around the beginning of the twentieth century.

It continued to be a challenge to define the Ozarks into the 1960s. Reporter J. C. Tillman wrote in an Ozark newspaper that "from conversations and interviews, it would appear that so long as you don't disdain a community that prides itself on being in the Ozarks, or praise some Petit Jean [a place far outside of the Arkansas Ozarks] group for its Ozark handiwork you're safe with a general comment [about where the Ozarks are located]."[28] His point was that the Ozarks end where people no longer regard themselves as Ozarkian. On another level, being southern is still being a type of American, as is true for being Ozarkian.

Beyond the cultural boundaries that constitute Ozark identity, there are mythical boundaries as well. Mythic lands and other paranormal phenomena such as UFOs are trickster-like in that they "are fundamentally linked to destructuring, change, transition, disorder, marginality, the ephemeral, fluidity, ambiguity, and the blurring of boundaries."[29] In chapter 3, I enter the mythical territory of Ozark identity by way of popular culture through the famous cartoon character of Li'l Abner and his town of Dogpatch. The South, and particularly the Ozarks, occupies two worlds—the world of myth where popular cultural creations such as Dogpatch and *The Beverly Hillbillies* exist and the real world, in which the inhabitants occupy socioeconomic arenas. Often, the mythic world, created primarily by outsiders, paints a picture of the Ozark people as buffoons. However, in the case of Li'l Abner, I argue that he is more a trickster than a dimwit. Li'l Abner's creator, Al Capp, found a character who was able to challenge social norms and make people stop and think about a number of basic assumptions in American life. In an interesting twist, modern folk stories about flying saucers emerged at the height of Li'l Abner's popularity. Al Capp used aliens deftly to ask Li'l Abner pointed questions about American culture, particularly religion, politics, and gender relations. Like Li'l Abner, the archetypical Ozarkian lives in a liminal world between isolation and community, between history and modernity. In the end, the hillbilly as the trickster offers us lessons about who we are and the way we can navigate the arising issues of modernity.

The next three chapters focus on the way the Ozarks established a niche in American life and popular culture centered on the culture of paranormal activities. The town of Eureka Springs is the epicenter of much of what is paranormal. In chapter 4, I take a look at Eureka Springs, where paranormal events are held against the backdrop of a very devout area. The *Passion Play* is a major draw on one side of the town, while Eureka Springs's more countercultural residents meet on the other side. Some people believe the town possesses an "energy vortex" like the one that is thought to exist in Sedona, Arizona. Perhaps because of these beliefs, one of Arkansas's major newspapers declared that the town was a "haven to eccentrics." I combed through various types of documents to learn more about the region's spirituality and ascertain whether residents and others do indeed consider the place sacred or liminal. I also focused on the intersection of community/conformity and individuality/isolation.

The general public may not realize how important UFOs are in popular culture. I certainly had no idea. I wondered whether the roots of Ozarkers reporting anomalous experiences, such as seeing flying saucers and/or being abducted by aliens, are but the latest variation of a long Ozark spiritual and folklore tradition. It is this rich tradition that offers answers to the various contradictions and issues of community and modernity. In chapter 5, I explore these and other questions. I relied on a number of information sources to learn the way mainstream and fundamentalist traditions in the area reacted to paranormal/UFO enthusiasts and activities, and I found that a very large number of paranormal manifestations (e.g., UFOs or ghosts) are reported in the Ozarks. I also attended a UFO conference in Eureka Springs in 2016, and my experiences there and research offer a glimpse of UFO culture, the UFO conference and attendees, and Ozark folk knowledge.

The Arkansas Ozarks also has a long history of cultic activity, highlights of which chapter 6 presents. Often rooted in apocalyptic ideology, many cults arise because of economic and societal uncertainty. Members seek to find or create some form of religious *communitas*.[30] With that in mind, I examine the Incoming Kingdom Missionary Unit that emerged in the early 1920s as an apocalyptic cult that believed most people would die in a battle between Protestants and Catholics in 1926. Obviously, there was no apocalypse, and the cult folded several years later. In the 1980s, an African American religious group, also known as the Nahziryah Monastic Community, moved into the same area. This group is unique in two ways. First, African Americans have rarely formed communal arrangements. Second, African Americans in the Ozarks are rare in any case, but an African American cult anywhere is particularly rare.

The next three chapters explore how the Ozarks attracted "prophets and artists" who Victor Turner argued were liminars and major agents of disrupting social norms, especially along lines of class and ideology.[31] This creativity and innovation was pivotal in fostering the rise of new genres of music, including rockabilly, and music was often interwoven with communal ideals and aspirations. Chapter 7 details the rise of the Dan Blocker Singers, later renamed "The Group." After a humble start in Odessa, Texas, the Group reached a level of fame in Hollywood, then they decided that life in mainstream popular culture was not for them. Many members moved to the Arkansas Ozarks to live communally. Using various documentary sources and a number of in-depth interviews, I go into greater detail about these interesting bands that transformed into two types of communal groups.

Chapter 8 is entitled "When Electric Music Came to Arkansas: The Rise of Rock and Roll in the Ozarks," and it provides a detailed examination of the long history of folk and traditional music in the Ozarks. The region produced a number of rockabilly or hillbilly rock bands that launched the careers of some well-known artists, such as Jerry Lee Lewis and the Band. They even inspired Jim "Dandy" Mangrum of Black Oak Arkansas to want to be like them when he grew up. The Ozarks pretty much escaped the psychedelic period of the 1960s, but when the wave of back-to-the-landers came in the late 1960s and 1970s, they helped open the area to rock and roll. Indeed, the first rock concert in the Ozarks was held in 1970 on a farm near Fayetteville. In some ways, the music scene adapted to the region by addressing regional culture and identity. On the other hand, popular music and other aspects of popular culture connected the region to the wider American culture. One of those bands was Black Oak Arkansas (BOA), which was on the forefront of the emergence of hillbilly rock and roll. BOA's music, and its lead singer, celebrated hypersexuality, one of the facets of a trickster, counterpointed by a fascination with religious themes. Another facet of the trickster is the paradox BOA highlighted between exalting the southern male and violence, while at the same time embracing many elements of progressive communal- ism. In contrast, the Ozark Mountain Daredevils (OMD), from Springfield, Missouri, manifested the wanderer facet of the trickster by writing about leaving home, the journey, and returning home but being ready to leave again. Their songs offered complex lyrics that often focused on social justice. I spend time discussing the origins and stories behind each band's music, offering another opportunity to explore why the Ozarks is a special place.

In the previous chapter, music represented the lives and aspirations of its participants, who began their lives playing music that they then used to spread ideals important to them. In chapter 9, I explore the way a number of environmentally minded communalists in the Missouri Ozarks came together to practice community. These counter-culturalists created commu- nity that sparked artistic expression such as music. Not only did they create a complex web of interactions greater than any one of the communities, but they also planted the seeds of sustainable living that would become accepted in mainstream culture, such as cooperative food arrangements, organic gar- dening, solar energy, and other alternative energy solutions. One of the major intentional communities that shared in this process was Seven Springs, a group of back-to-the-landers that formed in part to provide alternative edu- cation for their children. Planning meetings for the school as well as other times when members could get together led to extended music jams, which, in turn, led to the Hot Mulch Band's formation. Often, their songs conveyed, in clever and amusing ways, what life was like in an intentional community and the principles of sustainable agriculture and energy production. Several years after our arrival in the Ozarks, I had the good fortune to hear one of their better-known songs, "Ozark Mountain Mother Earth News." To many, including me, this song is the anthem of the back-to-the-land movement. The band performed this song and others, in which they spun stories of communal living in a bluegrass-rock way within the circuit of communal groups located in southern Missouri in the mid-1970s. I had the pleasure of meeting with a number of the band's members and other key people who were part of the communal scene in southern Missouri in the 1970s. In addition to my conversations and communication with various people involved with Hot Mulch, I used a variety of documents to flesh out the narrative. The story that emerges is of such communities as Edge City, Seven Springs, the Garden of Joy Blues, New Life Farm, East Wind, and Dragon Wagon, which created a network that met all the communities and their members' cultural needs (e.g., food, entertainment, news).

In the late 1960s to mid-1970s, a number of people from other states, typically urban areas, moved to the Ozarks. These hipbillies, as historian Jared Phillips refers to them, found the inspiration to make such a leap in *Mother Earth News*, *Stranger in a Strange Land*, *Walden Two* and other popular back-to-the-land literature.[32] In chapter 10, I explore the back-to-the-land movement by looking at three families, one of which is my own. My family was one of many who moved to the Ozarks to establish a more self-sufficient, value-based life. Often, the immigrants were grossly underprepared, such as was my family's case. Other people brought skills and revitalized the communities they moved to in the 1970s. I share the stories in which each of our families contended with weather, poverty, and integrating with the local people. Given the scale of communal activity in the region, it is ironic that many of us were unaware of other Ozarkian communards. Most communes did not last very long, while others have survived but find it difficult to attract members of the younger generations. These stories showcase the devotion to communal ideals that kept many of these people in the Ozarks when so many others decided to leave. Moreover, this communal lifestyle had an influence on those of us who were children of the back-to-the-landers.

Exploring Regional Identity in Arkansas
The Salience of the Term "Ozark"[1]

My ancestors settled on these banks
perhaps by accident, delivered here
by high winds or high water,
and they put down roots so deep
that they became the identity of this place—
but few locals now know the name
of this stream, and its seasonal rise
wears away the course of the past;
yet I remain, misshapen by my seeking
of fissures, by my grasping of stones,
becoming the contours of resistance,
the contortions of my resilience,
holding in place what little remains
of a soil that once held me secure.

—Phillip Howerton, "The History of Tree Roots"[2]

In order to place the Ozarks into the tapestry of American culture, it is important to try to make sense of what the region is in social psychological terms. As a one-time resident of the Ozarks, I regard the Ozarks as a unique cultural region in the United States. The closest parallel I could find was the

American southeast, where there is no doubt by natives and outsiders alike that a region that includes Alabama, Mississippi, and other Deep South states, was The South.

The ambiguity about southern identity is a persistent topic of discussion, particularly when the regional character is a "quilt" or emotion defines its boundaries.[3] Added to the ambiguity is the loss of identity attributable to modernity that some southerners suggest is taking place. In his 1970 book about southern history and identity, C. Vann Woodward begins with an interesting question that guides the remainder of his essay: "When will a southerner stop referring to himself as a southerner?"[4] Many scholars have argued that southern identity has declined in recent decades.[5] In a 2012 national survey conducted by the University of Arkansas, 38.4 percent of respondents who lived in the South identified themselves as being southern.[6]

Southern identity, a regional sentiment, is not the only identity in the South, as Appalachian, Cajun, and other identities exist there as well. In this chapter, I explore the Ozark identity. One way to understand the strength of Ozark identity is by looking at Arkansan businesses and local events that use the term "Ozark" in their names compared to other terms, such as "southern," "Dixie," and "American." I assume that counting these regional terms will provide a substitute measure of regional identity.

One of the earliest scholars to recognize the importance of regionalism was historian Frederick Jackson Turner, who wrote that regions emerge as a result of attitudes, politics, and particular to a certain geography.[7] Later, Alvin Bertrand argued that regional sociology should focus on socially identifiable places, and researchers should use a comparative methodology.[8] Taking a more individual-level perspective based on symbols, language, and interactions between individuals (symbolic interactionism), he argued that the theory should focus on "all forms of human association within the given regional environment."[9] Regional sociologists were interested particularly in life in African American regions of the nation.[10] Examples of such areas are the Mississippi Delta, the Alabama Black Belt, and the I-95 "Corridor of Shame" in South Carolina.

Some research about regionality harkens back to Frederick Jackson Turner's concept of the frontier, in which culture died and was renewed continually. Odum was particularly explicit about the frontier assumption. He asserted that "the Frederick Jackson Turner theory that the American frontier has conditioned American culture and, therefore, the study of these frontiers is necessary to the understanding of American culture."[11] Writers such as Charles Morrow Wilson argued that the isolation and lack of networking with other regions made the Ozarks an "arrested frontier," to borrow a term from Brooks Blevins.[12] Other studies looked at the South as a colony, rather than a frontier, of the industrialized North, foreshadowing Immanuel Wallerstein's concept of the core and the periphery, where industrialized areas separate resources and talent from less developed areas.[13]

Place is an important ingredient in understanding any region. One early French sociologist that many regional scholars referred to was Frederick Le Play. He asserted that place effects the economy (e.g., resources, conduciveness to industry, etc.) and ultimately families in the region.[14] Rupert Vance, a colleague and protégé of Howard Odum, argued that place influences the culture of the people living there.[15] Later, David Haenke, an environmental leader in the Ozarks, argues that the Ozarks form a bioregion that shapes the culture of its people.[16]

In much of *Homo Geographicus*, Robert David Sack links place to identity. He wrote that Place [. . .] becomes an agent in the formation of self [and] Individuals and place can merge identities."[17] He argued that place worked the same way for groups in forming a collective identity. Focusing on the South, Samuel Wallace, a well-known sociologist from Missouri, argued that place was tied to southern identity.

In recent decades, researchers have turned away from descriptive and regional analyses to broader behavioral approaches.[18] Keeping the work of Odum, Vance, and others alive, Reed focused on the South from a social-psychological perspective.[19] Of particular value is Odum's citation from *American Regionalism* that "a region may be described loosely as an area of which the inhabitants instinctively feel themselves a part."[20] More recently, Thomas Gieryn argued for the inclusion of "place" in sociological studies.[21] Griffin's "The Promise of a Sociology of the South" offers readers a more detailed account of Reed's work as well as other more recent sociological studies of the South.

Following Odum and Heberle, Reed asserted that a southern regional identity was "the part of the country where people think they are Southerners."[22] Self-identification is one aspect of understanding who is or is not southern. According to Reed, assimilation is important.[23] Those in-migrants and natives who accept the norms and expectations of the region "fit in" as southerners. Those people, native or not, who do not accept or follow those regional norms (e.g., conservative politics/religion, and heavy dialect) are "misfits," or more academic terms, anti-structuralists, thin-boundaried, liminars, and tricksters. Strangers and freethinkers don't have biases one way or the other, thus, tend to occupy the middle ground between insiders and outsiders.

Phillip Howerton wrote about the relationship of the people to the Ozarks: "They put down roots so deep, that they become the identity of the place."[24] Over time, place and people get conflated which may cause some trouble. According to Sack, "Resurrecting a deeply mythologized past, they strive to attain an ethnic, religious, and racial purity, an identity, and a thickening of place."[25] That "thickening of place" is at the root of southern identity that is tied invariably to its history. Victor Turner noted that "structure is rooted in the past and extends into the future through language, law, and custom."[26] In the case of the South, the term "Dixie" is often used when referring to the region. The Mason-Dixon Line, which settled a border dispute between the colonies of Pennsylvania and Maryland, became the dividing line between free and slave states. Thus, "Dixie" refers to those states below the Mason-Dixon Line that were slave-holding states prior to the American Civil War. Cox argued that because "Dixie" refers to the South prior to and during the American Civil War, when used in advertisements or business names in the South as a brand, the term tends to make it "martial in spirit."[27] Certainly, the term and the symbols that connect the contemporary South to its history promote the sense that it has an identity separate from that of the rest of the nation. Cobb maintained that the latter half of the twentieth century has seen the "Dixification of Dixie," the regional tendency to celebrate and even invent differences in cultural norms simply because they separate the South from the rest of America.[28]

Counter to Dixification is the idea that regional culture will converge with mainstream society, a notion shared by a number of scholars such as Vance and Reed. For Vance, popular culture and economy were the main culprits in the South losing its distinctiveness. He wrote,

> Those who do not migrate to these focal centers have the urbanizing cultural forces beamed in their direction—services that run the gamut from pre-mixed biscuits and precooked rice to television's mass pabulum of horse operas and soap operas. Once, like Vermont, we in the South too had unique rustic personalities— somewhat cross-grained at times. Today we have mass. Culture and minds, and the only way a man and his family can remain "hayseed" is to be brought up in a *mountain cove* with communication cut off by land, sea and air. [My emphasis.][29]

Thus, popular culture has a homogenizing effect on regional and cultural differences between groups. A number of academics such as Walter Cralle, a sociologist from the Missouri Ozarks, described the risk of loss of cultural uniqueness in the Ozarks in the 1930s.[30] In 1977, Southern Missouri State historian Robert Flanders referred to the incursion of popular culture and migrants into the Ozarks as the "Californication" of the region.[31] Another Missouri sociologist, Samuel Wallace, addressed the Mid-South Sociological Association in 1980 about the "demise" of the South.[32] Outside the academic world, however, the view was not as dim. Life and culture in the South and the Ozarks persisted in some ways and changed in other ways.

Testing cultural convergence, Reed argued that one way to explore the geographic boundaries of identity is through the use of names of businesses and other entries in telephone directories.[33] The identifiers he focused on were "Southern" and "Dixie" as a percentage of "American" entries. The values obtained were then interpolated between sample cities. None of the sample cities was located within the Ozark region, and only Little Rock represented Arkansas. Reed found that the "Old South" had the largest number of Dixie entries, and the "New South," the largest number of "Southern" entries.

Most Arkansans who responded to the Southern Focus Poll in 1992 and 2001 identified themselves as southerners.[34] However, Arkansas and Missouri are border states to the Deep South and the West, making a strong affiliation with any region ambiguous. In a sense, inhabitants of the Ozarks, like people living in other liminal spaces, have to live and work "slant-wise" to dominant culture. That is, Ozarkians don't outwardly resist dominant culture but "maneuver in indirect, oblique manner in relation to social structures, narrow social identities, legal norms, cultural value systems, and other forces that would restrict or oppress them."[35] The Ozarks operate well outside the dichotomy of either the New (southern) or Old (Dixie) South. Cora Pinkley-Call, a writer from Eureka Springs, wrote, "Just overlapping the South of 'You all' and the West of 'Howdy Stranger,' Arkansas lies, a world as different as a continent apart."[36] In both geographic and cultural ways, the state occupies a liminal place in American life.

Reed conducted a follow-up study in 1988 and found that the term "Dixie" had fallen into further disuse and that the region that still used "Southern" to identify business names in telephone entries was shrinking.[37] Cooper and Knotts replicated Reed's work and found a continued decline in Old South terms such as "Dixie," a decline that they termed "de-Confederatization."

The authors contended that African Americans' re-immigration into the Deep South in recent decades was a contributing factor in the decline. Thus, according to Cooper and Knotts, racial composition and sheer population dynamics contribute to regional identity.[38] Blevins also suggested that the changes in the US role in the world and the increase in communications technology dampened interest in regional types as Americans began to compare themselves as a nation to other national types.[39]

Ozark Identity

Following E. Joan Miller and other scholars, I accept the notion that the Ozarks constitute an alternative and transformative cultural tradition in the South and the United States.[40] "Ozark" is a more precise term than is Reed's "pure" measure of southerness—"Dixie." Griffin noted that early on, Reed cautioned that differences within an area need to be explored (e.g., regions of Arkansas).[41] This caveat was overlooked to some extent by the interpolated values used to describe regions not covered in Reed's work and that of others later. Griffin also pointed out that Reed failed to look at the many differences between mountain and lowland southerners. Finally, Reed's South and southerner tended to be white and individualistic. In essence, much of Reed's work assumes a homogenous South.

Like Griffin and others, the South is not homogenous. Griffin is correct that other identities (e.g., Jews, Asians, etc.) might trump a southern identity even on the part of those with long-standing ties to the South. Here, I explore the regionality effect on business/event names with special emphasis on the Ozarks. I argue that Ozarks/Ozarker describes the region and people who live between being southerners and something else. An integral part of Ozark culture is that identity is tied to physical geography. Over 15 percent of 2,502 place names in the Ozarks include the words "knob," "hill," "ridge," or "mountain."[42] In his exploration of the Arkansas image, Blevins considered the lack of attention paid specifically to Ozark culture.[43] Through a brief survey of articles listed in the March 1963 to February 1965 *Reader's Guide to Periodical Literature*, Blevins observed that the term Appalachia appears in 18 articles, 15 of which are devoted to topics of reform. The term Ozark was mentioned in only 3 articles, and Blevins suggested that the smaller geographic area the Ozarks represent made differentiating Ozark identity from Appalachian identity inconsequential. However, Ozark identity can be differentiated from both Appalachian and southern identity.

There are many facets that constitute Ozark identity. The principal ones Francaviglia noted included self-sufficiency, insularity, and a negative perception on the part of outsiders.[44] As Francaviglia observed, Europeans whose farms and communities were self-sufficient and did not rely on slave labor or large external markets as did cotton-based agricultural communities in the lowland South settled in the region. Such an orientation made the Ozark settlers insular. The topography also isolated the people migrating into the Ozarks from other regions of the country. The isolated mountain folk inspired a "combination of fascination and revulsion in outsiders."[45] Yet, that combination lay at the heart of the interest nonsoutherners showed in true trickster spirit of individualism and nonconformity that the South—especially the hillbilly South—represented. Thus, the sense of identity was strengthened as a result of increased marginalization by outsider stereotypes and derisive labels, such as "Hill Billy," associated with those living in the Ozarks. Although the hillbilly label plays a part in regional identity, Blevins suggested that the iconic mid-twentieth-century hillbillies were used to represent the discomfort with modern life all Americans felt rather than to explore or highlight aspects of regional identity. As well, Francaviglia noted the irony in the separateness of Ozark identity even though the region was an area contested highly between Union and Confederate forces during the Civil War, a fact noted earlier by Charles Morrow Wilson.[46] In fact, Huber pointed out that mountain communities during the Civil War often supported the Union, making the association of the Ozarks or Appalachia with Dixie or the Old South rather imprecise.[47] The Ozarkian as a resourceful, independent, nonconformist serves as a positive identity for the residents of the Ozarks, as well the foundation for the negative hillbilly image outsiders apply. Thus, the Ozark label, because of its "between and betwixt" nature makes it unique from other labels such as "southern" or "Dixie."

Both Appalachian and Ozark hillbilly culture are presented as essentially the same in the commercialized version of the hillbilly. Southern tourism, much like southern identity, can be subdivided according to regional identities. These regional identities have been shaped by the fact that "the national increase in consumerism, affluence, and automobile travel after the Second World War rapidly expanded the South's modern tourism industry."[48] Whether considering Cobb's "Dixification of Dixie" or the commodification

of the hillbilly image, the influence of images of the Ozarks defined exter-
nally and used commercially has had an effect on the image of Ozark culture
overall. When Cox discussed "advertising as a medium that can both reflect
and reinforce cultural values," she referred to the use of "Dixie" in marketing
southern products.[49] This point is significant, in that the marketing of hillbilly
products has had a similar influence on the image of the Ozarks accepted,
and images of the South, Dixie, and the Ozarks has changed over time in
response to their commodification. Although the hillbilly image remains
much the same today as it was in the 1930s, with representations of hillbillies
that focus on their ignorant, violent, and sexually deviant nature, the hillbilly
as part of the Old South or as a supporter of racialized Dixie is a product
of recent shifts in the Ozark image.[50] The result is that popular culture and
advertising may weaken and veil the links other Americans may have with
the people of the region. If there is any constant regarding Ozark identity is
that of its ever-shifting and often paradoxical nature.

John Williams Graves argued that the state could be divided from the
northeast Mississippi Delta, predominantly slave-holding counties diagonally
to the southwest timberland counties. Ozark counties, with few slaves, would
be above Graves's imaginary line. Intrastate divisions such as Unionist and
Confederate sympathies arose between these two areas. Later, Blevins, divided
the state into mythic hillbilly Arkansaw of the Ozarks and the real Arkansas.[51]

In *Hillbilly Hell-Raisers*, J. Blake Perkins, chronicles the inter-regional
tensions between locals who tended be progressive in outlook and the local
elites who were more self-interested and less progressive. Often, federal policy
makers would leave out the common man in various policies and acquiesce
to local elites about managing local draft boards, agricultural dictates, and
New Deal programs. Much of the animus that the typical Ozarker had was
not so much at the program but how unfairly it was administered by local
elites. That all changed with President Johnson's War on Poverty initiatives.
Local elites were able to foment racial resentment to effectively misdirect the
animus of citizens to those progressive efforts in the 1960s.[52]

Almost from the beginning, race was an issue in the Ozarks. According
to Huber and Drowne, early on, the term "Hill Billy" indicated an unso-
phisticated person who lived in the Appalachian or Ozark Mountains.[53]
However, the term became defined more narrowly to label Ozarkians. For
African Americans, the word was associated with bigotry beginning in the
late 1890s.[54] Moving forward, the Ozark region has been host to a number

of communities from which African Americans were forced out, now commonly known as sundown towns, a name that derives from the fact that minorities and outsiders were threatened to leave town before the sun set. As Blevins pointed out, Orval Faubus spent much of his six consecutive terms as governor of Arkansas in the 1950s and 1960s claiming a connection between the Ozark hillbilly and the racist South.[55] Given these racial dynamics, the question of the degree to which Ozarkians share a sense of the southern or Dixie identity with other regions of the state of Arkansas arises. In this respect, the Ozarks do fit Reed's conceptualization of the South and Dixie as being primarily white and individualistic.

Although Blevins noted that the interest in the hillbilly type in the 1950s and 1960s may have reflected anxiety over the migration of southerners from mountainous regions to the north and west, another interpretation of the trend is that the hillbilly represented the best of southern identity at a time when the South was associated increasingly with racism.[56] The negative and positive characteristics that Blevins associates with the Arkansas image include "violence, ignorance, shiftlessness, laziness, with generous doses of racism, moonshining, clannishness, inbreeding, barefootedness, floppyhatedness, and general cussedness . . . independent, resourceful, nonconformist, close to nature, unpretentious, generous, and non-materialistic."[57] Some of these characteristics generally reflect the ideal American type—the independent frontiersman. Although the representations of the hillbilly were comical, they were far less threatening than were those of southerners shouting at, or attacking, African American students attempting to integrate southern schools.

The Socioeconomics of the Arkansas Ozarks Region

To understand the socioeconomic context of the Ozark region better, USDA county-level data for Arkansas were aggregated by regions and analyzed. Those results, together with complementary research, are reported below. Boundaries are based on "Internal State Regions" (ISRs) Polidata developed in 1996. These boundaries are mirrored in http://www.arkansas.com /places-to-go/cities-and-towns/.

Compared with the other regions of Arkansas, the Ozarks are racially homogenous, have relatively modest incomes and education, and are represented heavily by the elderly and veteran populations.[58] According to the

USDA data, there was an increased presence of African Americans in Ozark counties between 2000 and 2010, but they continue to constitute a small fraction of the population.[59]

Of all of the counties in the Ozarks, only Newton County was classified as having persistent poverty. Kuehn and Bender (reported growth in the manufacturing sector in nonmetropolitan Ozark counties in the 1960s and 1970s.[60] This expansion remains the case in the Ozarks currently, where most counties depend on manufacturing and unspecialized activities. The region's relative isolation, coupled with considerable issues associated with transportation (infrastructure, drive-time, etc.) make gainful employment difficult for many in the region.[61] Nonetheless, unemployment does not seem to discourage Ozarkians from seeking jobs.[62]

Grinstead-Schneider and Green wrote, "It is not unusual for Ozark and [Arkansas] Delta communities to contain as many as 25 percent functional illiterates (those with five or fewer years of formal education)."[63] However, according to current numbers that are aggregated by Arkansas regions, the Ozarks has slightly higher percentages than does the state at all levels of education.

Finally, the Ozarks has the highest percentage of veterans of all the regions, at 9.8 percent, followed by the Ouachitas at 9.4 percent. One possible explanation for this higher level of education may be retirees' immigration to the Ozarks. At the same time that natives of the Ozarks emigrated, Midwestern retirees were settling in the same rural counties. Johnson noted that the region is a retiree magnet.[64] If it were not for immigration, the population in the Ozarks would be very small because of the large numbers of older people in the region. In fact, in 2000, the USDA classified eight of 18 Ozark counties as Retirement Destination counties. A large elderly population is a major contributing factor to the number of Ozark counties that have modest per capita income levels.[65] By the 1950s, Mountain Home in Baxter Country was one of the most popular destinations for retirees, and the county had more than 150 lodges, hotels, resorts, and restaurants.[66] Blevins's overview of the retirement community boom in northern Arkansas in the 1960s and 1970s indicated that most of the retirees were from the Midwest, with many from Illinois, Missouri, Indiana, Iowa, and Wisconsin. Although many of the retirement communities are somewhat isolated from the rural native Ozark social structure by their very nature, Blevins pointed to a number of significant changes that have occurred as a direct result of the immigration of Midwesterners, especially the influx of Lutheran and

Roman Catholics, who have worked to end bans on alcohol sales in counties in which evangelical Christians once dominated, like Baxter and Carroll. The immigration of retirees continues to affect the demographics of these rural counties. Glasgow and Brown showed that, since the 1960s, immigrants in nonmetropolitan destination counties have had a measurable effect on the literacy rate of those with large retirement communities.[67] Despite potential economic hardships, many people are attracted to the Ozarks for a wide array of non-pecuniary reasons.[68]

Incoming retirees became a force for nostalgia-laden and conservate efforts in the Ozarks. Phillips wrote, "Such communities challenged the Ozarks to understand how to deal with incoming retirees, a group who, despite their alleged desire to return to the America of yore, had little regard for the traditions of the region." Old-timer Ozarkers, many more progressive than the retirees moving in, were able to work with and share cultural traditions with back-to-landers, a group not as appreciated by the retirees.[69]

Increasing one's income is a major motivation for leaving the Ozarks.[70] Both immigration and emigration would seem to dilute the sense of community.[71] However, poll data on southern identity and the sense of region of long-term residents living in the South who don't identify as southerners or "lapsed Southerners" is canceled out by more recent immigrants who adopt that identity. Perhaps the indeterminacy of the Ozark term fills the gap in identity for Ozarkians.[72]

Measuring Ozark Identity

A number of popular cultural memes have grown up around the Ozarks, particularly the Ozarks as the home of the hillbilly. At the same time, the Ozarks as home to the rugged individualist has a connection to the southern, Confederate nostalgia, or anti-establishment Dixie. The heyday of the hillbilly image, from the 1940s to the early 1970s, coincided with Egerton's 1974 pronouncement that we had entered the time of the "Southernization of America."[73] Although Cobb claimed that Edgerton's expression was merely a convenient, and not entirely accurate, explanation for the rightward swing of American politics, cultural products of the Ozarks from the latter half of the twentieth century suggest otherwise.[74] Formerly southern interests—country music, political conservatism, NASCAR, and the NRA—have become nationwide interests.[75]

Ozark fiction writers have explored the motif of the Ozarkian as a rugged individualist. Woodrell's collection of short stories, the *Outlaw Album* (2011), is populated by characters who are nonconformists in every aspect of their lives. Harington's novels, set in the fictional town of Stay More, Arkansas, live in a typical Ozark community filled with independent, resourceful, and unpretentious citizens whose isolation and unity fit the positive stereotype of the Ozarkian. The characters in the Stay More series are not haunted by the ghost of the Old South. Rather, they represent the fabled self-sufficient and capable Ozark hillbilly, one who sets him/herself apart, in some ways an outsider, from social conventions and embraces individuality.

Hillbilly tourism has taken on a special flavor in the Ozarks. Silver Dollar City opened in 1960 in Branson, Missouri, playing somewhat to the stereotype of the hillbilly, and the Ozark Folk Center was established as an Arkansas state park in 1973. Dogpatch, based on the Li'l Abner cartoon series, opened in 1968. Blevins wrote of Dogpatch that it is "a surreal and unintentionally postmodern entity."[76] Even as the theme park operated on the hillbilly image, it allowed visitors to interact with that image in whatever way they deemed, as parody, regional Americana, or celebration. *The Beverly Hillbillies* television show served a similar purpose for a national audience. Created by Missouri native Paul Hennings, the show used the well-known image of the Arkansas Ozarks to provide social commentary on consumerism and its effect on regional identity.

Musically, the Ozarks has produced a number of influential groups, including folk singers known well outside the region. *Newly Discovered Early American Folk Songs* (1959) by Jimmy Driftwood was a successful album nationally, and Driftwood was conscripted to help organize the 1963 Arkansas Folk Festival in Mountain View, which quickly became the state's largest tourist attraction.[77] Cobb's essay, "From Muskogee to Luckenbach: Country Music and the 'Southernization' of America," addressed the way the South's music represented elements of American culture that were deeply religious and socially traditional.[78] He highlighted the conflict between the New South and the hillbilly values early country music stressed often. Country music and even early southern rock—Black Oak Arkansas and the Ozark Mountain Daredevils—embraced the view of southerners as traditional and independent. Cobb argued that these musical factions represented fans who "had long been the enemy of crusaders for social change."[79] A product of the Arkansas Ozarks in particular, Black Oak embraced the "hillbilly outlaw image" with songs like "Revolutionary All-American Boys" and "When Electricity Came to Arkansas."[80]

Region	Ozark	Southern	Dixie	American
Central	45 (0.27)	79 (0.48)	24 (0.15)	165
Delta	2 (0.05)	′ 25 (0.61)	3 (0.07)	41
Ozark	463 (2.91)	67 (0.42)	15 (0.09)	159
Ouachitas	8 (0.53)	34 (2.27)	2 (0.13)	15
River Valley	85 (1.15)	21 (0.28)	5 (0.07)	74
Timberland	1 (1.00)	0 (0.00)	0 (0.00)	0
Grand Total	604 (1.33)	226 (0.50)	49 (0.11)	454

Table 2.1 2014 Arkansas Region with Aggregated Select Businesses with Ozark, Southern, Dixie or American in their Titles.

Although the Ozarkians may not define themselves as hillbillies, the general theme of independence and self-sufficiency that the hillbilly motif suggests is very much a part of all cultural expressions of the Ozark identities. The connection to the South or "Dixie" as part of its identity may well reflect that aspect of regional identity.

To understand whether there was any geographic variability in identity, I analyzed data from the Arkansas secretary of state about corporations and exempt organization data from the Internal Revenue Service (IRS). The region with the largest number of Arkansas entities that incorporated the term "Ozark" in their names was obviously the Ozarks, where the term was used 2.9 times more than the term "American." The River Valley, adjoining the Ozarks, had the second highest count of entities named "Ozark." The term "southern" was used more than any of the other terms, 34 times in the Ouachitas, approximately 2.3 times more than "American." "Dixie" is a term used rarely in any of the regions' business names. In all regions, "Dixie" was used 49 times compared to 226 times for "southern," 454 times for "American,"

Region	Ozark	Southern	American
Central	1 (1.7%)	6 (28.6%)	4 (23.5%)
Delta	0 (0.0)	4 (19.0)	2 (11.8)
Ozarks	54 (90.0)	5 (23.8)	4 (23.5)
Ouachita Mountains	2 (3.3)	0 (0.0)	2 (11.8)
River Valley	3 (5.0)	0 (0.0)	4 (23.5)
Timberland	0 (0.0)	6 (28.6)	1 (5.9)
Total	60	21	17

Table 2.2 2014 Events in Arkansas Regions with Specific Words in Titles.

and 604 times for "Ozark" (see table 2.1). The term counts by region for businesses are given in table 1 and for events in table 2. Proportions of the term "American" are given in parentheses beneath the actual term count.[81]

It should come as no surprise that results from Missouri show the highest frequency of "Ozark" as part of a name for any tax-exempt organizations that are located in the Ozarks region.[82] Missourian Ozarkers are about 1.4 times more likely to refer to their tax-exempt institutions with "Ozark" than with "American." What may be more interesting is that unlike Arkansas, where "Ozark" has gained wider acceptance in non-Ozark regions, there is seems to be almost no use of "Ozark" in any of the other regions of Missouri. Moreover, the use of "southern" and "Dixie" is virtually nonexistent. Besides "Ozark," it is likely Missouri regions other than the Ozarks might identify as "Midwest" and similar labels.

Table 2.2 reports events in each ISR that included "Ozark," "southern," and "American" in their names. Data were collected from http://www.arkansas.com/events/. Related Ozark terms, such as "hillbilly" and "mountain" (excluding mountain bike and similar uses) were counted. No "Dixie" events were listed, even when I expanded the search to Civil War events. Finally, derivations of the term "American," such as "America" and "national" were counted as American. By far, the term "Ozark" is the most popular in Arkansas events, especially in the Ozarks. The term is used 54 times in the name of events held in the Ozarks, 90 times more than the term "American." All other terms are much rarer in event names (see table 2.2).

Concluding Remarks

Brooks Blevins noted that in the nineteenth century, the definition of the Ozarks was much broader than it is today and that it included even an acceptance of the Ouachita Mountains.[83] The results support that broad conception of Ozark identity today. For example, in the counts for Ozark-named events, the River Valley shares an Ozark identity to some extent. Moreover, the term "Ozark" is much more common throughout the state than is "Dixie," "rebel," or similar terms. The acceptance of "Ozark" as a label for a type of southern identity is widespread in Arkansas but confined to the Ozark region in Missouri. Another finding is that both the central region (e.g., Little Rock) and the Ozarks tend to identify themselves as both southern and American at higher levels than do other regions of the state. On the other hand, some evidence suggests that for Missourians, "southern" is rarely used. These baseline findings suggest that rather than becoming less southern and more Americanized, Arkansas regions are identifying increasingly with Ozark culture as a variation of southern identity. For Missouri, Ozark identity seems to remain in the Ozark region of that state.

The opportunity to investigate Ozark identity using other novel methods and sources of data needs further exploration. Exploring the term "Ozark" using Google Books Ngram allowed me to see how often the term was used in the millions of books that Google has scanned. In the both fiction and nonfiction books from 1650 to 2000, it is most often linked with the terms such as "mountains," "folk," and "region." "Ozark region" was fairly common for much of the twentieth century, until "Ozark Mountains" surpassed it in the mid-1960s. Another term emerging over time is "Ozark folk" such as in Ozark folk music, arts, and so on. Another Google tool, Google Correlate, offers the researcher the ability to see how aggregate Google searches correlate with other searches. For instance, people using the search term "Ozark" are also likely to search for lakes, boat rentals, and so on. Using Google Trends, I was able to see the trends of searches for "Ozark" and then compare it to search terms such as "southern" and "Dixie." Beyond the trend lines for each of these terms, I was able to compare states and regions on the prevalence of searches according to those terms. The use of these tools and other emergent technologies for research will offer exciting ways to understand a wide variety of social phenomena.

Patterns of immigration and emigration also affect regional identity. In the Ozarks, emigration has been concentrated largely in areas that have the least fertile farmland and are isolated geographically. Quite often, the small communities that have the greatest emigration are those that are distant from employment opportunities as well. Blevins noted that almost one-third of the population of the 13 rural Ozark counties left the Ozarks from 1940 through 1960.[84] Cooper and Knotts demonstrated how race and population density shape the way regions are identified.[85] The Ozarks also has not experienced an influx of African Americans as have other southern regions. On the other hand, economic and political circumstances have led to other ethnic groups, such as Asians and Hispanics, migrating into the region. The way these or other emerging ethnic clusters will shape Ozark identity will be interesting, especially as the number of Hispanics has increased in all areas of the state. What influence will virtual affiliations have on in-group identities? What role do reconfederation efforts play in shaping identity?

Ironically, reconfederationization efforts in the Ozarks might be accelerated by a sense of the loss of a "mythic past" in a region that was, in fact, not very sympathetic to the Confederacy. Garreau wrote, "The influx of people like that [retirees, back-to-the landers, urbanites, etc.] for better or for worse, has whiplashed, if not Future-Shocked the Ozarks.[86] That phenomenon—being Future Shocked or the threat of being so—is in the 1980s, what ties the South together." Perhaps Garreau is being hyperbolic, as both African Americans and whites regard themselves as southerners, and racial conflict is not an exclusively southern conflict. When Cobb echoed Zinn's earlier claim that the uncouth, traditionalist, and racist South was simply the mirror of darker sentiments in all of America, he reduced one aspect of southern identity, the connection to that mythic and racialized past, to a footnote of American identity.[87] Culture in the Ozarks, the South, the United States, and even in other countries has reached a place that postmodernist Jean Baudrillard called hyperreality.[88] Hyperreality emerges as a condition where it is hard to discern between an imagined or simulated (e.g., Branson, Dogpatch, Civil War reenactments) reality and what is truly real.

Homogeneity in the Ozarks was long a defining characteristic of the region. Now immigrants who want to be southern cancel out southerners who want to be something else. Too much is made of these differences. On the other hand, differences between mountain folk and others are real and persistent.

The Ozarks also is also a homogenous region in terms of socioeconomic measures. Far too many Ozarkers are often marginalized and in terms of income, occupation, and education underperforming when compared to other regions of the country. Thus, the region and its people are ripe for religious or liminal experiences or ideology that offers some promise for *communitas*. Some people will find comfort in deepening their faith. Other people will turn to more racially and ethnically exclusive groups.

Recent events concerning the Confederate flag, racism, and related issues will raise many questions for researchers about the direction of the orientation of the people of the South. Following Hall and Wood's notion of the "Janus-faces of the South," will southerners continue to focus on the hyperreality of real/imagined pasts and continuity or will they turn toward the future and progressive change?[89] The popularity of the term "Ozark" for Arkansas might offer an alternative path where heritage and future can be melded to offer a unique identity that many Arkansans even outside the Ozark region can share.

Perhaps the movement toward reconfederation needs to be addressed directly by pointing out that many of the people in mountain regions in the South were not at all sympathetic to secession from the Union—unlike what many Ozark/Appalachian people now accept as the past. Understanding why today's Ozarkians and Appalachian people find the Confederacy so appealing will allow researchers to understand the way "imagined pasts" gain more salience than the past as it was. Such research also will shed light on the way interest groups mobilize people to support ideas that may offer little in terms of socioeconomic benefits than providing or reinforcing a sense of in-group identity. It will be interesting to see whether the surge in the popularity of the Dixie flag will persist and provide greater exposure for other things Dixie. However, it is doubtful that business and event names with Dixie will ever surpass those that use the term "Ozark."

While technology, transportation, and education bring different groups of people closer together, they also may repel those who are resistant to change or difference. Modernity "thins" culture and makes cultural boundaries porous for different perspectives.[90] The region is more appealing for many residents, tourists, and others because it offers a unique regional identity. John Shelton Reed's "fits" or fully assimilated southerners and those who don't fit in both have a place in the Ozarks. Indeed, the motto of Eureka Springs is "Where Misfits Fit." The Ozark culture is contradictory and complex. In the future, research should address that complexity, as well as the way Ozark identity fits with other identities. For example, it is likely that Ozark identity will have to adapt as more ethnic diversity increases in the region. How will Cambodians refer to themselves as they establish themselves in various communities in southern Missouri and Northern Arkansas? Will contact with Cambodians or other groups challenge what white Ozarkians consider Ozarkian?

Researchers should track the way people regard themselves in the region according to technology, population, and other factors that have led to changes in the region. Many academics predicted the "demise" or "Californication" of the South and the Ozarks. Reed's work does show a decline in Deep South identification with the term "Dixie." I am skeptical about the decline of the South as a region. In some way, regional identity is alive and well in social networking sites such as Facebook. Likewise, the South and especially the Ozarks has hosted a number of waves of in-migrants such as the back-to-landers. Rather than killing off the native culture, the incoming people helped perpetuate old cultural practices dealing with agriculture, crafts, and music. Cultures change and adapt to emergent technologies and trends. Sometimes, interesting amalgams result.

In a more empirical way, I followed John Shelton Reed's insights and methodologies and found that the people of the Ozarks prefer to call their businesses, events, and nonprofits "Ozark" more so than any other label. Yet, I suspect, especially for Arkansas, people think of themselves as southerners, but of a different sort. They are Ozarkers, and maybe they identify more with people regardless of region who live in around or in the mountains.

In this chapter, I tried to find an answer to Woodward's question of "When will a southerner stop referring to himself as a southerner?" It seems that the term "southerner" is slippery and elusive. It means many things to many people. Mississippi author Willie Morris wrote, "I became firmly committed to the idea that the South ends where a man's feel for the guilt of the land fades away, wherever that might be."[91] I think what Morris was getting at was that the past, even in the Ozarks, is forever a part of the present and future for the South. This fluidity of time adds to the liminality of the region.

Li'l Abner the Trickster

Mythical Identity in the Ozarks

Good old boy . . . A little bit of wit, a little bit of grit, and a whole lot of shit. He's funny and he's a trickster.
—Baxter Hall and Cecil Wood

In the last chapter, I explored the way in which the identities of the South and the Ozarks are more nuanced than many people might realize. Identity is complex. One aspect of modernity is that identity or community is no longer tied to a location or even anything "real." The same modern ephemeral nature of collective identity is true for the southern identity. Reed, a sociologist who spent much of his career trying to understand the social-psychological boundaries rather than geographic ones of southerners, wrote, "The South is no longer geography—it is an attitude and a philosophy of government."[1] According to Hall and Wood, the South is unique because "the gateways to the South today are as metaphoric as they are geographic, for the South was born of myth."[2] Later, Anderson agreed with Reed that an "'imagined' south is replacing a geographic south," and in many ways, popular culture has filled the gap between the South's real and imagined worlds. Inge observed that, "It is no exaggeration to say that culture in the United States, high and low, had been obsessed with things Southern and Appalachia since the turn of the [twentieth] century."[3] Chief among the major cultural influences on the public's perception of the South for decades was Alfred Caplin's, later Al Capp's, *Li'l Abner* cartoon strip, which offered an imagined, mythical identity about mountain people, particularly those in the Ozarks.

Beginning in the 1930s, the South became a more commonplace geography in comic strips. It also was the "heyday of the hillbilly" according to historian Brooks Blevins.[4] *Li'l Abner* was so popular, especially in the 1940s-1950s, that the cartoon strip reached a worldwide audience.[5] It also was long-lived, and ran from 1934 to 1977. Thus, "Capp arguably had a profound influence on the way the world viewed the American South."[6] I would go further and argue that Capp's *Li'l Abner* and Billy DeBeck's *Snuffy Smith* shaped popular culture and opinion about the Ozarks and mountain people in general.

As a boy, Al Capp was an avid reader of southern and mountain stories, such as John Fox's *The Kentuckians* and Harold Bell Wright's *The Shepherd of the Hills*.[7] As a young man, he read Charles Dickens, Bernard Shaw, Mark Twain, William Cowper Brann, and other social critics.[8] Quite a few of the books about mountains and the South were made into silent movies that Capp had an opportunity to watch as a boy, and a hitchhiking trip he made to the Appalachians when he was 16 was influential in *Li'l Abner*'s development. His brother wrote, "When 'Li'l Abner' became a success, Alfred would resolutely maintain that the trip to Memphis was but a preliminary tour of the hillbilly country so that the future cartoonist could research the characters who wound up populating his wildly successful comic strip."[9] Last, as an adult, Capp watched vaudeville shows, such as *The Hill Billies*, that were playing in New York City in the early 1930s and also inspired *Li'l Abner*.[10]

Li'l Abner was introduced to some Arkansas and Missouri newspapers in the late 1930s. Other cartoon strips that shared space with it in some Ozark newspapers at the time were *Diana Dane, Tarzan, Scorchy Smith*, and the *Gay Thirties*. In the 1940s, *Blondie, Alley Oop*, and *Red Ryder* appeared in a number of newspapers. However, *Li'l Abner* was offered consistently over time and was quite popular in a number of newspapers in the Ozarks.

Cartoonists, both in the past and today, use comics in a variety of ways, including to parody and satirize social issues. Satire is fundamental to political cartoons. However, many cartoons have a critical edge to them that may go unnoticed by many readers/viewers (e.g., *The Smurfs*). In many ways, cartoons became an ideal way to criticize power because the messages are hidden or conveyed as metaphors. More pragmatically, cartoons avoid censorship or public outcry precisely because the "real" message is hidden. Pop culturist James Black wrote, "Comic strips offered hidden transcripts and built-in alibis for the expression of dissent during the 1950s at a time when others [media] could not."[11]

Allegories provide a form or structure within which cultures operate. Myths, folklore, and other aspects of culture associated with a group of people is the content that fills in the form. The things with which we fill our daily lives tell a great deal about who we are and what we value. Comic strips grew in popularity after World War I and became a genre that people followed and talked about with their friends and family.[12] Thus, cartoons contribute as well to a people or region's myths and folklore.

Al Capp, Billy DeBeck, and other cartoonists recognized that folklore mirrors a particular culture.[13] Indeed, Ozark folklorist Vance Randolph inspired Capp, and the two corresponded. Such stories, or folklore, offer both insiders and outsiders a way of understanding a culture. According to anthropologist Alan Dundes, we are "seeing culture from inside out" through folklore.[14] Moreover, according to sociologist Emile Durkheim, shared folk beliefs and traditions provide a group a sense of social solidarity. The various contents of which folk life consists can help researchers understand cultural boundaries, like those of the Ozarks, even better.[15] Such stories exist at the national, regional (e.g., South), state, and even such specific locales as the Ozarks.

To some extent, the state of Missouri and northern Arkansas form a distinct north-south cultural dichotomy.[16] This "middle landscape" caught the imagination of all manner of people[17] and, as a place, has inspired many of the popular cultural myths outsiders generated. Fazio wrote, "The South was seen from the outside not only as a holdover from simpler times but also as a mysterious, special entity, a repository of ancient virtues and of regional identity."[18] Perhaps this is why nonsoutherners created so many comic strips, such as *Li'l Abner*, *Snuffy Smith*, and *Pogo*. As historian Karen Cox noted, "This geography of production represents an important opportunity for historians [and other humanities scholars] to consider how perceptions of southern identity have been shaped from *outside* the region."[19]

Commercial interests also use myths to exploit regional stereotypes, such as the hillbilly, in the Ozarks and Appalachia.[20] Beverages such as Kickapoo Joy Juice or Mountain Dew, create and convey a commercial folklore through comics such as *Li'l Abner* and *Snuffy Smith*. These products' creators found it lucrative and suffered few repercussions when they depicted Ozark and Appalachian people to sell their products. Indeed, people living in the region often "bought into" the commercialized stereotypes by selling all sorts of knick-knacks to tourists. Altogether, the material culture commercial folklore created then feeds into people's collective identity even if people outside the region produced it.[21]

One of the largest commercial enterprises involving the hillbilly motif is the theme park Dogpatch, which was located near Harrison, Arkansas. In the late 1960s, Little Rock entrepreneur Jess P. Odom approached Al Capp with the idea of building a theme park in the Ozarks based on *Li'l Abner's* town of Dogpatch. Capp agreed enthusiastically, and the park opened in short order in 1968. However, some people were worried that the hillbilly-themed park would damage the work the state had done to promote its image of progress and development.[22]

The park encompassed 825 acres and included 75 buildings, a number of parks and lakes, a tram, and a number of other elements to made it on par with other theme parks, such as Six Flags. There was even a 1,500-foot ski slope and 30 alpine chalets at the associated Marble Falls Resort. In addition to the rides and other attractions, there were plans for an annual Dogpatch festival, Sadie Hawkins Day races, and other events.[23]

The California firms in charge of Dogpatch's economic plan predicted 400 thousand visitors in 1968, 800 thousand in 1972, and over 1,000,000 in 1978. The planners argued that all of these potential visitors would be a boon to the region and the state's economy. However, the visitation numbers were never as high as predicted and the park went through a number of owners before it closed in 1993.[24]

Myth of the South and Hillbillies

One of the most enduring myths in the South is the Lost Cause.[25] This particular myth is founded on the notion that there was a very old, chivalrous system in the South that was destroyed as a result of the Civil War and Reconstruction. In broader terms, the Lost Cause is a variant of the lost community theme used often to address modernity and social change.[26] Hall and Wood noted that much of what is called the "Old South" is not very old in historical terms. Indeed, much of the South was frontier until a few decades before the Civil War. Instead, what was lost and is yearned for is a rather ambiguous and ephemeral sliver of history.[27]

Part of the desire to find that Lost South was attributable to its frontier spirit. Frederick Jackson Turner focused on frontiers, which he regarded as places that lead and shape American culture. Turner's thesis has met controversy, as there is little empirical evidence to support it; however, according to cultural geographer Wilbur Zelinsky, more generally, the thesis and frontiers affected the American mythos profoundly.[28]

Folklore and mythic traditions offer insights into the way groups cope with such dilemmas and paradoxes as community and modernity.[29] Myths reified often lead to nostalgia for a false past and can feed ethnocentrism.[30] The actual term is "anemoia," which means being nostalgic for an imagined past. Anemoia focuses on the feeling that many people have that modernity is alienating, and thus they imagine a past that never existed. Many people in business, politics, and religion have capitalized on this form of nostalgia—a past imagined and often at odds with what actually *did* happen in the past. Nostalgia also can be dangerous because too many people want to "return" to that imagined past. The common American myth of the rugged individualist has done much harm to the way we regard each other and extends into various facets of government policy. In the case of the South, Hall and Wood's warning "Beware of a Southerner with something to prove" undergirds the pernicious myth of the Lost Cause.[31] Capp, who was sensitive to race and religion, was able to portray the Abners as patriots rather than Confederate sympathizers, and thereby shone light on the myth of the Lost Cause.

Often, what people understand about the South involves an interplay between myth, reality, and kinship. We even reshape our lives according to accepted myths.[32] Notions about origins, history, and mission accepted commonly may or may not be consistent with historical realities and family stories. Frequently, authors characterized these facets of mythical southern identity in various ways. For example, Hall and Wood argued that there was a southern trinity that involved three archetypal groups. The first was the well-heeled blowhards of the political and business world. Next, what would the South be without the religious rabble-rousers?[33] However, in addition to southern politicians and the rabble-rousers, a third face emerged during the Jacksonian period in American history, a common country person to whom Hall and Woods referred as the "good old boy," otherwise known as the "mean sumbitch."[34] The good ol' boy can be a trickster too. In more colorful terms, the good ol' boy trickster is "a little bit of wit/a little bit of grit/and a whole lot of shit."[35] Perhaps this is the good ol' boy to whom Robert Morris referred when he described a type of Arkansan who exhibits "saucy dialog . . . [and] crooked answers."[36]

Sometimes the good ol' boy had little wit, but made people laugh nonetheless because he was considered a fool. From such a view arose a major genre of mountain folktales and stories built around the Celtic myth, which among other things linked hillbillies to buffoonery.[37]

When the buffoonery was mixed with politics, fantastic stereotypes emerged, such as was the case in an 1852 article in the *Hannibal Journal*. While attending a meeting of Missouri Democrats for presidential candidate Franklin Pierce, the author—who was neither sympathetic to Pierce nor Democrats—listened to a lecturer who boasted that he could discern a Whig (elite class and precursor to Republicans) from a Democrat, in that Whigs had bumps on their heads, while Democrats were smooth or "flat-headed." The author accepted the lecturer's notion and argued that he thought flat-heads were prevalent throughout the South and especially in the Ozarks. The bumps indicated that their bearer aspired to higher levels of attainment, while flat-heads were content with their lot. Because the Whig sought to use all means, including public resources, to benefit his private situation, that in turn, would benefit everyone else. Specifically, as the Whig brought benefit to himself, the effect would trickle down to others, including the flat-headed Democrats. An elite, cosmopolitan attitude would spread and change the free-riding Democrat "who catches a new idea—a bump begins to sprout on his turnip shaped cranium; he sees more of life; gets the papers; his bumps grow, and finally, if he is an honest man, he becomes a Whig."[38]

In 1929, a columnist for the *Springfield Leader and Press* remarked about the practice of reporters who treated Ozarkers in stereotypical fashion as aliens, slackers, and fools. Reacting to one article that aroused his ire, he wrote: "The writer found a strange race of people [Ozarkers] not 100 miles from St. Louis and he might save railroad fare if he had looked around town a little where Ozarkers go quite frequently. To make the Ozark stories interesting we must be pictured as a different race with a different language."[39]

Arkansas historian Robert Morris noted the common practice of treating Arkansans as rubes who are "creature[s] of jokesmiths."[40] Indeed, Walter Blair indicated that many jokes arose out of stereotypes about mountain people, such as being dirty, lazy, and ignorant. He termed this genre as the Humor of the Irresponsibles, examples of which are Paul Webb's cartoon characters, *Li'l Abner* and *Snuffy Smith*.[41] Finally, Ozark commentator Fred Starr quoted from an Ozark publication: "One of the most popular numbers in the standard brands of humor has always been the hillbilly joke. The hill folk staged before a backdrop displaying a one-room shack stuck like a barnacle on a rocky hillside, with a rickety porch festooned with stone churns, skinny hounds and razorback hogs, has always been a bonanza for the joke writer."[42]

On the other side of the spectrum were romanticized Rousseauian notions of hill people as "strange wildflowers of human spirit, hardy, wayward, shy, fantastic, beautiful, and doomed to extinction."[43] For example, Morris portrayed the Arkansan as a pioneer who was exaggerated and colorful like the bear, deer, and other animals with which he associated closely.[44]

Last, there is Blair's category of humor, which concerns the notion of rugged individualists.[45] Elements in this category include a nostalgic sense of the past and even a reverence for "old-fashioned" things.

Tricksters

There are characters known as tricksters who inhabit the world of myth. Within Appalachian folklore, the trickster's role is portrayed in stories such as *The Jack Tales*.[46] In many of the Jack Tales, Jack is a trickster who uses his wits, often in dubious ways. Arthur Berger, author of *Li'l Abner: A Study in American Satire*, wrote that trickster stories in Appalachia indicate the way tricksters as *picaroons* (e.g., *Don Quixote*) rely on their smarts and deceptive powers or more often, on the winds of fortune, to get what they want.[47]

The trickster usually is insatiable and ever changing.[48] He or she tends to be a wanderer.[49] Typically, tricksters of all sorts (fools, heroes, mortals, and gods) are outsiders. Berger wrote that "the fool is almost always alienated, set apart from society."[50] A common theme for cartoonists, Capp included, is the country bumpkin, an outsider visiting an urban setting. Alternatively, city slickers are those outsiders who spend time in the country. Indeed, until Capp could populate and flesh out mythical Dogpatch, many of Li'l Abner's antics occurred outside his town.[51]

Moreover, tricksters are portrayed frequently in picaresque terms, such as villains or rogues who violate norms and rules.[52] The trickster challenges authority in folklore and myths that often showcase acceptable behaviors and what happens when the normative culture is violated.[53] Mythologist Karl Kerenyi argued, "Like every other trickster, Hermes, too, operates outside the bounds of custom and law."[54] The trickster also personifies the times when cultural norms are turned upside down and some disorder is at play. These upside-down moments or cultural inversions act not only as a social pressure release valve, but make explicit society's hierarchy and power.

The Greeks even made Hermes, a deified trickster, the "patron saint of liars and thieves." As such, deity or mortal, tricksters are ambiguous and liminal. Tricksters often possess dual aspects of nature and inversions.[55] In their articles about *Li'l Abner*, both southern cultural scholars M. Thomas Inge and James Black identified oppositional attributes associated commonly with the mountaineer identity, such as "friendly" but "vengeful."[56] Clearly, the mountaineer character is ambiguous. Similarly, Berger argued that it is difficult to classify *Li'l Abner* "fool, hero, superman, chump, greenhorn."[57]

Examples of tricksters are found throughout popular culture. There are many in literature, including Jack from *Jack and the Beanstalk*, Tom Sawyer, Huckleberry Finn, and Br'er Rabbit. Charley Chaplin, the Marx Brothers, Ferris Bueller, and Borat are some noteworthy tricksters in film. On television, tricksters such Hawkeye Pierce, Bugs Bunny, and Homer Simpson question and side-step authority in witty ways. Last, in cartoon strips, the tricksters Snuffy Smith, Blondie, and Li'l Abner have entertained readers for a long while.[58]

Li'l Abner as the Trickster

Al Capp's Li'l Abner personifies the Ozark trickster well. *Li'L Abner* was a popular cartoon about a clichéd backwoods Ozark man who lives in the mythical Dogpatch with a wide range of interesting characters. *Li'l Abner* and other cartoons offer considerable social commentary and critique. In essence, Li'l Abner was "a tool who allows Capp to judge society."[59]

The idea that Arkansans, and particularly hillbillies, can serve as tricksters is common. However, when the hillbilly trickster is added to a geographical setting steeped in paranormal beliefs and myths—where more recent legends of UFOs were emerging—the result is rather interesting.[60] In "An Open Letter to The Hill-Billies of Arkansas" written during the height of the flying saucer craze in 1950, the *Madison County Record* published a letter to the editor from Simp-Li-Me, who wrote: "Now, as to this remote controlled-saucer contraption. It is the finest method we have ever found to transport mountain joy to far places, where joy is badly needed, right over the heads of the Revvies."[61] Hillbillies, whether moonshiners or not, have a long history of skirting rules and authority figures. In this instance, moonshiners demonstrate the cleverness and humor often associated with the trickster, and these trickster qualities also appear in the comic strips during the period.

Moreover, Capp recognized the utility of using UFO stories to help flesh out contradictions in society. He did this by having aliens act almost as sociologists—as outside observers who posed awkward questions to which Li'l Abner always had a quick answer from his insider perspective. As James Black wrote, the aliens "furnished Capp with a straight man for some fine Panglossian dialectic" with overly optimistic Li'l Abner.[62] A July 10, 1950, cartoon strip features such a dialog between alien beings on a ship with Li'l Abner, who is along for the ride.[63]

Religion and race are controversial topics and were especially so during the McCarthy era. Scholar M. Thomas Inge noted that Al Capp usually steered clear of race and religion.[64] True enough, African Americans do not exist in any meaningful way in Dogpatch's world—a sad parallel to their actual representation in the Ozarks' population.[65] However, Li'l Abner, with the help of three-headed aliens or in the case of Mammy Yokum's magic, did mock authority, highlight social problems, and even offer solutions. Moreover, Capp did address racial and ethnic bigotry in meaningful ways. The Anti-Defamation League published and distributed a booklet throughout the country with Capps's cartoon strip that follows the story of Dogpatch's oval-eyed citizens (us) trying to drive square-eyed people (them) out of town. The only one who stopped the angry Dogpatch mob from harming their neighbors was Mammy Yokum, who showed that the square-eyes were humans as well.[66]

The second example of the "Idiot Era" that the aliens and *Li'l Abner* discussed concerns politics. Again, Abner is riding in a saucer with three aliens running through mountain peaks and careening through space as they all discuss political representation's nuances. According to Berger, "Capp's political philosophy and his psychology of humor are both Hobbesian."[67]

The last contradiction Abner and the aliens address is gender roles. The aliens, peering intently over their saucer at two pretty ladies sunbathing talk to Abner about what they perceive to be the idiocy of gender relations.[68]

There are other examples in *Li'l Abner* in which Capp satirizes gender roles. One such example is the Sadie Hawkins Day in Dogpatch that allowed the community to act out cultural inversions such as reversing gender roles. Both in the mythical and real worlds, holidays and celebrations often are based upon inversions of gender, class, and power.[69] Sadie Hawkins Day is an actual day described as follows: "On this day, as in Dogpatch, the girls, widows, old maids, and all unmarried who wish will be given an opportunity to chase the unmarried men down the main street."[70] The event is held

Figure 3.1 Li'l Abner and War, July 10, 1950.

Figure 3.2 Li'l Abner and Politics, July 11, 1950.

Figure 3.3 Li'l Abner and Gender, July 12, 1950.

Figure 3.4 Snuffy Smith and Crop Circles, Baxter Bulletin 2005.

on the first Saturday after November 11. From the 1930s through the 1940s, Sadie Hawkins Day events became popular in Missouri and Arkansas and even across the nation.

Li'l Abner was aware that getting married would mean that he would lose his freedom and suffer diminished masculinity. Thus, he spent many years somehow avoiding Daisy Mae's marital schemes.[71] In a sense, the Sadie Hawkins celebrations expand the trickster from the mythical Lil' Abner to all of the eligible bachelors who, like Lil' Abner, flee from being captured and "domesticated" by women.

In contrast to the way in which Capp uses Li'l Abner and the aliens to address social problems, Snuffy Smith seems more an "irresponsible character" than Li'l Abner. Two cartoon clips from 2005 and 2010 highlight the difference.[72]

We find this in the second strip:

Modernity and the Need for a Trickster

As a youth, I usually passed over *Li'l Abner* in favor of what I thought were funnier cartoons, such a *Beetle Bailey, B.C., Hagar the Horrible*, or *Snuffy Smith. Li'l Abner* simply was too complex for my taste. I was unaware of Sadie Hawkins Day when girls asked boys out. As a teenager in the early 1980s, I had the chance to visit the Dogpatch theme park. As the decades passed, I remember my visit to Dogpatch fondly, when "Daisy Mae" told me I was cute. Although the park is closed, people still go there occasionally to take eerie but beautiful pictures of the park's decaying structures. Similarly, I learned it was extremely popular to dress up as Li'l Abner or other characters

Figure 3.5 Snuffy Smith and Abduction, Baxter Bulletin 2010.

from Dogpatch, well before Cosplay was even a word.[73] I learned that Sadie Hawkins Day used to be so big that it was celebrated around the country each November.[74] In addition, a race horse was named Dogpatch, as was a US military base during the Korean conflict.[75] The Iowa town of Mount Pleasant celebrated Dogpatch Day every February.[76] School and community theaters across the country took part in *Li'l Abner* musicals and plays.[77] There was even a Miss Dogpatch USA competition to which scores of states sent their various Miss Dogpatches to compete each year.[78]

As I scanned newspapers over the decades, I sensed that all things dealing with *Li'l Abner* and Dogpatch are a shadow of what they once were. Thus, in a way, their years as a fixture in American popular culture and then their ultimate decline and demise, that of the comic strip in 1977 and the theme park in 1993, highlight the complex interplay of cultural identity and Capp's dated views about gender and his own personal history with women. Perhaps the hillbilly cliché no longer captured the imagination as it did for so many decades. Capp's health was an issue as well. Finally, he also became more conservative in his later years and even scornful of younger people, which may have hastened Li'l Abner's demise, as well as that of Mammy Yokum, who could no longer exist in Capp's world. [79]

The trickster, Li'l Abner, taps into identity and modernity in a number of ways that invite further exploration. The Ozarks hill people share the same general culture of other regions such as the Appalachians. The contours of such a general Appalachian culture are sufficiently distinct to invite characterizations in the popular culture over much of the last century and into this one with such shows as *Ozark* with Jason Bateman and Laura Linney. There is a long history of outsiders such as Al Capp defining the Appalachian people and their culture. The region's people often embraced that mountain image, but they reshaped it to fit their needs. It seems the relationship remains one-way, in that there is no dialectical feedback loop in which outsiders change their views as they learn more about those they caricaturize. Thus, Li'l Abner as a personification of outsiders' views of the region wears an ever-changing mask not of his own creation.

The comic *Li'l Abner* also is symbolic of the moral order as Capp saw it. Whether Abner becomes a "normative figure, with whom the reader can sympathize but who certainly is no model for imitation is a fool" is open to interpretation.[80] The question remains: Is Li'l Abner a fool or a trickster? Black wrote that the "Caricature, like every revolutionary, is sustained by the system it attacks."[81]

As a trickster, Li'l Abner takes on the role of a mediator of opposites—having a foot in both mainstream popular culture and civilization versus a mythical hill culture far from the city.[82] The cartoon strip also exposes the postmodern dilemma of the socially constructed version of history and that history that emerges through scholars' efforts.[83] Often, counterhistory is minimized as revisionist history because of its tendency to challenge notions of the past accepted commonly. Arts and humanities often provide "oppositional counter memories" by exposing imagined pasts to reveal those that actually occurred. Such goals counter narratives that lack introspection and context.[84] Southern writer W. J. Cash focused on history and counterhistory in his examination of the Old and New South's historical continuities.[85] As a humanistic endeavor, Arthur Berger contends, "If democracy involves, as Niebuhr claims, accepting proximate solutions for insoluble problems, then *Li'l Abner*, by ridiculing formalists and absolutists, is a good democratic strip."[86] In essence, *Li'l Abner*, like other counterhistory endeavors, seeks to challenge notions accepted commonly, and particularly those cast in absolute terms.

Like growing up, the civilizing process has a disenchanting effect on modern life and points to the need for modern day tricksters.[87] Jung wrote,

> The so-called civilized man has forgotten the trickster. He remembers him only figuratively and metaphorically, when, irritated by his own ineptitude, he speaks of fate playing tricks on him or of things being bewitched. He never suspects that his own hidden and apparently harmless shadow has qualities whose dangerousness exceeds his wildest dreams. As soon as people get together in masses and submerge the individual, the shadow is mobilized, and as history shows, may even be personified and incarnated.[88]

Cultures with a rich folkloric tradition realize the need for tricksters. However, somehow, the modern person has forgotten this archetypical character's importance. More than ever, we need a trickster to expose the ironies and contradictions inherent in modern life. Jung believed that the trickster never really goes away, but is there for us, even in the form of "annoying accidents, jinxes, gaffes, slips, and faux pas."[89]

According to Jung, modern men and women are as superstitious as were those of the past.[90] He also saw the trickster as a personified collection of a culture's traits. His assertions are untestable, but I believe certain marginalized groups function as the trickster in the way he describes. Minorities, unconventional thinkers, really anyone who defies social convention, becomes the other, and communities' members understand who they are in reference to that other.

Are the hill people so different that essentially they are outlanders in their own nation?[91] Or is the Hillbilly "doomed to extinction" as well? Really, the trickster is simply a facet of ourselves—portrayed as poor little men, as "frustrated bunglers."[92] Thus, modernity will not dispel the Arkansas trickster; she or he will reemerge over and over again.

A major issue in looking at popular culture's image of the Ozarks and its people, particularly in cartoons, is finding the work of a cartoonist of the region to compare and contrast with Al Capp's work. There are a number of famous political cartoonists, such as George Fischer, Jon Kennedy, and John Deering in Arkansas, and *New Yorker* cartoonist George Booth in Missouri. However, although few cartoonists who live in the Ozarks have depicted life there, three who lived in the region in the 1960s through the 1970s, Columba Krebs, Cat Yronwode and Ronn Foss, deserve further study.

Columba Krebs, originally Anna Belle Culverwell, finally settled in Willow Springs, Missouri after leading a rather colorful life all around the country. She was a cartoonist-painter who was deeply devoted to paranormal ideas that she shared in lectures around the country all the way back to the 1930s. Her book *Skuddabud*, a cartoon book about aliens from the planet Skuddabud that end up living on an uninhabited island on earth, was published in 1936. Over the years, she would provide illustrations and paintings for a number of paranormal and science fiction covers. Columba visited the Ozarks frequently during the 1950s and 1960s to attend Buck Nelson's annual "Spaceship Conference" in Mountain View.[93]

Cat Yronwode originally came to the Ozarks to visit Buck Nelson and Columba Krebs but found the region so beautiful she decided to stay. She was a founding member of the intentional community Garden of Joy Blues and was known for her calligraphy, maps, and drawings of the region. Later, she became a well-known authority on comic books[94] and was coauthor of a book with Trina Robbins entitled *Women and the Comics*.

Ronn Foss was an avid fan of comic books as a high schooler in the 1960s.[95] Eventually, he ended up creating several fanzines and comics. In the early 1970s, he moved to the Missouri Ozarks and was part of the countercul-ture there. He also was editor of *Your Times X-Press*, a counterculture newslet-ter that provided information to communal folks in the region. He also drew pictures of people and events in the Ozarks, such as the Hot Mulch Band.[96]

Eureka Springs,
Where Misfits Fit

By its nature, the metropolis provides what otherwise could be given
only by traveling; namely, the strange.
—Paul Tillich

There are towns that are quaint, odd, idiosyncratic, or even just plain weird.
It is not easy to tell whether some towns are really odd or whether eccentricity is a gimmick to lure tourists. One candidate for a town that I believe
is truly quirky is Eureka Springs, in Carroll County, an Ozark county that
borders Missouri to the north, while its immediate neighbor to the nest is
Benton County, an Ozark county that borders Oklahoma. In some ways,
Eureka Springs is similar to Hot Springs, a resort town to the south and also
in Arkansas. Both towns have natural springs and tourists.[1] Both have colorful histories. However, Eureka Springs is unique compared to most places,
including Hot Springs, in that eccentricity and creativity permeate much of
the little alpine town.

One theoretical thread that this chapter follows is the role of place-making
in understanding Eureka Springs. Place-making is a dialectical process in
which a particular geography shapes people, and the converse. Theology professor Douglas Burton-Christie wrote that place-making entails geography,
autobiography, and metaphor.[2] The Ozarks are interesting and picturesque
geographically. However, what makes them so compelling is that people
and folklore are intertwined so closely with the land. A place's meaning and
importance may vary greatly between people and groups.

Place-making involves the interplay between geography and sociology.[3] Part of that interplay involves what Howard Campbell called "slant-wise" behavior in ambiguous or liminal places.[4] Slant-wise behavior may mean losing a past identity and taking on a newer identity linked to the Ozarks and in this case Eureka Springs. Thus, place-making can be deeply personal, as what we consider most important about a place has its origins in our day-to-day lives and experiences.[5]

The connections between place-making and psychology are obvious, such as identity formation and geography. One area of psychology that is especially well suited in understanding the uniqueness and metaphysical feel of Eureka Springs is how physical environment contributes to a place influencing people's reports of anomalous activities. After surveying personal stories and related stories of adventurers and explorers, Peter Suedfeld and John Geiger found that many people reported feeling some type of "presence" while out in the wilderness and particularly in the mountains.[6] That extraordinary feeling is expected in church or religious settings, where the numinous Other tends to reside. However, researchers were able to recreate such sensations through experimental settings where props were set a bit awry, lighting was off, and other artificial manipulations that induced subjects to "feel" the presence of something or someone in the room with them, even when there wasn't anyone there but the subject.[7] Although the terrain of Eureka Springs is not as extreme as that of the Himalayas, it is mountainous. In addition, the layout of the town is the definitely a bit awry. As Sean Wilsey noted about the eccentric town of Marfa in west Texas, even "mundane interactions unexpectedly take turns for the surreal."[8] All these things may contribute to making the place seem magical to many people.

History

Cora Pinkley-Call, author of *Stair-Step-Town*, wrote that in the year that Eureka Springs was named, the twenty families that set up camp there had little idea what was to come. The land was too hilly for more than a few houses, and the water the first settlers used to make coffee and cook soon would attract long lines of people seeking perceived relief from their various maladies.[9] Nonetheless, the history of Eureka Springs begins in 1880 with the fluke find of the supposedly all-healing spring water, and in short order, newspapers across the nation wrote about the amazing qualities of the water in this remote spot. One of the more extravagant accounts of the water in Eureka Springs appeared in the *Springfield Leader and Press*:

> You drink the water as you would wine. You drink it because you love it. You drink it and bathe in it, and declare there is no such other nectar on earth. You drink it, and feel its life coursing through your body. You drink it, and youth comes again, with all its gladness and strength. Disease is scattered as the sun scatters the night. You are well once more, and want to work and play as you did years ago.[10]

With descriptions such as the one above, it is no surprise that in the course of one year, Eureka Springs became a health resort boomtown. One commentator wrote, "I hardly know how to describe the place; it is so different from anything I ever saw; it is a city of log cabins, tents, and fine hotels which seem to have sprung up by magic."[11] Another writer noted, "A few months ago the gulches and hills about Eureka Springs was a 'waste of howling wilderness,' inhabited by bear, deer, and other wild game, but as if by magic a city sprung up, numbering now five thousand inhabitants."[12] In the same year, daily coaches began to ferry people back and forth to the town. Eureka even opened a public skating rink.[13]

Often, boomtowns attract unpleasant people, but a commentator reassured the reader that was not the case for Eureka Springs. He wrote that the casual outsider might have the impression that the town was filled with "all manner of out-breaking reprobates, rowdies, rascals, thieves, robbers, gamblers and drunkards. Doubtless all these are represented, but not very noticeably. Grey beards and baldheaded prevail."[14] Apparently, the town was overrun with old men of humble means searching for the fountain of youth. He warned that one should not scorn the testimonies of the healing properties of the water "unless one is anxious for a good drubbing." One Kansan decided not to heed the warning and wrote that the town was full of "Arkansawyers" who were "leeches" to tourists who were "suckers." He wrote: "The water in Eureka Springs is the only thing that's free. I have been accustomed all my life to living in a country where the air was free also, but at Eureka they don't have any. Visitors breathe the gas that escapes from the mouths of the natives as they praise the imaginary virtues of the most desolate country on earth."[15]

In addition to attracting people seeking relief from various ailments by drinking the spring water, the town attracted a number of homeopathic healers, quacks, and medicine scalpers.[16] These various groups fought each other but really had little regard for mainstream medical doctors as "they denounced all pathic doctors as murderers."[17] In trying to explain what caused the water to have such healing properties, some people claimed that as it coursed around the roots of pine trees, the healing qualities of the pines, hills, or radiation somehow leached into the water.

Most of the trees were cut down in the rush to build up the town and offer two-thirds of its residents "box huts." All this razing and wide-scale rapid development led to growing concerns about sanitation and contamination of the springs.[18] The *Chetopa Advance,* a Kansas newspaper, described the town structures this way: "In architecture Eureka Springs is a law unto itself, and many of the dwellings are rude structures temporary and not even comfortable."[19]

By May 1880, Little Rock's *Daily Arkansas Gazette* reported that there were 10,000 inhabitants in Eureka Springs.[20] Another paper put the population at 15,000 during May.[21]

Such growth in Eureka Springs led to one of the first complaints against unbridled progress in the region,[22] and indeed, Eureka Springs had issues in its formative year. As one medical doctor reported, "If one's case is pronounced incurable, then Eureka is the place. The consequence is thousands of poor, deluded mortals spend their last dollar to get here, live in misery and squalid wretchedness while here, and return home in disgust and disappointment."[23]

Eureka Springs became more settled around the turn of the twentieth century, when people from around the country and foreign countries visited the town of 4,000 for the healing waters.[24] Beginning in the summer of 1913, an advertisement for the Basin Park Hotel grew over the years to become one of the town's many slogans—"Switzerland of America."[25] By 1914, there were approximately 5,000 residents and 50,000 visitors annually.[26] However, the town "barely survived World War I," and "by the 30s Eureka was looking pale indeed. By 1940 only the ghost of the gay old days remained—indeed ugly, vacant buildings standing like scarecrows."[27]

An influx of retirees flooded the area after World War II. Many people read Marge Lyon's column in the *Chicago Tribune* that touted Eureka Springs—so much so, the town added "Little Chicago" to its long list of nicknames.[28] Some

Figure 4.1 "Sweet Spring, Eureka Springs, Ark." Postcard of photograph by Lucien Gray, early 20th century.

early Bohemians who sought "establishment of a magazine for the Ozark area and continued plans concerning the Ozarks art colonies planted the seeds for Eureka Springs' rebirth."[29] By the late 1940s, Louis and Elsie Freund, both natives of Missouri and well-known artists, established the Art School of the Ozarks and also helped establish an artist colony in the town.[30]

Eureka Springs Today

To obtain a better understanding of Eureka Springs in the past few decades, I read hundreds of recent articles about the town. After reviewing them, three themes emerged. The first is that Eureka Springs has a dual personality that often manifests as a schism between the people in the core of the town and those who live on the outskirts.[31] The second is that Eureka Springs is a quirky and creative place. The third is that there is something mystical about Eureka Springs that leads many people to believe that the town is a center of energy.

Dual Personality

One facet that many observers noted right away was that the town has a dual identity. City clerk Mary Jean Sell called the town "fractured and fractious."[32]

Some of that discord may be attributable to competing visions of the "upscale resort" or "religious Mecca" sides of the town.[33] Many commentators also noted that there is a fundamentalist and antigay and a progay schism.[34] There also is the mainstream folks versus "yuppie culture [which] has invaded even these hills." [35] Even what appears to be a contradiction in terms, hippy capitalists, such as former mayor Richard Shoeninger, who is a motorcycle freak and anarchist, invites debate.[36]

The newspaper articles point out a schism between the town proper, with its many counterculture in-migrants, and the town's outskirts retirees and more conservative out-of-staters occupy.[37] Outside the town, the *Passion Play* is a major tourist attraction for evangelicals and fundamentalists. The same is true of the *Christ of the Ozarks* located on the town's outskirts. Gerald Smith, the founder of the *Passion Play* and the *Christ of the Ozarks* was a well-known conservative, America-Firster, and anti-Semite who moved to Eureka Springs in the late 1960s. Many leaders in the town fawned over him and his projects and considered him largely a town benefactor. The city Chamber of Commerce offered a declaration of their gratitude to him that led Georgia Stratton Ziffzer, a former teacher, Peace Corps volunteer, and the Chamber of Commerce treasurer, to resign. The mild-mannered Ziffzer worried that Eureka Springs's full embrace of Smith, someone she considered a bigot, would ruin her beloved town's reputation.[38] Ironically, many of the people who worked in the *Passion Play*, such as actors and set designers, held political and social sentiments opposite those of the founder, his cadre, and the tourists who attended the event.

Whatever Bohemian class that existed expanded greatly with the hippies' arrival in the early 1970s. Many of these in-migrants were back-to-the-landers and other communally oriented people with relaxed and liberal personalities. On the other hand, development and money making are very important as well. Despite their differences, both groups coexist and work together, particularly to attract tourist dollars. That cooperative spirit has led to many conferences that cater to a wide range of tastes. For example, in addition to the UFO Conference, there are conferences each year about mushrooms, paranormal activities, and bikers, as well as LGBT events.

With respect to politics, Eureka Springs is deeply progressive. Looking at the Federal Election Commission's report for the city, most of the $43,295 in contributions between 2017 and 2018 were to progressive causes. One of the major recipients was Act Blue, which received 56 percent of all contributions on the part of Eureka Springs contributors. By comparison, for the few conservative recipients, the donations were larger, but vastly fewer. Many of the progressive contributions were for candidates and causes in other states and at the national level. Thus, many Eureka Springs residents seem to be very engaged in all levels of politics.[39]

In addition to civic engagement, the town is known as a haven for creative types. Richard Florida devotes a good deal of his book to the argument that one vital ingredient in making a place livable and thriving is creativity.[40] What fosters creativity in communities in part is that different people come together to share ideas. The question of diversity in the Ozarks or even much more broadly the South usually focuses on racial diversity. American geography often is racialized, in which rurality is white and urbanity is African American. However, what makes the Ozarks unique is the region's stark whiteness—both in its cities and rural communities. In 1959, Charles Morrow Wilson wrote: "The loss of the Negro was unquestionably the gravest sociological loss suffered by the Ozarks region."[41] Ironically, whites seemed unaware that they shared much with their former African American neighbors in the Ozarks and even in the South overall.[42] The region became one of many areas in the United States that sociologist James Loewen calls "Sundown Towns" because African Americans were warned not to be in town after the sun went down.[43] In fact, as W. J. Cash noted, "although there had been few slaves in the mountains, he had acquired a hatred and contempt for the Negro even more virulent than that of the common white of the lowlands."[44] Little has changed with respect to diversity, and in some cases, it has become even worse with the emergence of racist communities in the 1980s.[45]

Although the Ozarks is among the racially homogenous regions in the country, the area is not homogenous in other ways. It is a region that appeals to nonconformists, communards, bohemians, gays and lesbians, and other people marginalized elsewhere in the country. The same is true for Eureka Springs. The town is a place that has attracted, and continues to attract, all sorts of interesting people, such as Frank and Jesse James, Carrie Nation, and more recently, actor Tim Curry.[46]

Eureka Springs has experienced some recent conflicts, particularly with respect to LGBT rights, but most town leaders realize that being inclusive is good for business, and the data suggest that Carroll County is more attractive to same-sex couples. Among all households in the county, it had a larger percentage of same-sex couples in both 2000 and 2010 than is the case for other

	Number Same Sex 2000	% Same Sex 2000	Number Same Sex 2010	% Same Sex 2010
Central	1,072	24.2	1,317	31.1
Delta	677	15.3	520	12.3
Ouachitas	536	12.1	425	10.1
Ozarks	1,085	24.5	1,151	27.2
Carroll County	78	7.2% of Ozarks	112	9.7% of Ozarks
River Valley	407	9.2	398	9.4
Timberlands	645	14.6	415	9.8
Arkansas	4,422	99.9	4,226	99.9

Table 4.1. Same Sex Couples in Arkansas, 2000 and 2010

Arkansas counties. Underscoring the county's level of diversity, it ranked in 38th place in the US in LGBTQ representation. Moreover, the Ozarks are more LGBTQ inclusive than are most of the other regions in the state. There was a higher percentage of same-sex couples in the Ozarks than in other regions in 2000 (24.5 percent), while the central region was a close second at 24.2 percent. By 2010, the central region reached 31.1 percent of all same sex couples, and the Ozarks had 27.2 (see table 4.1).[47]

Fortunately, there are pockets of intense and diverse social interaction in the Ozarks. These are known as "free places," where people have the chance to meet all sorts of other people in public.[48] Indeed, as stated above, theologian Paul Tillich argued that "the metropolis provides what otherwise could be given only by traveling; namely the strange."[49] In an interview about the town, one woman said, "This is a polyglot community, a micro-metropolis. It's different from other towns in northwest Arkansas."[50] Such "polyglot" towns are places that allow people to explore freely and perhaps develop different ways of thinking about, and reconnecting with, past ideas. Evans and Boyte wrote that free spaces are "dynamic, foster counter-cultural movements."[51] Eureka Springs is such a place. A *genius loci*, or some sort community spirit can even arise in places that have a bit of conflict, are inclusive, and allow for public eccentricity.[52]

Ralph Turner coined the term *communitas*, which refers to moments when social differences do not matter to participants and they become more connected with each other. He wrote that "prophets and artists tend to be liminal and marginal people" and that these people fill the ranks of the creative class. These 'threshold people' and places exist between established, routine reality and something more transcendent." Turner continued to explain that *communitas* "generates imagery and philosophical ideas." But *communitas* is elusive. It seems the more people search for something special or liminal, the harder it is to find, even when such things or moments are manufactured.[53]

A Quirky and Creative Place

All sorts of characters, such as public characters and counterculture types, play roles in creating unique places. The town may even become a character in the story. Interesting towns have interesting people. Some of these interesting people, following Jane Jacobs's term, are "public characters."[54] A public character is a person who is a connector or brings people from various backgrounds together. One such public character is longtime resident Crescent Dragonwagon, who told a reporter that Eureka Springs was the "strangest small town."[55] Capturing the essence of the town has been difficult. It has been referred to as Little Switzerland, Stair-Step-Town, and Up-and-Down Town.[56] Indeed, the town's current motto showcases this very theme: "Where Misfits Fit." Some of these articles refer to the various eccentrics who live in the town. Like Great Britain, eccentricity is not scorned, and eccentrics are very much a part of the community.

Perhaps the idea that Eureka Springs is an energy vortex is sufficiently quirky. However, I think the town is unusual for other reasons too. Eureka Springs is filled with incongruous and contradictory cultures,[57] such as bikers and gays,[58] social liberals and the devout,[59] and hippies and fundamentalists.[60] These incongruent cultures interact in ways that add to the town's uniqueness (e.g., bikers and UFO abductees). In a town of only 2,000, 10 to 20 percent of residents are artists, and yet ministers of all stripes make up 20 percent of the population.[61]

Another ingredient in the recipe of the town's quirkiness is that it doesn't really look like other American towns. Otto Rayburn wrote that his town was "a crazy quilt [. . .] made up of pieces arranged without pattern or order."[62] The town leaders may not have read Jane Jacobs's book *The Death and Life of Great American Cities*, but they were wise to recognize the value of Eureka Springs's mixed architecture, especially its many older buildings.[63] One of the town's monikers, "Little Switzerland," is fitting because of its European

Figure 4.2 "Spring Street, Eureka Springs, Ark." Postcard by Hawley & Co., early 20th century.

ambiance.[64] Then there is the town's hodge-podge or haphazard plan.[65] Reporter Keith McCanse wrote in 1923:

> There isn't a straight street nor a square street corner in Eureka Springs. It is said that cowpaths were the cause of the crookedness of the streets of Boston. If any animal is to be held responsible for the unusual character of the streets of Eureka Springs it must be the snake for the streets of this resort city, wind and twist all over the steep side of the mountain on which the city is built.[66]

Urbanist Jane Jacobs recognized how important streets are in shaping a town's identity. She wrote, "Impersonal city streets make anonymous people."[67] In other words, interesting streets make for interesting people. In Eureka Springs, there are 360 intersections, only one of which includes a right angle.[68] More generally, places like Eureka Springs that are filled with contradictions and anomalies generate eccentric spaces.[69] According to noted religious historian Mircea Eliade, what emerges in some cases is something more sublime.[70]

Author Eric Weiner argued that "genius places" are havens for odd people to come together and share new ideas.[71] Towns like Eureka Springs are built in part on fuzzy rules that dilute or "thin" the day-to-day structure of community and open up pockets of ambiguity or liminality, and it is that ambiguity that can attract creative folks who think in novel, occasionally quirky, ways. Lyn Lofland wrote, "Eccentrics . . . appear to have no conception of how one is 'supposed' to act in the city, but . . . this ignorance maybe more apparent than real. It may be, in fact, that they discovered a great urban secret: in the city, he who behaves most oddly, is often treated most kindly."[72] Eccentrics, then, become public characters who attract like-minded people, tourists, and others to a place.

Fred E. H. Schroeder, author of *Outlaw Aesthetics: Arts and the Public Mind*, argued that towns can be typified. One type of town he discussed was a subtype of the tourist town he called the arts center.[73] Eureka Springs is a tourist town and the history and data also suggest that Carroll County, and by inference, Eureka Springs, is a haven for Bohemians. Artist havens have the curious quality where the inhabitants become the art and vice versa. Sean Wilsey noted that what described the quirky west Texan artist colony of Marfa best was that it was "a work of art that was not graphic but demographic."[74] Such may be the case for Eureka Springs.

In the 1930s, WPA muralist Louis Freund and his wife, Elsie, started the Summer Art School in Eureka Springs.[75] In the 1950s, historian/folklorist Otto Rayburn noted that the town was a "Writers and Artists' Mecca." Vance Randolph, another Ozark folklorist, also lived in the town.[76] From the 1960s to the 1970s, hippies, back-to-the-landers, and others swept into the Ozarks and Eureka Springs. Louis Freund reported to Ruth Weinstein McShane that Eureka Springs citizens were really worried about all the new in-migrants: "The fear that they would be murdered in their beds was prevalent among many locals of Eureka Springs during the hippie invasion of that Arkansas town. Louis and his wife Elsie, together with several others, served as advocates of the hippies through an organization known as the Brotherhood Coop."[77]

By the 2000s, the result was that there were "more artists, writers and ponytails per capita than most other places."[78] A decade later, resident Lyla Allison reported to Dianne Keaggy, "The environment here is so creative it just makes people want to learn new things."[79] The level of creativity that is manifested in all sorts of interesting endeavors made each visit I had to the town like it was my first visit.

It long has been observed that the arts and other creative endeavors usually are found in urban areas. Thus, the central region, with Little Rock as its hub, has 24.2 percent of the share of the state's creative people and the Ozarks, 21.2 percent. Both regions are slightly lower than the 25.6 percent

	All	# Cultural Creatives	% Cultural Creatives	# Bohemian	% Bohemian
Central	301,585	72,965	24.2	2,950	0.98
Delta	173,255	27,670	16.0	894	0.51
Ouachitas	144,870	27,280	18.8	874	0.60
Ozarks	324,820	70,585	21.7	2,559	0.79
Carroll County	12,045	3,110	17.5	155	1.3
River Valley	135,355	24,385	18.0	635	0.47
Timberlands	162,370	24,400	15.0	674	0.42
Arkansas	1,241,955	263,055	21.2	10,701	0.86
USA	141,800,515	36,333,695	25.6	1,618,588	1.1

Table 4.2. Cultural Creatives & Bohemian Classes in Arkansas, 2007-11

for the United States. However, what is interesting is that 1.3 percent of the people in Carroll County are classified as Bohemian, which is above the 1.1 percent for the United States. Thus, the data suggest that the Ozarks is a region of high creativity, and Carroll County is its epicenter (see table 4.2).

Mystical Attraction

As noted often in nature-based religions, some places are considered inherently mystical or spiritual in their nature.[80] These locations are centered on geographic features such as mountains or water. Such is the case for Eureka Springs, where much has been written about the town's spiritual or mystical draw. For example, consider this quote about Eureka Springs: "Locals say the town has a mystical pull, that it grabs a hold of some people and won't let go."[81] Resident Ken Rundel told Anderson that Eureka Springs was "a magical world in the North West corner of Arkansas."[82] Mary Springer, also a resident, told Mehta, "There's something really magnetic about the place."[83] Perhaps some people feel that the place has a sense of timelessness or the town is like a time capsule.[84]

Many people believe that Eureka Springs actually has magnetic properties that bring people together.[85] Some reporters have written that it is astrological—alignment lures people with "stronger and creative personalities.[86] One reporter noted that Eureka Springs, like its cousin Sedona, is full of coincidences and epiphanies by nature.[87] Other writers, such as Erick Weiner, do not believe it is as much a mystical energy, but the town's people and culture.[88]

The idea that Eureka Springs, Sedona, and other such places have some concentration of energy, or a vortex, that makes each unique is a popular notion among the more paranormal minded. This idea originates with paranormal author and therapist Dick Sutphen, who, according to travel reporter Wallace Immen, wrote, "If you believe the theory, this valley [Boynton Canyon in Sedona, Arizona] is one of the primary power points of Earth, creating beams of energy that Sutphen describes as the perfect runway beacons for alien spacecraft."[89]

Apparently, Sutphen's book *Sedona: Psychic Energy Vortexes* introduced the vortex concept that the paranormal community later would accept widely.[90] However, despite considerable literature on the topic, vortex as a concept remains vague, and even the definitions given are contradictory. Energy vortices are thought to exist in such places as the Great Pyramids, Stonehenge, and Sedona. These spots energize those who enter them and "draw you back."[91] The New Age crowd has recognized this power as a center of mystical earth energy "vortices," but they often are tourist traps as well.[92] There also are other types of vortices, such as the water vortex that Eureka Springs is thought to possess.[93]

The folklore surrounding the water's magical properties derives from the late nineteenth century, and town leaders recognize its economic potential. With respect to Eureka Springs, Uhlenbrock wrote, "And the town born on magical strength of spring water still caters to those seeking metaphysical healing. You can buy new age crystals and herbal supplies. Spas, healers, and 'wellness' centers offer therapeutic massage, reflexology, reiki, polarity balance and ortho-bionomy."[94] Indeed, the town proper is a dazzling marketplace of metaphysical and artistic goods and services.

Concluding Remarks

According to German historian Oswald Spengler, the primary difference between a town and a village is that towns have a soul.[95] In less theological terms, perhaps Spengler meant that because of their scale and diversity, towns have personalities. In a more sociological sense, a town has a sense of shared identity. In contrast, it has become trendy for various companies and organizations to create a sense of what each community seems to be through some set of quantitative measures. The goal of several rankings is to find the right formula for what makes a town a good place to live. The rankings range simply from looking at home prices and several other indicators to very complicated, research-driven models. However, most rankings are unlikely to consider such qualitative measures as shared identity or characteristics as quirkiness.

Do moneymaking events that are produced well offer participants some level of liminality? Perhaps one reason they may not is that liminality does not follow a recipe; it is spontaneous and fleeting. Furthermore, liminal events cannot be manufactured—they happen on their own. It is a balancing act between authenticity and towns' continuous efforts to find a niche that makes them sufficiently unique to attract tourists.

There has long been consensus in a variety of newspaper articles across the nation that Eureka Springs is a special place. However, does the hyper-real side of business in the town transform Eureka Springs into something inauthentic? One reporter wrote: "When you get to Eureka Springs you discover that the whole town is a caricature" of a hillbilly place or something out of *Li'l Abner*.[96]

Eureka Springs showcases some aspects of Ozarkian identity discussed elsewhere in this book. No place is just one thing, and that is especially true for the Ozarks.

The friction between conservative folks and more forward thinkers in Eureka Springs suggests that place-making is a contested practice. Eureka Springs's unique nature is a reflection of that fight between the past and future. Blevins used the metaphor of "Janus-head" to refer to the split between the "real" Arkansas Ozarks and the mythical Ozarks.[97] Hall and Wood used the same metaphor earlier to make a broader point that the South possesses different identities that often are contradictory. They wrote of the "Janus-faced Southern psyche of love and hate, sin and atonement."[98] Woodward tied the Janus-faced motif to history: "Myths that support the notion of a distinctive Southern culture tend to be Janus-faced, presenting both an attractive and unattractive countenance. The side they present depends on which way they are turned and who is manipulating them."[99] Eureka Springs is an excellent case study that highlights the tension in the Ozarks, and even more generally in the South, between the past and the future.

One of lessons of Eureka Springs is that much like liminality, creativity cannot be manufactured. Some things, such as diverse groups of people, public spaces, and perhaps even a touch of patchouli go a long way to fostering creativity. Theologian Paul Tillich noted, "By its nature, the metropolis provides what otherwise could be given only by traveling; namely, the strange."[100] Eccentric places attract eccentric people—people willing to live and think in the margins.

5

Close Encounters
of the Ozark Kind

Doctors here reported a severe epidemic of sunburned tonsils in Mountain Home among people who have been spending the last few days gaping at the sky in hopes of seeing one of those flying saucers.
—Peter Shiras, Baxter Bulletin, July 11, 1947[1]

This study began when I learned that there were Library of Congress (LoC) transcripts of Arkansans who reported witnessing paranormal phenomena, such as unidentified flying objects (UFOs), in the Ozarks.[2] Later, I learned that Ozarkians have a long history of reporting all sorts of paranormal activity. Although not in the Ozarks, in 1897, two constables in Hot Springs reported seeing and cigar-shaped airship and met its occupants a bearded man and a woman. The man was visiting the area and but was returning to Nashville.

In his book *The Trickster and the Paranormal*, George Hansen wrote, "The paranormal, and the supernatural are fundamentally linked to destructuring, change, transition, disorder, marginality, the ephemeral, fluidity, ambiguity, and the blurring of boundaries."[3] Later, he asserted that UFOs and angels are transitional beings between our mundane world and something more otherworldly and mystical. In much of what I would learn about both aliens and their enthusiasts, the trickster concept seems to fit well.

In June 1947, Oregonian Kenneth Arnold started the first wave of reports of flying saucers.[4] One month later, the *Blytheville Courier* ran a story entitled "Farmer near Fayetteville Reports Saucers Flying Low on 2 Different Days." In the same month, a cylinder-shaped object was reported that "looked like airplanes without windows, wings, or tails" in the southeast Missouri town

Figure 5.1 North West Arkansas Times, "As They Might Appear Over Fayetteville," July 7, 1947, 1.

of Morehouse.[5] Another man from Pattonville, Missouri, saw a silver-gray circular object with a propeller that "kept turning in the manner of an airplane doing a slow roll.[6]

Between the late 1940s and mid-1950s, major newspapers in the Ozarks offered readers reports, stories, and opinions about the flying-saucer craze, which even extended into the mythical Ozark realm of Li'l Abner cartoons.[7] Another piece to this story is that for decades, Eureka Springs has hosted one of the largest paranormal and UFO conferences in the United States. Thus, I will explore why paranormal beliefs, particularly those about UFOs and aliens, flourish in the Ozarks.

The point of this chapter is not to debate whether UFOs exist, or even more broadly, whether paranormal phenomena are real. Instead, it is intended to offer insights into who UFO enthusiasts are as a group. I also consider the role of Ozark geography as a key element in fostering greater acceptance of paranormal beliefs. It is likely that people in the Ozarks have a tendency to draw from past narratives that they find are a way to understand unexplainable modern phenomena. Scholars in general have found that cultures use folk narratives often to interpret anomalous experiences.[8] Specifically, before the 1940s, people reported seeing UFOs or aliens, but they tended to use different words and ideas suitable for the times in which they lived, such as fairies, dancing lights, foxfire, and other terms and phrases to describe such extraordinary situations. Similarly, people today use more contemporary words and phrases that fit with the popular culture to make sense of phenomena such as UFOs.

I relied on a wide variety of sources to understand UFOs and their enthusiasts. Several interview transcripts from the LoC were reviewed. Survey data provided insights about the characteristics of paranormal beliefs and experiences. The National UFO Reporting Database, as well as websites devoted to hauntings and humming sounds, gave me a sense of the geographic distribution of paranormal reports within the state. Last, I used my observations at the 2016 annual conference in Eureka Springs to describe UFO enthusiasts and their culture.

UFOs and Ozark Folk Knowledge

Sociologists and anthropologists share a common disciplinary history as well as an interest in folklore and folk traditions. This shared interest between disciplines extends into the study of UFOs as well. Saliba argued:

> One of the most common approaches in sociology and anthropology is to examine UFO accounts as integral parts of society and/or culture. The underlying assumption is that UFO beliefs come into being and flourish in a culture that is congenial to their existence and draw their materials from already existing traditions. UFOs must be related to the matrix in which they occur and thrive.[9]

Similarly, many scholars have suggested that UFO narratives serve as a modern form of folklore.[10] Peckham (1950) noted that UFOs fit into a theme in general folklore, following Stith Thompson's index, D-1520—"Magic object affords miraculous transportation."[11] Thompson argued that "in an overall sense the UFO phenomena keeps its face pointed in two directions: events in time and space that seem to defy conventional explanations, and toward the symbolic/mythic milieu arising in and around these events."[12] Religious studies scholar Michael Kinsella wrote, "Legends as a folklore genre represent communal efforts to adapt old customs and beliefs to new situations. Simultaneously, legends frame emergent customs and beliefs by placing them in a historic continuum, thereby connecting the activities, behaviors, and beliefs of individuals and communities in the present to those in the past."[13] Thus, UFO stories offer the student a rare opportunity to witness the emergence of modern folklore out of earlier traditions.

Swedish folklorist Carl Wilhelm von Sydow proposed that folklore, like anything biological, adapts and changes to its environment. He referred to these cultural variants as "oicotypes."[14] Later, folklorist E. Joan Wilson Miller argued that the folk tales of the Ozark region do fit with von Sydow's concept of oicotypes. In other words, the Ozarks were producing new variations on traditional folkloric themes.[15]

Perhaps UFO narratives appeal to Ozarkians because they live in a region with a long history of friction and uncertainty about various aspects associated with modernity. Such paranormal phenomena and encounters fit well in the realm of trickster.[16] Folktales, legends, and UFO stories offer a way to explain social change and crises.[17] Blevins characterized Ozarkians as Janus-faced figures who are caught between a past based largely on stereotypes (e.g., rugged individualism, slow-minded, socially isolated), and the promise of the future, where people are more than ever connected with each other and more reliant on modern technology.[18]

Indeed, the Ozarks has a rich oral and literary history about paranormal beliefs. One Ozark newspaper article from 1897 linked the mystique of the Ozarks with earlier Native American legends.[19] That year, law officers saw an airship in Hot Springs. The ship landed, and the officer talked with a bearded man, most likely Professor A.W. Barnard, who was accompanied by a woman. The man mentioned that he had wanted to try the hot springs but he had to get back to Nashville for an exposition. Other people reported the airship as it traveled through the state and back to Tennessee. The airship and passengers, even though of this world, captured the imagination of many people and were the subject of many newspaper articles and even a poem.[20]

According to Underwood and Underwood, authors of the 2012 book *Forgotten Tales of Arkansas,* "a culture built on equal parts folklore and facts, stories and statistics. Where ghosts still haunt with unbridled vigor and tales of superstitious old-timers are faithfully retold to shape a new generations' worldview."[21] Throughout the book, the authors report a number of tales from the Ozarks that involve magical water, extraordinary mountains that change the nature of matter, monsters, and UFOs. It also may be the case that such narratives foster, shape, or reinforce one's identity. Further, Steward, Shrivers, and Chasteen report that metaphysical narratives following Erving Goffman's framing concept shape both individual and collective identity.[22]

One of the first writers to document some of the Native American legends in the Ozarks was James William Buel in 1880.[23] Many of the stories involve supernatural phenomena, often linked to certain mountains, caves, and springs. He wrote that "the superstitions which the wild and lonesome forests created in him [the Native American of the Ozarks] are worthy of perpetuation."[24] Buel's use of the Ozark term in the title and throughout the stories had a broader reach since most of the stories are actually located in Hot Springs and the Ouachitas. However, a sense of the geography and paranormal experience is accepted early on: "The wrath of the mountain and the elf of the valley spoke to them [Native Americans] in the whispering winds."[25] Thus, according to Buel, geography shapes a culture's beliefs, and those beliefs need to be passed on to newer generations.

Wilson's 1935 book, *Backwoods America*, discusses various interesting stories and superstitions Ozarkians hold. One of the major sections in his book addresses signs of impending death such as "sassafras wood crackles and splinters while burning," or "a rooster crows or a fox barks near a sick room," or "one sees his reflection in a house where death is."[26] Later, in *Ozark Magic and Folklore*, Randolph devoted an entire chapter to the topic of folk beliefs and superstitions about death and burial customs.[27] In one of the LoC transcripts from the Arkansas Ozarks, a 23-year-old man talked about using signs to tell when to plant his garden. He said, "Well, I knowed quite a few people that went by the signs, but they're dead now." Later, he admitted that he thought garden success had more to do with soil than signs.[28]

Monsters figure heavily in Ozark folklore, and Underwood and Underwood noted, "The Trantrabobus is the name given by Ozark hill folks to any needed monsters or devil creature."[29] One of the better-known stories of monsters in the Ozarks are those about the White River Monster, which date back to the Civil War. Another water monster is the Heber Springs Water Panther. There even is an Ozark Yeti known as the Peter Bottom cave monster.

Wilson (1935) reported that Ozarkians believe in ghosts and that they can be killed with silver bullets. Further, astral movement is highlighted in a superstition in which "in the Ozarks, many cover mirrors at night. This ensures that their souls will not wander into the mirror and become trapped there forever."[30] Two girls in the LoC transcripts mentioned other paranormal activities, including premonitions, while in another LoC transcript, a 77-year-old man reminisced that he and his father wore charms around their necks to ward off a disease that many of his neighbors had caught.[31] Underwood and Underwood wrote about the ghosts at the Crescent Hotel in Eureka Springs.[32] As for the occult, Wilson wrote, "Tales of witchcraft are as common as oak leaves."[33]

Prior to the 1940s, people did not really have words for UFOs, but they were able to explain odd things in the sky in a fashion that made sense for their time and place. Around 1910, a disk was observed in the sky in Kirksville, which is located in northeast Missouri.[34] Twenty years later "Grey entities" were reported on a farm near the Ozark town of Piedmont, but similar reports went back to the 1850s.[35] Much like Valle, and Thompson, Randolph noted that in ghost stories, such as those that refer to "Indian lights" or "fox-fire lights," ghostly lights are similar to what people would refer to later as UFOs.[36] He reported various colors (e.g., red, green, blue, etc.) that "hovered impishly" or moved around. These "dancing phantoms" appeared often in or near cemeteries. There also are common references to swamp gas.

However, some of these older phrases and descriptions of extraordinary things in the sky extended into the 1950s. In a 1955 issue of *Fate* magazine, Jack Henderson wrote an article about reports of mysterious lights that he and others saw in the Arkansas Delta.[37] This particular issue of *Fate* is noteworthy because of the number of articles about anomalous sightings, such as "bouncing blue lights" (Oregon), "Green Fireballs" (New Mexico), "Dancing Flames" (Arizona), and "Floating Fireballs" (Mississippi)." Writers also mentioned other paranormal activities that have a strong presence in the Ozarks, such as water divining—a topic about which I learned when I moved to the Ozarks in the late 1970s.

As the flying saucer craze swept the United States in the summer months of 1947, a number of theories were offered to explain what the objects were. An iron worker noted that what people saw as UFOs in Seattle was he and his coworkers melting down beer bottle caps.[38] Apparently, the process of melting the bottle caps down often causes some of the material to fly up into the air. Some people thought people mistaking the floating spider webs and spiders as UFOs.[39]

Underwood and Underwood wrote briefly about UFOs. They reported that "Arkansas has had its fair share of encounters with things from other worlds."[40] They continued to indicate that there is a long history of UFO sightings there. One of the authors "was informed that a contingency of people in the town [Eureka Springs] believes that aliens not only landed generations ago but also are the reason the spring water has mysterious healing properties. Further, they contend that some of these aliens still live beneath the city in the spring caverns." The last LoC interviewee was a middle-aged man who described seven different encounters he had in the Ozarks.[41] In another set of interviews, two Ozark back-to-landers reported having UFO and other paranormal experiences.[42]

UFO investigator Lee Prosser argued that UFOs and other paranormal activity are common in Missouri. He wrote, "Missouri holds many secrets, making it an ideal place of wilderness to camouflage UFOs and their alien passengers. Also, the state is centrally located within the United States, making it an ideal location to contain extraterrestrial bases to connect to other such bases."[43] He also believed that other paranormal activities such as "shadow figures"—some sort of transitory beings, lots of weird time anomalies (time slips, traveling, and missing time), alien implants, energy vortices, and ghosts plague Missouri. For some reason, many of these paranormal phenomena are found around the Branson area. Apparently, farmers and pets are not to be trusted either. He wrote, "If you are in your car or motorcycle driving down a Missouri road in the country, and you accidentally come upon a farmer, and it is getting close to evening, you may have to seriously ask yourself, if I have lost my way off the main road, and see this elderly looking man walking with a dog, is it truly a human man with his dog, or could it be an exploratory party of two extraterrestrials checking out the area for a UFO landing."[44]

The Missouri Ozarks were also famous for Buck Nelson's annual "Spaceship Conference," which began around 1956 and ended by the late 1960s. The event took place on Nelson's farm near Mountain View and was usually held the last week of June. Around 300 people attended at the height of its popularity. The same surge was happening around the same time across the nation. In 1959, George King, a Brit appointed by Venusians to be the "Voice of Interplanetary Parliament," visited an estimated crowd of 2,000 at the Giant

Figure 5.2 Buck Nelson at the 1966 Spaceship Conference. © Ken Steinhoff. All rights reserved.

Rock conference in California. Every year, attendees at Giant Rock would come from all over the country to hear and share their UFO stories. It was also a chance for Nelson to sell his self-published booklet, *My Trip to Mars, the Moon, and Venus.* The conference and his book made Nelson a minor celebrity and allowed him opportunities to lecture around the country and on television in New York City, Washington, and Kansas City.[45]

According to Nelson, in 1954 when he was 59 years old, black-bearded, overall-clad aliens came to Nelson's farm and used a ray of some sort that cured him of lumbago and neuritis.[46] The aliens were attracted to the farm because of the spring water and "lines of force [that] cross there." They returned in 1955, with "Bo," their 385-pound dog, and took him to the moon

Figure 5.3 Columba Krebs at the 1966 Spaceship Conference. © Ken Steinhoff. All rights reserved.

and Venus and Mars where he planted little United States flags as proof that he visited.[47] The aliens made it a habit to stop and visit Nelson, maybe because they liked him and also because he claimed to have a nephew on Venus. According to Nelson, Venusians observed "absolute segregation of all races and nationalities."[48] The aliens were very tall and lived a long time because they followed the 12 laws of God closely and ate organic food. He could also communicate with them via telepathy.

In 1961, it was reported that the aliens visited while the conference was in session. One of the results of the visit was radioactive fallout that produced little silver strands that attendees picked up as souvenirs, but the strands disintegrated by the next day. The radiation also caused people to itch.[49] One frequent attendee, Columba Krebs, contended that the farm was the "safest spot in the whole country just in case there is another radioactive fallout from a nuclear attack."[50] Krebs was interviewed by a reporter about her paranormal experience, "and there was a California woman in toreador pants who had become acquainted with a Venusian in Phoenix. She spotted him because he wore his hair long and drank a lot of orange juice."[51] Sometime in the late 1960s, Columba Krebs bought the adjoining land to Nelson to create a "Cosmic Art Shrine."[52]

In the mid-1960s, because radar was unpleasant to the aliens, visits from outer space dried up—in fact, 1963 was Nelson's last saucer ride. Paralleling the decline in alien visits, conference attendance declined for much of the 1960s.[53] Nelson thought he could attract more visitors by adding an actual carnival in 1966. Fewer people attended that year, and fewer were willing to pay for the rides. Adding insult to injury, rather than paying the carnies, Nelson forced them to give him a cut of their meager profits.[54] In 1969, while Nelson was away, his farm was destroyed in a fire.[55] Perhaps for health reasons and the fire, Nelson moved to California in the late 1960s. Nelson died 1988 at the age of 88.[56] Even though Buck was gone, Columba and others still believed the burned-down farm plus the aliens made the land special. Last, Columba would become friends with a newly arrived founder of the Garden of Joy Blues, Catherine "Cat" Yronwode.[57]

Besides Nelson, and Krebs, there was also Bessie Jan, with whom Cat became friends, who had a UFO contact that cured her cancer. Bessie was a transplant to the Ozarks. After the Great Depression, she and her mother left Chicago in their Model T Ford. Stopping at every crossroad they encountered, they let God decide which way to go. Ultimately, that divinely inspired process led them to Birch Tree Missouri.[58]

Geography of Paranormal Experiences

Literature related to the geography of paranormal beliefs and experiences is scarce. According to the Baylor Religious Survey (BRS), compared to other regions in the country, southern respondents were less likely to accept that various paranormal phenomena (i.e., ESP, ghosts, etc.) existed, while, as a region, western respondents were more likely to accept such phenomena.[59] With respect to actual experiences, the General Social Survey (GSS) asked particular questions about whether respondents had experiences with spirits and visions.[60] The western south-central region of the United States, of which Arkansas is a member state, had higher percentages than respondents anywhere else.

Finally, surveys by Bader are available for analysis from the Inter-university Consortium for Political and Social Research (ICPSR). Bader wrote a book based on his survey results.[61] He went to UFO and Big Foot conferences and surveyed enthusiasts.[62] According to his data, I found that UFO attendees from small towns and urban areas reported higher percentages of UFO sightings than did their rural counterparts. Tiryakian found that urbanity was conducive to astrology activities.[63] Weiner made the point repeatedly that in a general sense, urbanity was crucial for the rise of creativity.[64] More specifically, urbanity fosters conflicting viewpoints that may arise and be expressed because there is a high level of trust and interaction.[65]

Data from the UFO Report Database (URD) were analyzed to acquire a sense of the geographic distribution of UFO sightings in Arkansas and Missouri.[66] This database documents reports individuals submit about any UFO activity they encounter. Data in the report include the time and place of the event, as well as details such as shape, color, and so on. However, some reports are incomplete, and not all events are reported. For example, the LoC transcripts mentioned above are not listed, nor is the incident the 1947 *Blythville Courier News* article reported—the first Arkansas report in the database is from 1950.[67] Thus, it is likely that there are many more cases of UFO activity reported than the 816 valid cases in the database for Arkansas and 2,209 for Missouri.

The URD allows reporting of narratives for each event. For instance, there is a report from Prairie Grove, Arkansas, in August 1952: "Two observers saw silverish 30-foot disk maneuver above and below horizon at hover and supersonic speeds." Or more recently, in 2012, a "Teardrop shaped craft passes over the Ozarks." Of the 816 URD for reports for Arkansas, 781 indicated shapes of the UFO encounters. The highest reported shape were round objects (33.5 percent), then lights of some sort (32.4 percent), chevron/triangle/diamond (18.3 percent), other (9.1 percent), and unknown shape (6.7). The most reported color was orange (32.1 percent%) then white (22.6 percent), blue/green (17.0 percent), multicolor (15.1 percent), and other colors (13.2 percent).

URD data were also used to produce the map in figure 5.4, which shows the geographic distribution of UFO sightings in Arkansas. A total of 254 towns and cities reported 816 cases of UFO activity. Seventy-nine of those were located in the Ozarks. Compared to the Ozarks, the central region (e.g., Pulaski County) also had a large number of reports; however, far fewer towns/cities (30) were reported. Like the central region, the River Valley (e.g., Pope County) had a large number of reports but fewer towns (26) than was the case for the Ozarks.

Data about hauntings came from a variety of sites, but the most popular and largest is "Haunted Places." The website has a detailed list of haunted

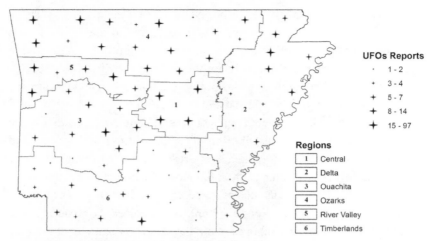

Figure 5.4 Geographical Distribution of UFO sightings in Arkansas.

places for each state.[68] In Arkansas, there were 157 listings, compared to Missouri, where there were 282. In some cases, a town may have multiple listings. The listings are detailed and occasionally offer redundant information, which I ignored. In the Arkansas Ozarks, Madison County has a large number of haunted sites. In the Missouri Ozarks, Greene County, with the city of Springfield, is home to many haunted places.

Besides UFOs and ghosts, another common topic in paranormal experiences is humming sounds. Hums are often associated with a wide variety of paranormal things, such as crystals, auras, and energy vortexes. Humming phenomena has gained interest outside the paranormal community. Professor David Deming explored the phenomena scientifically in a 2004 article entitled "The Hum: An Anomalous Sound Heard around the World."[69] In 2013, a German researcher suggested that the source of the sound is within the inner ear of the sufferer.[70] Later, a 2016 article in the newsmagazine *The Week* focused on the strange humming sounds heard by many people around the world.[71] The reporter even interviewed Glen MacPherson, who lives in Canada and works as a teacher and researcher. I looked at what I thought would be a logical source for humming—earthquakes or similar activities. The Ozarks are west of Memphis and the San Madrid fault line. Looking at National Oceanic Atmospheric Administration (NOAA) data, I found that there is a history of earthquakes in the Ozark region.[72] Of all the earthquakes in the NOAA data for Arkansas between 1795 to 1985, 458, or 29.9 percent of the reports, were

	UFOs	Haunted Sites	Humming Reports
Central	21.8%	24.8%	18.2%
Delta	10.7	14.6	0.0
Ouachita	11.0	11.5	9.1
Ozark	31.3	19.1	52.3
River Valley	15.8	12.1	13.6
Timberlands	9.4	17.8	6.8
Number	816	157	44

Table 5.1 Paranormal Reports in Arkansas Regions

out of the Ozarks. Thus, I cannot rule out that some humming sounds might be related to major geological activities, although I doubt this is the case.

Although humming sounds do not necessarily indicate paranormal activity, the paranormal community often sees the phenomena as such. The hum data I found came from http://thehum.info, a website where the World Hum Map and database can be accessed. The director of the website is MacPherson. He wrote, "After first noticing the Hum in spring of 2012 and discovering the Hum community, he [MacPherson] sensed the need for a unified, moderated, and serious place for discussions and research surrounding the world Hum."[73] On his website, a user can click on the individual reports shown as red dots on the map. In each report, any person who wants to report a hum phenomenon answers a set of questions such as how loud the sound was, did it pulse, location, own a smart meter for the home, hearing issues, and demographics.

The data for the Ozarks shows that 65.2 percent of the reports are by men, and 34.8 percent are by women. Both men and women tend to be in their mid to late 40s. The hum was heard mainly at night. Most respondents did not have a smart meter on their homes. Some of the respondents reported caves, water features (lakes, hydrological dams), and mountains/hills near the site they heard the hum.

The percentages of UFO sightings, hauntings, and humming sounds for Arkansas reported are shown in table 5.1 below.[74] The Arkansas Ozarks has the highest percentage of UFO sightings (31.3 percent) and the second highest reports of haunted sites (19.1 percent), while central Arkansas (e.g., Little Rock) has the highest percentage of haunted sites (24.8 percent). People in the Ozarks report humming phenomena at much higher percentages than do those in other parts of the state as well. These data show that reports of paranormal

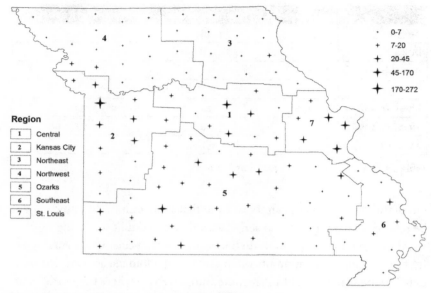

Figure 5.5 Geographical Distribution of UFO sightings in Missouri.

activity (UFOs, ghosts, humming sounds) are more common occurrences than is the case for most other regions in the state (see figure 5.5).

In Missouri, 475 towns and cities reported 2,209 cases of UFO activity. The Ozarks are second (28 percent) to the Saint Louis Region (32 percent) in UFO reported activities. The number of Ozark towns and cities reporting was 166 or 34.9 percent. Many of those Ozark reports came from Springfield and surrounding towns in Greene County. UFO reporting was much sparser in the northern region of the state.

There is a high level of reporting of other types of paranormal activity in the Missouri Ozarks. For instance, the Ozarks had more reported haunted sites (30.9 percent) than Kansas City (22.7 percent) and St. Louis (21.6 percent). In the hum reports, the St. Louis Region made up 41.8 percent of all the reported cases compared to the Ozarks, which had 27.2 percent (see table 5.2).

UFO Conference and Attendees

Businesspeople in Eureka Springs have found that they can profit by offering a place, services, and goods devoted to the paranormal, and they advertise all

	UFOs	Haunted Sites	Humming Reports
Central	10.3%	5.0%	3.6%
Kansas City	10.7	22.7	21.8
North East	2.0	2.8	0.0
North West	4.0	8.1	5.4
Ozarks	28.0	30.9	27.2
South East	4.0	8.9	0.0
Saint Louis	32.0	21.6	41.8
Number	2,209	282	55

Table 5.2 Paranormal Reports in Missouri Regions

sorts of festivals in their visitors' magazines. In addition to paranormal activities, these include festivals for mushrooms, bikers, and music. The town has been able to determine ways to combine these various interests successfully and attract people to the town. People come not only for the conventions, but they tend to stay in area hotels, eat at the restaurants, and buy a wide variety of souvenirs and paraphernalia.

Every year since 1988, Eureka Springs hosts one of the largest UFO conferences, the Ozark Mountain UFO Conference, which is attended by all sorts of people, including UFO believers, those who had encounters, paranormalists of all types, and even cults such as the Purple People.[75] The conference is run by Ozark Mountain Publishing, who also operates KGRA, "The Planet," where listeners can learn about "New Knowledge for the New World." Eleven speakers talked on a variety of UFO topics. The draw for many in the crowd was Whitley Strieber, author of *Communion* and Erick von Daniken, who wrote a number of books, including *The Chariots of the Gods*.

When I attended the conference, I found that vendors were plentiful and diverse. Many speakers, both past and present, had booths where they sold and talked about their publications. Ozark Mountain Publishing gave away free books with such titles as *The Divinity Factor*, *Awakening to Your Creation*, *A Journey into Being: Knowing and Nurturing Our Children as Spirit*, and *Beauty and the Priest: Finding God in the New Age*. Attendees were offered all types of services, such as tarot card readings, lini sound, reiki, chakra balancing, spiritual intuitive readings, quantum touch hands on healing, orgone generation, biorhythm analysis, individualized subliminal recordings, astrology reports, dowsing, Egyptian magic, neimology, esoteric tutoring, energy healing, and shaman readings. With respect to products, there were paranormal supplies, such as tarot cards, orgone generators, and many types of incense and oils. There also was jewelry, much of which incorporates crystals of some sort. Art, such as striking stained-glass depicting aliens, and music were available, as well as clothing and neck pillows. What is interesting is that there only were a few vendors devoted solely to UFO merchandise and novelties. Instead, many offered combined services and products, as was the case with the Purple People, who sold energy vortex jewelry, but also hawked their paranormal beliefs to willing listeners.

Demographically, conference attendees are older, and there is a general parity in the number of men and women.[76] I saw only three African Americans, two of whom were members of the Purple People. Members of this commune drive a purple van with a bumper sticker that reads "May Love Transcend on the Earth." The Purple People, a name they use for themselves as well, derive their name from the fact that they wear purple robes and clothes. There even was a group of bikers dressed in leather and their colors who visited the UFO conference and walked through the vending area. It was a unique experience to witness the interplay between leather-clad bikers as they strolled among the Purple People, New Agers, paranormal gurus, and UFO vendors.

I obtained a sense of the attendees' socioeconomic status by going out to the parking lot and surveying what they drove. The parking lot was full of Priuses. This and other observations fit with past research that indicates that paranormal believers are not marginal members of society. These UFO enthusiasts appeared to have a high socioeconomic status. I also learned that, in addition to the ubiquitous UFO bumper stickers, stickers for Bernie Sanders and other types of progressive issues were popular on vehicles, and it was clear that the attendees tended to be liberal. Thus, my observations were consistent with those of Swami and colleagues, who found that conservatism dampens UFO reporting.[77] On the other hand, one conference attendee emblazoned his vehicle with conservative stickers in addition to the standard UFO/Alien stickers.

Research by Emmons and Sobal, suggests that there are three types of paranormal believers.[78] The first are those who, if they are inclined toward religion and accept paranormal activities, tend to focus on ghosts, angels, and spirits. The second type, not as religious as the other groups, subscribes to paranormal activities such as telekinesis and UFOs. The third group accepts both religious and secular paranormal activities. This is the same group that Saliba categorized as religious UFO people.[79] He divided these into two further categories: those who believe devoutly in aliens as stand-alone entities and those who fold UFO stories into a Christian End Times narrative. Both types of religious UFO enthusiasts attended the UFO conference in Eureka Springs, and attendees and speakers combined the secular and the sacred using von Daniken.

The attendees were among one of the most dedicated groups of people I have ever observed outside a traditional religious context. Festinger and colleagues found that the level of commitment of individuals and groups that share a millennial outlook is strengthened when they are exposed to contradictory evidence.[80] As Festinger noted, "A man with a conviction is a hard man to change. Tell him you disagree and he turns away. Show him facts or figures and he questions your sources. Appeal to logic and he fails to see your point."[81]

McGarry and Newberry found that greater involvement in group activities leads to intensification of paranormal beliefs, as well as an increased sense that one can control his/her situation.[82] I certainly felt that members were involved heavily in UFO groups and activities, and this deepened their convictions. One of the speakers asked the audience how many of them had been to the conference only once, and I saw they were an extreme minority. Most attendees not only had attended several times, but many had attended more than half of the years the conference had been held. This fact signifies the loyalty these people have to this particular event and to the values and beliefs the group shares. Moreover, I overheard several conversations in which people reported their own sightings, contacts, and even abductions, and it was apparent that the audience members tended to keep abreast of the latest UFO literature.

The conference included sessions such as "The Flying Saucer Invasion of 1950—Farmington, NM and Beyond," "Now You See It Now You Don't," Strieber's "A New World If We Can Take It," "The Extraterrestrial Hypothesis: A Fresh Understanding for a New Century," and von Daniken's "Unsolved Mysteries of the Past (Part 2)." With respect to the sessions as a whole, a few general themes became apparent. The first is that many of the presenters folded paranormal experiences within a multitude of perspectives from various arenas such as religion and science and some used existing religious frameworks (e.g., Catholicism).[83] From a sociological perspective, UFO enthusiasts, like other believers, use ritual, beliefs, and symbology to convey what they consider sacred or at least very important.[84] Several speakers were ambivalent about science. They scorn science when scientists do not validate paranormal claims but accept the need to use science to get to the stars or project humanity into the future.[85]

Strieber, the author of *Communion*, is quite famous. Both he and von Daniken were Roman Catholics, so they were able to superimpose that framework on some of the ideas they had about UFOs. An interesting example is from von Daniken, who wrote what is basically UFO enthusiasts' Bibles—*The Chariots of the Gods*.[86] He said that UFOs are as old as Ezekiel. He indicated that the time in which Ezekiel lived was one when humans made contact with aliens and that aliens tasked Ezekiel to create written instructions on the way to make spacecraft. Another interesting idea von Daniken talked about was that aliens and humans mated sometime in the past, and at that time, people referred to aliens as angels. Quite often there seemed to be a sense that participants faced both the past and the future simultaneously. Moreover, the event had the feel of being at church, especially when attendees quoted lines of scripture together with cherished UFO ideas. Indeed, some of the people knew what von Daniken was going to say. In all, I felt that I was witnessing a religious event.[87]

Another theme that emerged during the sessions was social change and time.[88] A number of presenters talked about past extraterrestrial activities and predicted their return to usher in a new age well as well. Paranormal activity involves, in many ways, time. In this case, it was prophetic time. Festinger's *When Prophecy Fails* highlights the way particular groups prophesy that we are transitioning from current time into the end time. Robertson provided a detailed account of the extent to which UFO thinking revolves around a millennial, often apocalyptic, framework.[89] Further, they predicted that there was going to be an end time. Strieber and von Daniken pointed out that we were in the Age of Aquarius, in which they likened us to being in the womb or earthbound.[90] The end times would involve a period when aliens would come and help believers move past their earthly boundaries. They would save humankind, a type of redemption, if we just listened.[91] And the UFO enthusiasts are the chosen ones.

The third theme was in-group/out-group appellations. Rhetoric that emphasized that attendees understood and believed the truth—that there are aliens and they will return to help save humanity—highlighted the belief that members had special knowledge that they could use to benefit themselves and others, and those critical of this worldview would be left behind.

Conclusions

Perhaps being both southern and Ozarkian, these geographical and cultural identities possess contradictory qualities that help foster folklore and paranormal narratives such as UFO stories. Thompson noted, "If there is a 'teaching' of the saucers, perhaps it is to remind us of the multiple worlds we inhabit, a reality with which most of humanity has lived for centuries."[92] Folklore and myths also expose the various worlds in which people lived in the past.

One principal set of contradictory qualities is community versus individualism. Modernity has forced the transition from the former to the latter, and tradition, status, and other aspects of culture have become confused. Older explanations make way for newer ways to understand change. Stories about foxfire and swamp gas sufficed for an earlier time; however, with the advent of modernity, stories needed more modern concepts, and they will change as society changes.[93] Thompson posed this question: "If UFOs do disappear tomorrow, will we simply find another domain in which to continue what is inevitably a religious search [to] recover lost intimacy?"[94] Research by Michael Kinsella suggests that people will find the Internet a very hospitable and even liminal place for exploring, reporting, and sharing paranormal experiences.[95] It is also likely that UFOs will make way for another concept in the future as people continue to focus on modernity and community.

A final note on serendipity in research. I am not a UFO enthusiast, but I enjoy good science fiction movies—ones that make me think about society and social issues, such as *Her* or *Blade Runner*. Further, I also am an avid fan of science fiction books, especially those by such authors as Isaac Asimov, Frederik Pohl, Clifford Simak, and Roger Zelazny. Thus, it was a surprise when I learned that many of the LoC interviewees were from the same place in the Ozarks to which my family migrated in the late 1970s when we established an intentional community. A few of the people interviewed even went to the same school that I did. I never really paid attention to UFOs but I had a friend who showed me his copy of Van Daniken's *Chariots of the Gods,* fuzzy-image UFO trading cards, and similar things. Star Wars was big then too, so I thought this was all the same thing—a science fiction fad teenagers fell for in the 1970s and 1980s. However, in researching this topic I found a LoC interview of a 59-year-old man that proved me wrong. The man, who lived on Highway 21, told the interviewer he saw seven spaceships. He said,

> One come down and turned right there turned and looked at me. When I was shining lights at it when it was coming down. I had a big old five cell flash-light and and I was shining them. You know back and forwards like that try-ing to get him to come down. I wanted to talk to them. Well one did, it come down and just come down and set there and turned and turned just gradually turned. And just run off. I was standing there looking at it.[96]

These revelations piqued my curiosity and led me to this topic. Later, as I visited people in the Ozarks and told them I was writing about UFOs, family friends reported having encounters. I had no clue.

Serendipitous encounters with interesting topics is known as sideways sociology, in which something simply falls into a researcher's lap as s/he uncovers more information.[97] Even popular author Robert Persig spent con-siderable time exploring serendipitous knowledge when he wrote *Zen and the Art of Motorcycle Maintenance*.[98] Opportunities to engage in sideways research are rare and should be treasured. Not only did I learn about a rich and interesting story about a facet of Ozark life, but this story would lead me to another interesting story about the religious cults in Searcy County, Arkansas, particularly the Nahziryah, otherwise known as the Purple People.

The Cults of
Searcy County, Arkansas

Every so often the veil lifts and, for an instant, the dark matter in the spiritual universe becomes visible.
—Elizabeth Gleick[1]

As indicated in previous chapters, the Ozarks is a region that has a rich history in alternative living. People and groups have settled in the Ozarks to follow new faiths, engage in back-to-the-land living, and explore identities that often are marginalized elsewhere. Back-to-the-landers began to arrive in the Ozarks in the early 1970s and 1980s. The region's relative isolation may be the primary factor that causes these different people to be drawn to the area. Sometimes, for the very same reasons, cults have found the Ozarks appealing. One Ozark county, Searcy, experienced some of the wave of immigration from around the country. In fact, three communes emerged in the county in the 1970s, the Leslie community, Snowball, and Indian Camp. In 1920, John Battenfield led a group of people to settle in the county to prepare for the apocalypse that he had prophesied would happen in 1926. In the 1980s, the Nahziryah, a monastic community led by a charismatic figure, migrated to an area outside of St. Joe, in Marion County, neighbor to the north of Searcy.

I use the word "cult" sparingly, as the word has negative connotations of people who are brainwashed and engage in odd and even dangerous practices, sometimes even mass suicide. Usually, the word is used by powerful, established religious types to denigrate other faith traditions. Thus, the term scholars prefer is "new religious movement" rather than "cult." Although cults refer usually to particular religious groups, "new religious movement" fits both individual groups and wider innovations within the institution of religion.

I do acknowledge that there are special cases that the word "cult" describes best. I choose to use the term when a new religious movement requires members to change their identity, sever their ties with family and friends, and in which the leader makes all decisions, such that the members find that the leader has crafted their theological world entirely.

In both cults and new religious movements, power rests in a charismatic leader or prophet. Early German sociologist Max Weber described charismatic authority thus:

> The holder of charisma seizes the task that is adequate for him and demands obedience and a following by virtue of his mission. His success determines whether he finds them. His charismatic claim breaks down if his mission is not recognized by those to whom he feels he has been sent. If they recognize him, he is their master—so long as he knows how to maintain recognition through "proving" himself. But he does not derive his "right" from their will, in the manner of an election. Rather, the reverse holds; it is the duty of those to whom he addresses his mission to recognize him as their charismatically qualified leader.[2]

Prophets, according to Weber, are "charismatic-bearers." Unlike priests, who are part of the system, the prophet is a layperson who "claims definite revelations" and is usually not compensated like professional religious workers. Prophets often act as teachers of a new way of living and tend to be gifted orators. They and their prophecies tend to be on the margins of society and usually captivate those who are marginalized. They often spark new religious movements.[3] Using Victor Turner's terminology, they are religious edge-men and women.

According to sociologists Rodney Stark and William Bainbridge, new religious movements "do not have a prior tie with another established religious body in the society in question."[4] Innovative religious movements find themselves in conflict in society when they offer a new religious path that competes with more established faiths with respect to dogma or recruiting parishioners. However, they do not run the risk of conflicting with mainstream institutions when they simply provide paranormal or mystical services, such as card reading. An example of this is the common sight of palm-reading businesses throughout the Bible Belt. In the Ozarks, Eureka Springs holds a paranormal conference that offers a wide range of cult client services.

In this chapter, I describe various groups located in Searcy County that I consider to be cultic movements. One major group I focus on is the Incoming Kingdom Missionary Unit (IKMU) that emerged in the 1920s. IKMU was an apocalyptic-based group that believed a battle between Protestants and Catholics would lead to the end of the world. When that happened, IKMU would be ready to establish a new society. The other group, called the Nazir Order of the Purple Veil relocated to the Ozarks in the 1980s. They also are known as the Purple People. This group left New Orleans to establish a predominantly African American monastic community in the Ozarks. This is the group I will devote much time in describing.

Searcy County is in the central southern part of the Arkansas Ozarks. Folklorist Vance Randolph mentioned old time superstitions from Searcy County. The town of St. Joe is the epitome of Trump County and has almost no minority representation. The area is very evangelical, and approximately half of the residents are some type of Baptist. There also are sizable numbers of Assembly of God, Pentecostal, and Holiness adherents.[5]

An interesting thing about the Ozarks region is that it has attracted, and continues to attract, people who embrace alternative lifestyles and establish intentional communities. Communards came to the Ozarks to practice their faith with little interference or because they wanted to live in a more self-sufficient and sustainable way now known as the back-to-the-land movement. For some women, occasionally lesbian, who wanted to break from male-dominated mainstream society or even express their sexuality freely, the Ozarks offered them relative refuge to do so.

The Harmonial Vegetarian Society was one of the first intentional communities in Arkansas and was organized around Oneida beliefs and practices. From the early 1900s to the 1970s, most Arkansas intentional communities were formed for economic or religious reasons. At the end of the 1960s, the Alamo Christian Federation, often regarded as a cult, emerged in northwestern Arkansas.

Cultic Activity

One of the earliest cults in the Ozarks located in Searcy County was the IKMU, also referred to as the Disciples of Incoming Kingdom. The Disciples lived in Gilbert, Arkansas, in Searcy County, which is approximately 7 miles

J. A. BATTENFIELD

Figure 6.1 John Adam Battenfield in 1914. Battenfield
and Pendleton, *The Great Demonstration*, 12.

southeast of St. Joe, from 1920 through 1925. The Reverend John Battenfield
and many of his congregants migrated from the Louisville, Illinois, area
to establish a group that followed early Christian communalism and millennialist notions.

John Adam Battenfield was born in Napolean, Ohio, the seventh child in
the family. The boy was religiously precocious: "From earliest childhood the
Book of Revelation held John spellbound."[6] He memorized Revelations and
other parts of the Bible when he was a preteen, and by 16, he was preach-
ing. Around the turn of the century, he had ministered at two churches in
Illinois. The last church was not accommodating to his extreme ideological
views, causing him to leave the ministry and take up farming till 1903. He
returned to the ministry in 1907 and later, in a ten-day fast, he worked out
the details for his book *The Great Demonstration*, coauthored by Philip Y.
Pendleton. In that book which he set forth a number of prophecies based on

his understanding of Revelation.[7] I found the book dense and hard to follow both in writing, logic, and theology. Another critic listed several issues, chief among them being that Battenfield reckoned exact days for various things occurring in the Bible.[8] For example, he prophesied the millennium would end in 1972. After that, he believed there would be 1,000 years of peace.

Despite the critics, many people were attracted to Battenfield's worldview, many of them "discontent with liberalism" that they perceived was creeping into mainstream faith. Battenfield's beliefs and practices were very strict and like most Millennialist ideologies "were against Catholicism, jewelry, alcoholic beverages, and movies." Before moving to Searcy County, members spread Battenfield's message as they moved from job to job around the country.[9]

IKMU members, which were from "well-to-do" backgrounds, bought up more than half the town and 1,000 acres adjacent to Gilbert.[10] They also established "units" in Water Creek, Star Mountain, and other areas.[11] IKMU laid out a new community with 50 "modernly" constructed homes. Beginning with 70 people, each man received his own plot of land. All members worked together to plant and harvest the crops.[12] Members found communalism untenable—sharing was fine until it meant sharing one's own resources.[13] Like many other prophetic-led groups, IKMU was no place for slackers— "He who will not work will not eat."[14]

Members were expected not to cut their hair. On August 7, 1925, the *Neosho Daily News* reported, "Men of all ages with flowing beards and hair reaching their shoulders, are met at every turn, their faces bearing expressions of the deepest solemnity."[15] Apparently, IKMU leadership thought the hair and bearing mirrored the way the apostles conducted themselves.

Based on his interpretation of the Book of Revelation, Battenfield prophesied that the world would end in 1926 when Protestants and Catholics would destroy civilization. Thus, the Disciples were positioned well in the Ozarks, where they would be isolated from the battle and able to repopulate the world. Various aspects were thought about, and planned for, in the incoming kingdom. For example, clothing would be needed after the war. Thus, IKMU sought out 12 spinning wheels and the women to operate them.[16]

Battenfield and other IKMU leaders made major theological decisions through dreams and "radiomind." Reverend Battenfield proposed that minds were like radios and thoughts could be transmitted and received by others over great distances. Members also wanted to award each other and themselves with important biblical names, such as Peter, Michael, and Gabriel.[17]

The prophecy of the Great War did not come to pass, nor was Battenfield able to resurrect a dead member he said he could revive, even after several attempts. He also was unsuccessful in trying to part the Buffalo River. Quite like the resolve of cult members in Festinger's *When Prophecy Fails*, who refused to accept prophetic failure, Battenfield's failures did not weaken the members' resolve.[18] However, what did cause a rift in the group was his departure to a sanitarium and the subsequent division in the leadership and theology. Two factions emerged within the IKMU, those who had bankrolled the community and urged members to return to "old time religion" and Battenfield diehards, often referred to as visionaries. Then Incoming Kingdom's fabric ripped, as the two groups fought over whether Battenfield was transmitting instructions from his New York sanitarium as one member claimed. The great holy naming became an issue when one member thought another member was faking his visions about being Peter.[19]

All remnants of the cult ended in 1930, when the Visionaries' leader, Lee Graham, had a vision that he could combat an ailment with a 30-day fast, and died instead. When the last of the "old time religion" group of IKMU left Gilbert, the money dried up, and IKMU was disbanded.[20]

Another cult-like group located in the Ozarks in the early 1960s. This extremist religious group, referred to as the Conservative Christian Church, settled near Walnut Ridge, east of Searcy County. John Robert Harrel, a former fighter pilot, was a staunch conservative who was against integration, migrants, communism, and a number of other things.[21] He and some of his followers left Louisville, Illinois, the same place from which the IKMU moved approximately 40 years earlier. Harrel gave the townsfolk of Louisville considerable grief because of his ultra-right opinions. He lived with 130 people in a compound that sported a 40-foot-tall watchtower with armed sentries. Eventually, the FBI broke into his compound with an armored vehicle to arrest a marine deserter he was harboring. Together with harboring the man, Harrel, who was a rich man, had certain "issues" with the Internal Revenue Service. After the raid in 1961, Harrel went into hiding and later lived in the Arkansas Ozarks for over a year before he was captured in 1964.[22] After serving a lengthy prison sentence, Harrel returned to Louisville, where he continued to inspire his neighbors' ire. His compound was used for paramilitary operations until townspeople complained. To appease the townsfolk of Louisville, he moved his "paramilitary maneuvers" to Missouri. However, Harrel gained the admiration of ultraconservatives throughout the nation.

The Alamo Christian Foundation was another extreme religious group that emerged in California and then moved to western Arkansas in the mid-1970s.[23] Two failed entertainers/hucksters from Los Angeles decided that fundamentalist Christian evangelism was the next big scam that they should perpetrate jointly. Tony Alamo, originally Bernie Hoffman, was born in Missouri, and Susan Alamo, born Edith Opal, came from northwest Arkansas. Tony and Susan built a following and were part of the Jesus People movement that linked the counterculture with evangelical Christianity in San Francisco and Los Angeles in the late 1960s. The Alamos were successful and amassed a large following, many former drug addicts. Although their conservative religious and political message allayed some people's fears that they were a cult, the Alamos decided to relocate to western Arkansas in 1976. However, reports that members were abused continued to follow the couple. Tony spiraled out of control after Susan's death in 1982, which led to his conviction on multiple charges, and he died in a federal prison in 2017.[24]

The Nahziryah is the latest cult to make Searcy County home. To provide some context for how unique the Nahziryah is, it is important to spend some time on the topic of the African American communal experience. There are very few African American intentional communities in American history, and most were founded in the nineteenth century. Briefly, Davis Bend (later Mount Bayou) was a slave plantation Jefferson Davis's brother, Joseph, owned. Joseph was inspired to organize a plantation in 1827 based on a discussion that Utopian thinker Robert Owens had with Joseph and others on a stagecoach ride in 1825. Owens proposed planned "communit[ies] of cooperation" where everyone is gainfully employed.

In Tennessee, there was a short-lived mixed-race community called Nashoba, near Memphis.[25] Northerners established the Port Royal community in South Carolina to help African Americans after emancipation.[26] Elgin and Wilborforce were two intentional communities in Canada.[27] However, among all of the US communities, slaves at Davis Bend had the most control over their lives and community.

During the Depression, the federal government led a back-to-the land push in which over a hundred cooperative farms were established throughout the nation.[28] These government-sponsored communal arrangements were based on self-sufficiency and cooperation. The concept was to take displaced people and resettle them on farms where they would work and live together cooperatively, and many southern cooperative farms sought out African

Americans. Desha, Lakeview, and Townes Farms were located in Arkansas. Like the Davis Bend experiment, although the government sponsored these alternative living arrangements, there was little money or political will to help the programs survive.

Another African American intentional community that emerged in the early twentieth century was the Peace Mission.[29] This cultic community was a very successful religious community led by the charismatic Father Divine.[30] The group reached its largest number of followers, who were primarily African American, in the Depression era and then declined dramatically with Father Divine's death in 1965. At its zenith, it was headquartered in New York City, where its members provided domestic and other services throughout the city. The Peace Mission provided all its members everything, even literally a new family. Shared beliefs were few except that Father Divine was God. He stressed hard work, patriotism, sexual abstinence, and segregation. Furthermore, members were instructed to eschew tobacco, alcohol, profanity, and other vices. True believers were thought to gain eternal life if they followed Father Divine. However, he found himself in trouble with authorities often because of taxes, racist judges, and apostates. Although the Peace Mission still exists, it is a shadow of its former self.

Utopianism tended to manifest itself in the African American community more than in countercultural social movements that sought to change the existing social structure. Furthermore, the Black community viewed the church as the premier institution from which much social thought and action originated. Indeed, the very notion of Black liberation theology was the idea of the beloved community with the church as the hub for any progress.[31] Circumstances changed with the rise of the Black Panthers in the late 1960s, who advocated for separation from mainstream society. For example, the People's Farm community formed from the Poor People's March in 1968 and settled in southern Alabama. The People's Farm was a predominantly African American commune that, among other things, sought to grow food for school children primarily in the Alabama Black Belt.[32]

Liberty House was another example of an African American communal arrangement in Mississippi during the late 1960s and early 1970s. A major cooperative endeavor, Liberty House operated a number of different co-ops located in rural areas and small towns. Jesse Morris led the entire operation, which was headquartered in Jackson. These co-ops offered innovative and sustainable alternative niche, community-based markets that enfranchised their members. These Liberty House co-ops provided goods that were sold in New York City's Greenwich Village at a shop also called Liberty House, and some portions of the profits were distributed back to each respective co-op. However, state-sponsored spies within the Mississippi Sovereignty Commission monitored Liberty House and its cooperatives' activities closely and followed this group and others that sought to improve the economic standing of African Americans in the state. An interesting side note about Liberty House is that Abbie Hoffman was on its staff for a while.

Antioch, one of the few African American communes in the 1970s and 1980s, was located in Jackson, Mississippi. Members of Antioch, a racially mixed group, came together in 1983 to live communally and practiced early Christianity's radical communism for the next 12 years.[33] At approximately the same time, the Purple People were busy practicing their faith and selling their goods and services in New Orleans.

In addition to African American intentional communities, a number of African American messianic cultic groups emerged in the twentieth century. Like the communal movement in America, many of these movements occurred in the latter part of the century. Some were churches with an organizational structure rather than true intentional communities. Other African American messianic cults were organized as intentional communities. The Southern Poverty Law Center lists the Nation of Islam as a hate organization, but it has a presence in the larger urban areas in both Arkansas and Missouri, such as Little Rock and Kansas City. On the other hand, white hate groups make up most of the listings for both states.[34]

All of the African American messianic groups offered some version of a story in which their particular believers were the chosen people and should separate from mainstream white culture because white people were evil. In some cases, apocalypse entailed war between the two races: one Muslim and Black and the other Christian and white.[35] Donna Kossy, a long-time chronicler of fringe groups and ideas, wrote:

> Messianic religions almost universally offer new names and new diets to the downtrodden and displaced. The pantheon of North American Black Messiahs, including Noble Drew Ali of Moorish Science, Elijah Muhammed of Nation of Islam and Yahweh ben Yahhew of the Nation of Yahweh, provide all this and more. A convert begins his or her new life with not only a new name

and different eating habits, but also a genealogy, exotic rituals and colorful clothing; in short, a new identity.[36]

The messianic cult leaders Kossy described changed their names and heaped honorifics on their new selves as well. Noble Drew Ali of the Moorish Science Organization was B. Timothy Drew, a North Carolinian born to ex-slaves; Wali Fard Muhmamed of Nation of Islam, originally W. D. Fard, was a peddler in Detroit; Elijah Muhammad, Nation of Islam, was Elijah Poole, who came from a Georgia sharecropper family; Dwight York from Massachusetts became Isa Muhammad, leader of the Ansaaru Allah Community, and Hulon Mitchell from Oklahoma changed his name to Yahweh Ben Yahweh and led the Nation of Yahweh in the 1970s and 1980s.[37]

In addition to strict diets, such as vegetarianism for Moorish science, most of the Black Messianic groups had a proclivity for wearing clothing, often-times fanciful, which demarcated them from mainstream society. Women were expected to maintain subservient roles and usually wore loose-fitting clothes that concealed much of their bodies.[38]

Moving away from Black Messianic groups and back into mainstream culture, thousands of intentional communities emerged across the United States from 1965 to 1975. The South was particularly attractive because of cheap land and relative isolation to practice alternative living. Demographically, the surge in communal activity was attributable primarily to upper-middle-class to middle-class whites. However, many communes welcomed diversity. Historically, the handful of African American communes were located in the South, but there were not any in the Ozarks until the Purple People moved to the region.

The Purple People's story begins with their leader, Nazimoreh, or as he was known prior to leading the group, Duval Augustus Mitchell.[39] Mitchell was from Chicago originally and decided to break with his family and community at some point. He renamed himself Reverend Baba Nazimoreh Kameeayl Ben Kedem and started a monastic religious community two hours northeast of Jackson, Mississippi, in the town of De Kalb. Besides the name change, he required everyone to refer to him with the following honorifics "All Blessing and Respect Due" or ABRD for short. Since that time, he had three wives and 13 children.

According to Mitchell's account, he "comes [from a] long line of mystics" of which he asserted his father and grandfather were "adepts in esoteric knowledge." As a young man, Mitchell found a book in the "cellar of a large, old house" that "unlocked memories of former lives and figure out his spiritual path" as a "high adept" endorsed to "bring forth the ancient teachings in the capacity of leader and teacher."[40] It also has been reported that Mitchell's father passed his penchant for domestic abuse on to Duval.

By the mid-1980s, when it was located in New Orleans, the group became known as the Purple People, who operated the Nazir Arts and Crafts as well as the Veil of Truth Center for Metaphysics and Esoteric Learning. In 1989, a San Antonio newspaper reported that a popular TV reporter joined the "Cult."[41] Later, Mitchell began the process of moving the Purple People to the Ozarks. For some time, the group maintained the arts and crafts center while some of its members established their new residence in St. Joe, Arkansas.

In 1999, the Purple People were all settled in Marion County, near the town of St. Joe. Outside the work of reporter Jacqueline Froelich, not much is known about the community today other than what Mitchell provided on the commune's formerly accessible website. In 2002, Mitchell visited India. Some materials on the website suggest that the group is not as large as it once was. Froelich, a reporter for a public radio station in the Ozarks, reported on the commune and noted that Mitchell sold the land in 2016—the same year I encountered them at the UFO conference in the spring.[42] She also reported that other than one long-term member who acts as a caregiver to Mitchell, everyone has left the commune. Among those escaping Mitchell were his family, who suffered years of his physical and mental abuse.[43]

Like several other cultic communities, the Purple People are led by a charismatic authority figure who governs all aspects of the community. However, what is interesting about this particular group is that its members largely are African Americans. The community is monastic and reclusive, and Purple People travel in pairs or groups when outside the community. Their name derives from the fact that members usually wear all purple clothing, drive purple vehicles, and live and work in houses painted purple. The group also abides by very strict dietary rules (vegetarian, no drugs/tobacco, etc.). Mitchell believes that his members and family members, except for himself, should work hard. Like Battenfield, he advises his flock, "Do not expect something for nothing." Furthermore, members are never to engage in "frivolous talk" or activity, but can expect long periods of work, meditation, and silence. All members who fail to follow Mitchell's dictates are punished in a variety of ways, such as standing in place for long periods and three-day fasts. However, some of the more extreme punishments, such as beatings, were reserved for his children and wives.[44]

Gender in Naziryah, like other ascribed traits, is treated as something to overcome. Women are "spirit[s] traveling in female bodies."[45] The same is true for men, to whom Mitchell offered this rhyme: "I am not the Penis/I am not the hair . . . /Even though it is there." When people become attached to any particular identity, they are "crystalizing," which Mitchell considered to be bad. Crystalizing limits our potential, is selfish, and isolates us from each other and the "oneness." The leader's thoughts about women are antifeminist, as feminism can lead women to become overweight and lazy. Activities are gender-segregated, and women and men tend to associate with members of their own gender.

The Purple People have a belief system that fits in some aspects with the wider paranormal community. Spiritual vibration is one of the Purple People's major concepts, as it is with other paranormal believers. The Nahziryah and other vendors/attendees at the annual paranormal/UFO conferences in Eureka Springs, Arkansas, share this idea of vibrations, linked typically to one's spirit or "chakras." Moreover, a number of authors have written books the Ozark Mountain Press located in Huntsville, Arkansas, has published that address vibrations and other topics. For example, Christine Ramos wrote: "Universal energy is that which sustains all of creation on this planet." Later, she argued that it "transcends that which has limits of time and space."[46] Moreover, vibrations can be ranked and people can seek and attain higher vibrations or be led to them by those so attuned to them. The same phenomenon (variable vibrations) and process (attunement) can occur at the group and world-level. At the macrolevel, the process is cyclical and often catastrophic, but has the potential to advance humankind.[47]

Attunement or "at-one-ment" means that people are able to "harmonize the physical, mental, and spiritual aspects of our being."[48] Truth is the divine or spiritual essence. Mitchell contended that all faiths are "sublime" and truth itself is omniversal and leads to "one divine creator."[49] People who become more attuned create a "thought atmosphere" with their "thought energy," which creates "pockets" that allow for an "opening for bigger groups."[50]

Many paranormal believers, including the Purple People, believe that the color purple is indicative of the highest vibration of one's spirit and ultimately signals that an individual has transitioned into a phase of enlightenment and universal consciousness. According to Mitchell, the color purple represents "spiritual, peaceful and positive energies." The notion that the color purple has energy is common. For example, Maiya Gray-Cobb's *Seeds of the Soul* and Irene Lucas's *Thirty Miracles in Thirty Days*, both published by Ozark Mountain Publishing, provide detail about which colors are associated with which powers, who the guiding entities are behind each color, and essential key positive and negative attributes. Although there is agreement that the head or crown is the highest chakra or color and is purple, the notion that one's hair is like antennae that sense metaphysical vibrations is unique to the Nahziryah.

Another major concept important to the Nahziryah is that reality is cyclical. The "Involution-evolution" cycles fit into Mitchells's belief that "you get what you are." This kharma-like notion argues that the more focused and mindful people are in their duties, the more likely they are to reach at-one-ment. Time is an integral element in the Purple People ideology. Dates are referred to as dispensations and manifestations. For example, at some dispensation (time), a person might be some manifestation (male/female, African American/white, etc.). The Nahhziryah, as weary travelers, are on a "spiralic journey" involving ancient/new-time dispensations.

The Purple People are hardworking and industrious. Mitchell worked his people very hard. Over the years, they found a market for their crafts, scented oils, and so on. In New Orleans, where the group operated the Veil of Truth Center for Metaphysics and Esoteric Learning, they sold much of their handiwork or provided literature, training, and other metaphysical services to the public. While in New Orleans, the group had a booth at the New Orleans French Market Flea Market for a number of years. When they moved to Marion County in Arkansas, they spent much time engaged in intensive organic gardening and gathering wild plants. More recently, the Purple People were vendors at area events such as the Minority Business Enterprises conference in St. Louis and the UFO Conference in Eureka Springs.

Concluding Remarks

Shared religious beliefs are one of the most prevalent ideologies of communal living.[51] However, few religious communes form that reject mainstream society categorically and isolate themselves completely from family, church, school, and government.[52] Moreover, examples of African American cultic intentional communities are very rare. Members of cultic religious communities such as Nahziryah are deeply committed and share exclusive and strong internal bonds. Leadership and ideology are invested usually in one charismatic person. Thus, a test of a cultic community's longevity is whether the commune persists after the leader's death or removal.

Joseph Washington, a professor of religious studies at the University of Virginia, wrote in *Black Sects and Cults*, "Economic power is fundamental to the black cult-type."[53] By comparison, Fred Davis noted, "By and large, Negroes view with bewilderment and ridicule the white hippies who flaunt, to the extent of begging on the streets, their rejection of what the Negroes have had scant opportunity to attain."[54] Thus, by living together and sharing resources, Black cults offer a way for members to realize material gain they might not have access to otherwise. In summarizing his observations on a number of Black cults, such as those of Father Divine and Daddy Grace, Washington stated that the "central interest of the black cult . . . is to create a black ethos which provides blacks with dignity, integrity, freedom and power to become new wine in new wineskins."[55] However, the case of the Purple People, like other African American messianic cults, seems to fit better with that of white cults, where members live in poverty while the leader and his/her cadre live luxuriously.

It is astonishing how adept the Purple People were at gatekeeping information about themselves and their leader. Perhaps most cultic movements are highly skilled in presenting the leader and his/her group. It is true that all information flowed both ways through Mitchell. However, it would seem that members must have monitored each other to discourage anything but minimal interaction with outsiders.

The Purple People are an example of a cult, which Washington defined as "a new and syncretic religious movement in its early stages emerging in alienation from a traditional religious system and society. In the beginning, it is characterized by small numbers, search for a mystical experience, lack of structure, charismatic leadership, individual problem orientation, and presence in a local area."[56]

A syncretic faith is one that weaves into its belief system various theological strands of inspiration. Solving members' daily problems rather than redirecting their focus on the religious or spiritual world is what Washington means by an individual orientation. Washington's definition adds to Stark and Bainbridge's definition I presented earlier.

Some of Washington's criteria for cults, and especially those that are African American, fit with the Naziryah, as they are like other messianic African American groups in a number of ways. Even more generally, they operated much like other cults. When I first began studying the Purple People, I was inclined to treat their faith and religious life as an example of a new religious movement. Duval Mitchell did create a "new and syncretic" faith. However, he did much more than that. Over the years of his charismatic leadership, Mitchell was able to truly isolate his followers both geographically and socially by moving to the Ozarks. Naziryah were kept always busy and away as much as possible from the outside world. Like in other cults, members had to rely on each other in the group after leaving their family and friends.[57] He was able to exploit his members and even abused them for so long by keeping them isolated.

In addition to living in isolation in the woods, the Naziryah were forced to wear clothing that distinguished them from other people. Sociologist Rosabeth Moss Kanter refers to the practice of everyone in a group wearing the same clothing as a type of de-differentiating mechanism, or in other words, purple "uniforms" functioned in such a way as to strip each member of his/her individuality. According to Kanter, lack of privacy is another type of de-differentiating technique, something Purple People endured.[58] Finally, members become entirely dependent upon the leader and find it difficult to leave the group. Thus, I would categorize the Naziryah are a cult.

The story of the Purple People, like that of the IKMU, suggests that there is something about Searcy and Marion Counties, maybe even the Ozarks more generally, that fosters utopian and cultic activity. The region also is known to be home to a large number of back-to-the-landers and communal folk. Perhaps it is because Marion and Searcy Counties are agriculturally fertile and yet, an isolated region. It is true that John Battenfield sought a remote place away from the impending apocalypse based on his literal interpretation of the Book of Revelation that the people of Judea fled to the hills because of impending war.[59] Duval Mitchell found that the county fit his goal to isolate both his family and followers from the outside world. However, the county actually is no more isolated than some other places in the Ozarks.

Much more is known about Duval Augusta Mitchell after he changed his identity and became the Revered Baba Nazirmoreh K. B. Kadem. Unlike John Battenfield, the story of Mitchell's life as a boy and young man is missing. Similarly, B. Timothy Drew of the Moorish Science Organization, W. D. Fard and Elijah Poole of the Nation of Islam, Dwight York of the Ansaaru Allah Community, and Hulon Mitchell of the Nation of Yahweh lost or obscured their prior identity. Like the rest of these charismatic leaders, what was Mitchell like as a boy? What pivotal events led him and others down the path to become cult leaders? Other than a propensity for titles and colorful clothing, one common denominator seems to be that most of these men came from very humble backgrounds. Perhaps they fit somewhere along the spectrum of narcissistic personality disorder because they believed they were gods or God's messengers. It is clear that they expected total obedience and adoration and played on people's fears to convince them they offered their only way to salvation.

On the other hand, perhaps many of these men really were tricksters and hucksters. Through charisma, they attracted people looking for hope, now, and in this world. Often, these leaders have found themselves in trouble with the law and surrounding community. Members of the Nation of Yahweh and their leader were convicted of extortion and even murder, while Isa Muhamad and members of the Ansaaru Allah Community generated money through begging.

Interestingly, when I saw the representatives of the Purple People at the UFO conference in Eureka Springs, I didn't feel that they were gullible and weak. True, the women seemed reserved and were dressed from head to toe in purple garb. It is difficult to tell what the truth is because the group is reclusive, and Duvall Augustus Mitchell provided much of what little information we have about them. Much more is known about Mitchell and the hardships he exacted on his wives and children in the group because of the work of Jacqueline Froelich. As for the former members of Mitchell's cult, I wish each and every one of them the best.

The Group

In the early 1960s, a charismatic and talented musician named W. Dixon Bowles formed a group of singers out of Odessa, Texas. The singers later changed their name to the Dan Blocker Singers after Dan Blocker offered his name and support in securing the singers opportunities in Hollywood. They made it big in Hollywood in 1966 and 1967, appearing in a number of television shows and venues such as *The Milton Berle Show* and stadiums and night clubs. But all of the performances and rehearsals, as well as concerns about the Hollywood lifestyle, ultimately led the singers to call show business quits. In the late 1960s, the Dan Blocker Singers moved to the Arkansas Ozarks to live communally. Under the leadership of Bowles, the commune was very strict and entrepreneurial. The Group, as they became known, operated a guest ranch around the Clarksville area of Arkansas, as well as a set of hotels, a butchery, a local newspaper, and other businesses at Mount Magazine in Greer's Ferry. But after a series of misfortunes, as well as hostility from local citizens, the Group left the Ozarks in the early 1970s.

The Dan Blocker Singers

In 1964, a group of mainly young people from Odessa, Texas, banded together and began what would be a several-decade experiment in communal living. One of the twelve people was Dixon Bowles, a DJ, program director, and musician with K-BSN radio in 1964. He was also a college student in Odessa. Every weekday at 3:00 p.m., listeners could hear *The Dixon Bowles*

Road Show on AM 970. The group also had a program on Saturdays called the *K-Basin Collegiate Review*.[1]

In 1965, Bowles gathered 40 high school and college musicians and singers into a group that he named the W. D. Singers. After four months of rehearsal, the singers had their first public appearance, and their second public appearance drew 3000 people. "For over a year the singers have rehearsed three times a week in addition to giving 22 major concerts."[2] Each member performed on a volunteer basis. Any money that was earned was used to sustain the music business. The choir performed a "hootenanny" in Amarillo in early August. The band, according to one member, "sang folk and spiritual, foot stomping music."[3] One evening, the singers provided chorale backup for Dan Blocker, who gave dramatic readings.[4]

Later in August, the W. D. Singers headed to Hollywood but soon returned to Amarillo. One issue was that the large size of the group was unwieldy, so Dixon had to pare it down from 50 to 25 members. Sometime later, the name of the group was changed to the Rhythm Folk.

Dixon and his group returned to Hollywood in January 1966, but then they headed back to Texas soon afterwards. Later, in June, the group went to Hollywood again, but this time sought out help from Dan Blocker. It was around this time that Dixon Bowles changed the name of the choir again, adopting the name of the actor who played the character of "Hoss" on *Bonanza*—Dan Blocker. At some point when the singers were back in Odessa, Blocker visited the community college, and he liked what he heard, so he allowed the group to use his name.

The group's third try at making it in Hollywood was successful. While seeking help from Dan Blocker and his organization, a producer for *The Milton Berle Show* saw them and was impressed.[5] Reporter Jack Smith wrote that Dixon had laid out his plan for members to live in Hollywood. "We had a long indoctrination session in Odessa to prepare everybody to live in this house together under my puritanical dictatorship."[6] Some of the rules included avoiding areas of the town that Dixon had deemed bad, and members always had to travel in pairs. Romantic relationships between the men and women of the band were forbidden, and Dixon made all of the decisions about who the members could even date outside the band. Drugs and alcohol were forbidden.

The Dan Blocker Singers settled into a two-story house near the Sunset Strip that had once been owned by Errol Flynn.[7] The house had 10 rooms for

Figure 7.1 The Dan Blocker Singers, 1967. Photograph by Ben Olender. © 1967. *Los Angeles Times*. Used with permission.

the 18 band members. Part of the house was used as an audition hall because it was the only space large enough to fit all of the band members at the same time. Because of this arrangement, talent scouts actually came to the house, rather than the band going out to auditions.

With so many people doing so many different things under one roof, management was pretty strict. Most of the money coming into the house was used to sustain the band. Aside from gigs, five people made additional money in other lines of work and donated 10 percent of their earnings to the group. The *Herald* went on to say, "Under Dixon's drill sergeant direction, they maintain a daily routine, dividing up chores." Everyone helped with the household tasks, aside from cooking, which was done by a dedicated cook and soprano named Linda. Although there were a lot of mouths to feed, the food was simple, usually just meat and potatoes.

Of the many band members, only Dixon and his brother were married. The parents of some of the younger members were put at ease when Bowles assured them that he would take care of their children. According to Dixon Bowles, during their time in Hollywood, neighbors were indeed at first apprehensive about so many young people living in one house, but they later grew to accept the Singers. The band members were model citizens. Dixon specifically noted that there were "no pregnancies, not a single arrest."[8]

The singers, basically a folk music band, signed a four-performance contract with *The Milton Berle Show* with an option until 1968.[9] The debut was advertised in newspapers throughout the country.[10] The show premiered on September 9, 1966. The other guests that night were Lucille Ball and Richard Harris. The reviews of the performance by the Dan Blocker Singers were positive. One noted that they were "a lively group."[11] Another observed that "Blocker's group is called by some the fastest rising group in the country."[12] Jack Smith noted that the members "sing songs of joy and songs of sadness and protest, but it isn't a protest group."[13] In fact, some of the songs that they sung were quite traditional and included religious themes and imagery, such as "Swing Low," "When the Saints Go Marching In," and "Gonna Cross that Chilly Jordan."[14]

The *Reno-Gazette-Journal* reported, "One of the biggest up-and-coming folk-spiritual groups working today [. . .] present a wide range of vocals, covering tender ballads, lively spirituals, and even bombastic rock 'n' roll." Some songs on their playlist were "Joy in My Heart," "Dominique," "Deep River," "Johnny, I Hardly Knew You," "Bo Diddley," "Try to Remember," and "Confusion."[15]

Of the eighteen members who moved from Odessa, only two of the original members remained at this point. Everyone else was new. However, such turnover did not dampen the success of the band. The Dan Blocker Singers appeared with Dan Blocker at the Royal Tahitian on September 17 and 18 in San Bernardino.[16] Dixon Bowles appeared on the *LaLanne Affair* on September 30.[17] At the Beverly Hilton Hotel, the singers performed with Lorne Green, Danny Thomas, and Wayne Newton.[18] In Redlands, California, at the Hollywood Bowl, they participated with Don and the Good Times, Dick Dale and the Cougars, and Sheriff's Rhythm Posse.[19] In November, Dean Martin and Sammy Davis Junior also performed with them.[20] *The Milton Berle Show* featured the group working with Roy Rogers and Dale Evans on December 2. Dickson Bowles married Tina Van Horn on November 18, and the group's last *Milton Berle Show* performance was January 1967, where they appeared with Lucille Ball. Around Christmastime, they also performed for airmen at an air base in Amarillo.

Everyone was working hard carrying out the day-to-day chores of communal living. There was also the constant grind of performing. The band eventually burned out, and Bowles and other members worried how the Hollywood lifestyle was affecting them. The *Bonham Daily Favorite* noted that the band had "achieved commercial success but spiritual failure."[21] Another account noted, "The competition was ferocious, the morality negotiable."[22] Former member Dan Hazel remembered that Dixon and others talked about getting excited and then heartbroken; that the music had changed. But the core group wanted to remain together, but not in Hollywood.[23]

The band would close out their time in Hollywood doing a few stage shows, and they even performed a March 16–29, 1968, gig at the Nugget in Reno with Dan Bolger of *Wizard of Oz* fame. While in Los Angeles, Tina's mother saw an advertisement about available land in the Arkansas Ozarks, which Dixon and others found attractive.[24] Dixon Bowles recalled, "We came down to look at it [a lodge]. It was in the middle of the woods with friendly people . . . honest people . . . good people."[25] By the fall of that year, the idea to move to Arkansas was put to vote, and that's when some of the Dan Blocker Singers became the Beacon Street Irregulars. This iteration of the band would go on to perform with John Banner, "Sgt. Schultz" of *Hogan's Heroes*, at a USO event in Vietnam in April 1968. Some singers headed back to Odessa and other places. Meanwhile, Dixon and Tina Bowles, and the rest of the other former Dan Blocker Singers, would head southeast, caravan style with three or four cars, to Arkansas and become known as the Group.[26]

The Group

Later in 1968, members of the renamed and reconfigured commune signed a lease in which they were to pay $400 per month and maintain the Big Piney

Guest Ranch in Johnson County, Arkansas. The ranch was on a 90-acre wooded area outside the small town of Lamar, Arkansas. During this period of time, the Group's population was over sixty people. And as ever, the Group were industrious. "They worked as farm laborers, in a local pants factory and continued to do some singing."[27] The singing act was 20 to 30 minutes in duration, and then members would rotate in from other duties to do skits in the style of *Laugh-In* and other popular themes. They were not like the drug- and sex-fueled hippy communes, a point that they emphasized with *Memphis Commercial Appeal* reporter Thomas Bevier.[28]

Many people in the Group connected with other people in the community through trade, work, or the arts, such as in the case of Dixon directing a local high school play. Some members who sang or played musical instruments linked up with similarly talented people in the area to form the Arkansas River Valley Singers. But despite the community outreach efforts and the strict lifestyle followed by its members, the commune endured some vandalism and calls to the sheriff from outsiders who falsely accused the Group of marijuana cultivation.[29]

In 1971, the Group signed a 10-year lease with the United States Forest Service to maintain a lodge and 400 acres of land at Mount Magazine, Arkansas.[30] They intended to run a lodge and restaurant there, and they put much of their financial assets toward that goal. One member remembered the early years in the Ozarks as very busy times. Members were expected to work day and night in assorted jobs at Mount Magazine and in the surrounding area. Often, they would return to cook, entertain guests, and clean each night.[31]

Early in 1971, misfortune hit the commune when the Big Piney lodge was destroyed in a fire on Wednesday, February 3. The situation worsened further that Friday after several members of the Group were returning home after a long day of working for Governor Winthrop Rockefeller. A tractor trailer plowed into their VW van when it swerved into their lane, injuring or killing several of the passengers. But Bowles's charismatic nature prevented the community from collapsing.[32] Several years later, Bowles testified before a Federal Trade Commission meeting in Atlanta regarding the fact that two local funeral homes had engaged in shady practices and exploited the Group in the aftermath of the car crash.[33]

The tragedies, a shortage of jobs, and work on a church poverty project forced some members of the Group to leave Arkansas around 1971 to form a satellite group in St. Louis, Missouri.[34] Regarding the church project, members of the Group were working with a priest from St. Louis who sought their help to do good works in the area. They were also there to start restaurant and work in various day jobs. Thirty-two members of the Group moved into a nunnery next St. Henry's Church in East St. Louis. The house was a three-story building with one bathroom, and the floors were sex-segregated except in the case of married couples.

All members had to share one car, yet somehow the men were still able to work day jobs. Many members of the Group joined local churches and had a theologically guided sense of purpose that centered on the "fulfillment of Christ consciousness." This vision drove the members to do good works in the community, such as operating a telephone service for elderly people and running a lead poison prevention program for inner city children. But in spite of their industriousness and community outreach efforts, it appears that the local elites pressured the diocese to evict members, giving them only two days to leave. Local leaders also refused to issue a permit to the Group for their restaurant. Powerful interests fed a cover story to the paper that the house was too small for the number of people who lived there, even though it was a large building, and the restaurant didn't meet the city health code.[35]

One columnist who believed and perpetuated the cover story was George Benson[36] from Searcy, Arkansas, who opposed the commune. In an article in the *St. Louis Post Dispatch*, he stated, "In St. Louis they got into trouble with authorities and subsequently the house they had leased for their 'communal' living was condemned. An article in the *St. Louis Post-Dispatch* featured Bowles' autocratic rule." What Benson overlooked, though, was the traditional orientation and strong work ethic of the members of the Group. Instead of acknowledging those attributes, he cast a negative light in one area of the article when he stated that Connie Rosenbaum had characterized Dixon Bowles as a "benevolent but authoritative father figure."[37]

The Group, both at Mt. Magazine and in St. Louis, was getting hassled from all sides—by columnist George Benson and his syndicated column, the authorities, and then by neighbors who regarded them "with apprehension and trepidation."[38] However, when people got to know members of the commune, they inevitably changed their views. As a very large communal enterprise of out-of-staters with different and perhaps new ideas, the Group was seen as a threat to people in an area known for keeping to its own. Adding to the ambivalence of some in the general community was the fact that leaders within the Group enforced endogamy and socializing with nonmembers was discouraged. The endogamous nature of the Group even extended to the practice of children attending their own independent school, rather the schools provided by the community.

During these times, there was no overarching religious or secular ideology guiding communal life among members of the Group—just Bowles's charisma. Thomas Bevier reported in his 1971 piece, reprinted in *Mother Earth News*, that a communal Christianity was integral to notions of sharing resources, but all faiths offered insights to members. Bevier did note a Far Eastern philosophical leaning in at least some of the books that members read. New members from the northeast had also infused the commune with big city worldviews and New Age ideas.[39] Founding member Ed Eudy remembered that teachings were humanistic and based on doing good works. He said that members learned how to think critically and creatively. Regarding religion, they studied the commonalities that all faiths shared that they could follow. At first, these newer members seemed to bring a more hippy perspective, but Dixon blocked that direction, wanting to keep the Group "straight."[40]

The Group was very resourceful and talented from the very beginning, and wherever members went, they were involved in money-making enterprises. Music and entertainment, cooking, entrepreneurship, and architecture and building added to the creative pool that the commune possessed. A *de facto* two-class system existed: those who were sent out to work, and the people who remained at Big Piney to run the commune. At home, nearly everyone chipped in when it came time to do the chores.[41]

Dixon Bowles remained at the top of the hierarchy. One member told me, "Although he was small in stature, he was a very strong, very, very extremely bright. I think I heard of Dixon that [his IQ] was somewhere around 180." Coupled with his intelligence, however, was a streak of authoritarianism. Bevier described him as ascetic. It wasn't a wise decision to ever challenge Bowles and still remain in the Group.[42] Regarding Dixon's natural leadership, another member said that Dixon was "the wisest man I ever met. He understood people and listened to them. He was on a quest to learn more. Unusually great as people go. However, you could disagree with him. He may have had a little ego, but it was more of righteous anger than anything."[43] Given all these traits, it is not surprising why quite a few people decided to continue following Dixon and remain in the Group.

Another former member remembered that the Group was divided into thirds: one-third of the members were mainly women who maintained households and took care of and taught the children. Another third of the Group were out making money. The last third were also entrepreneurial but were more focused on the key philanthropic goals and mission of the Group. These members were out trying to make a difference and sought opportunities working for politicians and other elites aligned with Group values.[44]

Bowles relied on a council—many of them women—to ensure that things got done. This core group would remain the same over the years, even if members came and left. Tina, his one-time wife, was next in line in terms of authority. One former male member recollected that the women seemed quite more dominant than was typically the case in mainstream society. In some ways, the commune was between "a hippy camp and an establishment camp," in that the group was able to straddle a more egalitarian kibbutz model.[45] Whatever the reason, many men and women found the relaxed gender role expectations to be an attractive feature in terms of becoming or remaining a member.

Just like life in the house on the Sunset Strip in Hollywood, the members continued to follow strict codes of behavior in their new home. In what was the opposite of the common conception of communal life during that time period, there was no free sex taking place, and drug/alcohol use was forbidden. The Group was aware of other intentional communities, and even briefly interacted with a few. However, the authoritarian nature of the Group was antithetical to the ways in which many other communes were organized, which was often around some form of group consensus. Hippies looking for drugs, sex, or a place to lounge around found them sinhospitable. Local people also learned that the commune was stricter than what they had previously expected.[46]

Back at Greers Ferry, while the Group members kept to themselves in their compound, they did become integrated into the fabric of the community around them. *New York Times* reporter Roy Reed noted that members of the Group "became the entire volunteer fire department of the town, which has a population of 388. Other members became leaders of Boy and Girl Scout Troops."[47] A number of members also joined local churches and were involved in politics, media, and other spheres of activity in Greers Ferry. However, many townsfolk felt that the members of the commune were intellectually aloof, and this perceived arrogance was buttressed by the fact that the commune's children were educated within the compound and not in the public schools. Moreover, some people also felt that the Group actually wanted to take over the town.[48]

The Group became so successful that many of the more established residents grew to resent them—and their power. Reed wrote: "The town held an election last fall [in 1972] and for the first time since moving to Greers Ferry in 1971, the members of the group voted. It is important to note that members were never urged to vote as a block by leadership and could vote however they wanted. However, the Group's number of voting members did turn the balance of power between to fiercely contesting factions.[49] The losing faction turned its anger on the commune, and on the night of Aug. 23 [1973] The Group's home was attacked by a stone-throwing mob."[50] And in addition to the mob, the Group had endured all sorts of harassment, ranging from very negative and false newspaper articles by George Benson—who was mentioned earlier—to actual physical intimidation within the community.

Late on a Saturday night, August 25, 1973, some local residents showed up at the commune compound cursing and throwing rocks. In an interview with the *Hope Star*, Dixon Bowles "said the persons attempted to provoke a fight, but that the members of 'The Group' did not respond. 'Our people did nothing throughout the entire thing except stand there and dodge.'" Bowles did give some members weapons in case the commune was overrun by the hooligans. State police rounded up 21 people who were later charged with night riding. All of the charges were dropped, but the police officers were roundly criticized for siding with the Group.[51]

Eventually, the tension dissipated, but Dixon and others decided change was needed. He argued that there wasn't much to gain by staying at Greers Ferry. He pointed out that if the Group moved to Little Rock, they would be absorbed into a bigger community. Moreover, fitting in would mean being more effective in making a positive difference towards the world. Besides all that, their businesses were suffering because of declining tourism. So, in late 1973, the Group announced that their Snug Harbor Dinner Theatre would close down until further notice.[52] In February of the next year, Bowles announced that the business was closing—except for the 12 members who were staying to manage a coffee shop, hotels, a newspaper, and other businesses.[53] The remaining 55 members moved to Little Rock.

The move to Little Rock happened quickly. One of the members started looking for housing in Little Rock. Soon, people started moving in. Meanwhile, Dan stayed in Greers Ferry for a year to fulfill contract. His wife waitressed at the Narrows Inn Coffee Shop while he did the cooking. Some members still were around to staff the volunteer fire and ambulance. Most locals in Greers Ferry were sad to see the group leave.

Little Rock was one of Dan's favorite places. Initially, the Group had a location outside of Little Rock. There was a black member who stayed in Little Rock during the Greers Ferry years because of the fear of how he might be treated by locals in that town. Someone started a satellite in Little Rock, in a poorer part of the town called the Quapaw Quarter. The houses were rather large—four homes covered half of a city block. Members put a fence up around the homes to be able to walk between houses. Whenever Dan could return to Little Rock from working in the Memphis satellite for the winter, he felt like he was back home and with the family.

Like Steve Gaskin's Farm in Tennessee, the Group had detachments of people who set up "satellites" in other areas of the United States. Besides St. Louis, Group members established satellites in Memphis and Little Rock. The satellites were usually ten people or fewer. Former member Dan helped operate the one in Memphis. In Memphis, however, more people were needed to do all sorts of things such as entertain, operate a restaurant, and run a comedy club. The restaurant almost went bankrupt but eventually was able to do well.

The entrepreneurial spirit and dogged determination helped make the restaurant a success. According to Dan and Ed, who ran the restaurant in Memphis, food was cheap, with steak and potatoes at $2.99. It didn't hurt that another member was a butcher. Local bands brought people into listen to the music but more importantly to buy drinks. That's where the profits came from. The Group would give concert tickets to loyal customers. Acts such as Duke Tomato and the All Star Frogs played there. Even country singer Larry Gatlin, a long-time Odessa connection played there. There was also a live radio program. Soon, record companies put people in club and didn't have to pay a lot.

In the late 1970s, the Group started looking for a new place to live. The Quapaw district at that time was a rough area of town, and members found themselves always on guard. The decision was made to create a satellite and then move everyone to Portland. Housing in Portland didn't meet the Group's needs. The local authorities in Portland didn't want them—again they encountered strict city codes. And the price of everything in the area was too high. Given all that, the Group decided to stay in Little Rock.[54]

The Group still currently owns a couple of neighborhood blocks in an older, more affluent part of the city. They also have a vacation home out in the country with a mansion, pool, and other amenities on 100 acres of land. They are deeply enmeshed in the social fabric of Little Rock. However, some longstanding, well-connected members have left in recent years.

Dixon Bowles's "benevolent dictatorship" loosened up over time. Long-held prescriptions against various behaviors, such as alcohol usage and socializing with outsiders, also loosened or were even discarded altogether. Dan thought that members were too dependent on Dixon. When Dan returned for the 20-year reunion, he noted that Dixon had withdrawn some from operations. He had taken on too many responsibilities and finally allowed businesses to run on their own. A split arose in the Group after Dixon died, and Sharon and Clayton left. By late 1970s, Dan and Ed decided to leave the Group.

The council remained in charge after the death of Dixon Bowles in 2010.[55] The Group remains very successful, and the Quapaw district in which they live has increased in value over the years. They have their own internet service and a number of other businesses. Moreover, they are also well-established in various aspects of Little Rock society.[56]

Making Sense of It All

The story of a singing group leaving the mainstream and settling in the Ozarks to live communally is unusual. The Dan Blocker Singers had their musical roots in the 1960s folk music world. The Dan Blocker Singers found fame and touring to be an alienating and superficial experience. They then stepped away from the commercial music industry. Dixon Bowles went on to create communities in the Ozarks. Later, when the Group moved to Little Rock, they would become a major cultural force in the city.

The Group was never really received very well wherever they went in the Ozarks, or even in other areas such as St. Louis and Portland. Too many people resented them for remaining separate from other members of the community. Some people thought that the power of the commune to sway local politics was too much of a risk to keep them around. Elites used a variety of tactics, such as harsh, unfair health codes, negative press, and eviction to force them to leave their towns.

A major lesson of the stories of the Group is that the Ozarks became a refuge not only for back-to-landers, retirees, and others, but it also for burnouts who had previously been on the edge of major success as generators of popular culture. The Group had a focused set of leaders who were willing to break with the mainstream in order to seek a new way of living. Being able to have people buy into that vision is a testament to Dixon Bowle's charisma and the planning of the Group's core leadership.

When Electric Music Came to Arkansas

Nobody does Arkansas like Black Oak Arkansas.
—Ozark historian Brooks Blevins[1]

Before I moved to Arkansas in the late 1970s, the Animals, the Zombies, Deep Purple, and other bands were always playing in my life's background. However, I came of age, musically speaking, in Arkansas. My journey was a bit odd. I had an old portable record player and a transistor radio. I played whatever was around, including classical music; Mitch Miller; Peter, Paul, and Mary; Leon Russell; and Frank Zappa. With the radio, I could pick up faraway stations in places such as Chicago. One of my favorite radio shows was *Dr. Demento*. I started listening to the Beatles and became hooked. In high school, I couldn't get enough of Led Zeppelin, Black Sabbath, and newer bands such as Judas Priest, Iron Maiden, and Motley Crue. Southern rock was omnipresent but not really my thing. Riding the school bus every day, we listened to Billy Squire, REO Speedwagon, Alabama, and Foreigner. But the first time I heard Black Oak Arkansas, Jim "Dandy" Mangrum sounded like Captain Beefheart, whose voice I did not enjoy. Moreover, I thought the Ozark Mountain Daredevils, with their hit song "Jackie Blue," were too "AM radio." The year I graduated, our class made an essential compendium, in our yearbook, of popular culture as we understood it, and Arkansas music did not feature anywhere.

It was the year of Live Aid and Farm Aid. It was also the year of wrestling, videos, 501 Levis, neon colors, Rocky 4, Madonna, VCR's and satellites, big earrings, spiked hair, cropped pants, and jean jackets. Albums of the year were Bruce Springsteen's *Born in the USA* and George Strait's *Does Fort Worth Ever Cross Your Mind.*

To be sure, music is an important part of people's lives. In the United States in the 1960s and 1970s, rock and roll helped spread communitarian sentiments through the music of the Grateful Dead and other groups. Although the Ozarks ultimately became important to the emergence of rock and roll, it took a while for rock to become acceptable there. That changed in 1970, when a number of rock acts performed at the Ozarks Rock Festival held near Fayetteville in June. It was the first major rock festival in the region. Years later, Sedalia, Missouri, would become famous for its own rock festival. Likewise, one of the first rock bands in the Ozarks was Black Oak Arkansas (BOA).

As southern rock bands grew famous and rich, they often became progressive change agents. Author Ronald Brownstein noted, "Concerts by the Allman Brothers and their Southern rock confederates, the Marshall Tucker Band and Black Oak Arkansas, raised crucial early money for Jimmy Carter."[2] As BOA grew famous, the band gave much to charity and later helped with the presidential campaign of Bill Clinton. BOA also established a commune deep in the Ozarks, twenty miles from Mountain Home, Arkansas. The group's lyrics showcase its communitarian ideals and at the same time its neo-Confederate identity. The other famous Arkansas band, the Ozark Mountain Daredevils, stressed ideals more attuned to spirituality and social justice.

As a sociologist, I recognize that music relates to various facets of social life. Musicians convey big ideas on important topics, just as we do in the academic world.[3] However, the audience for musical artists is much wider than for that of academics and often serves as a catalyst for social movements. Music also shapes our identities and binds us with other like-minded people. Music brings people of similar backgrounds together and bridges different cultures and groups. In the words of one Ozark back-to-lander, "I honestly believe the music drove that culture pretty heavily. People gathered to hear music, people put the 8-track cartridges in their cars, bought albums as soon as they came out. It was a measure of where you were in the culture."[4]

As Pierre Bourdieu argues, class differences are demonstrated in the art, literature, and music we tend to enjoy.[5] Yet Bourdieu's point is not news to anyone who has observed American culture. Years earlier, social commentator and *Harper's* managing editor Russell Lynes observed that highbrow people listened to "Bach and before, Ives and after," while people of the lower-to-middle classes preferred "light opera and popular favorites" from such artists as Nelson Eddy and Perry Como.[6] At the bottom of the social scale, lowbrows got their music from jukeboxes. Rockabilly did not even make it onto Lynes's list; other commentators placed it near the bottom.[7] Regarding musical pecking order in the 1970s, Kemp wrote that white southern musicians "suddenly reveled in their white-trash heritage: Elvis, rhinestones, busy sideburns, moon pies, beehive hairdos, Black Oak Arkansas, velvet Jesuses, trailer parks, Myrtle Beach post cards."[8]

Rock music not only is agent of antistructure; it can also act as a deregionalizing force[9] in that it helps spread ideals, such as communitarian sentiments, across all sorts of geographies. At that time, many musicians sang songs that challenged mainstream society, including my favorite band, the Beatles.[10] From rockabilly to BOA, rock challenged norms while also reaffirming southern identity. Ozark Mountain Daredevils (OMD), on the other hand, tried to blur identity by focusing on crossing boundaries and cultures. The trickster is represented well by BOA, and earlier Ronnie Hawkins, who were known for their "unbridled sexuality" in their music and performances. OMD, on the other hand, with many of their songs about leaving home and searching, represents the wanderer aspect of the trickster. Both operated at the margins of culture and even their musical genre.[11]

Background

Marlon Brando, James Dean, the Beat Poets, and the fusion of "white" and "black" music all helped usher in rock and roll.[12] The Ozarks had a major part in the rise of rockabilly with Ozark Jubilee and early rockabilly stars such as Billy Lee Riley and Ronnie Hawkins. Many early rockabilly musicians had a start or were influenced by the *Ozark Jubilee*, a show that aired on ABC for much of the 1950s and was popular across the nation.[13] *Ozark Jubilee* entertainer Red Foley observed that "the kids sing the latest rock and roll songs. They don't even know how to square dance anymore." According to Foley, rock was taking over what was once country and western music's territory. Accordingly, he recommended that singers change with the times or get left behind.[14]

This type of Ozarks music resembled what was originally known as "hillbilly music" but later grew outside that music's humble mountain origins. Archie Green's definition of hillbilly music includes styles such as "old time, familiar tunes, Dixie, mountain, sacred, gospel, country, cowboy, western, country-western, hill and range, western swing, Nashville, rockabilly, [and] bluegrass."[15] It was music for white people—often poor white people.

Some social commentators worried that old-time musical traditions were being replaced by rock and roll. Tom Dearmore, the "Ozark Outlook" columnist for the *Baxter Bulletin*, wrote that fiddling was dying out in the Ozarks because "radio and TV bring a never-ending stream of rock n' roll, bop and other modern music to every hill home."[16] The obsolescence of folk music was the theme of the first edition of *Hillbilly Comics* in 1955. In the comic "Mountain Music," some big city music executives try to trick some hill musicians from Porcupine Junction into a record deal, but the executives end up being tricked when the band learns the mambo from the radio that the executive outsiders bring to the hills.[17]

However, traditional folk music, or even the kind of primitive hillbilly seen in *Hillbilly Comics*, did not disappear in the Ozarks. Newspaper notices from the period indicate no threat to country or old-time music. More often, events hosted singers representing all sorts of genres, including rock and roll. For example, in 1956 the Eureka Springs Folk Festival advertised: "Ballad singing will range from authentic old English ballads through the various Ozarkian variations of ballads to the modern rock n' roll."[18] Whether performed by balladeers, local beauty queen contestants, or bands from the *Ozark Jubilee* or other venues, rock had come to the Ozarks.

The Ozarks were home to rockabilly artists few people know today, but whose band members later became famous or influenced major artists. These rockabilly singers rarely mentioned the Ozarks or Arkansas in their lyrics. One major rockabilly singer who faded into obscurity was Billy Riley from Pocahontas, Arkansas. Riley learned about the blues and harmonica playing when his family moved to the Arkansas Delta and worked with fellow African American sharecroppers. He and his band became famous by exploiting the UFO craze of the 1950s. He fronted a band called the Little Green Men, whose members he actually forced to dress as little green men. The group had a hit called "Flyin' Saucers" on Sun Records in 1957. "Red Hot" was another popular song, covered later by the Beatles. At that time the band featured an unknown piano player named Jerry Lee Lewis.[19] Later, producer Sam Phillips chose to promote Jerry Lee Lewis over Billy Lee Riley, a move that kept Riley from greater opportunities. Later, Jim "Dandy" Mangrum, as a boy, saw Jerry Lee Lewis perform at a festival and decided he wanted to become a performer too.[20]

Another forgotten Ozark rockabilly artist is Ronnie Hawkins, who came from Hawkins' Holler near Huntsville, Arkansas.[21] "Down in the Holler, people spent their time hunting, fiddling, and drinking whiskey," according to the Band biographer Barney Hoskyns. Hawkins learned about the blues from an African American barber he and his father visited when he was growing up. Ronnie Hawkins's band, the Hawks, included Levon Helm on the drums and Robbie Robertson on guitar.[22] A signature part of the band's performance was "the monkey act" where Hawkins would add theatrics, many sexually suggestive, to the songs they played. The monkey acts, Hawkins's prior experience as a liquor runner, fondness for the blues, and other elements made him an early rock "incarnation of Dionysos, master of revels."[23] Helm later peeled the Hawks away from Hawkins to form the Band. Hawkins moved to Canada, bringing rock and roll with him. Although he faded into obscurity in the United States, his admirers included the Arkansas band the Cate Brothers, who would later work with the Band.[24] He had fans as far away as Great Britain, including John Lennon. The Guess Who and other Canadian rockers acknowledged his influence on their music.

In keeping with the puritanical half of W. J. Cash's hedonistic/puritanical southern psychic dichotomy, another variation on the trickster motif, leaders across the spectrum worried a lot about the suggestive nature of the new genre. To play in universities and other settings, Hawkins and the Hawks and other bands were expected to behave and refrain from "monkey acts" or other suggestive behaviors.[25] The genre was worrisome to those in power because it brought blacks and whites together in a society that disapproved of such interaction. The music also questioned the status quo on a number of other fronts by questioning sexual norms and challenging authority figures. According to one informant, "the counterculture started in the 50s and it was on the radio station when they started playing rock and roll and there was a lot of music like 'Stagger Lee.' Joplin radio stations wouldn't play that, even though that was the number one tune in the country. They said it was not the type of music they wanted to play."[26]

Concern about rockabilly peaked, and by the end of the 1950s, Ozark leaders grew hostile to the genre. At one radio station in St. Louis, Missouri, employees destroyed the station's collection of rockabilly music.[27] More puritanical types of people reacted to rockabilly as a "a mix of apocalypse, paranoia, bitterness, the old peckerwood resentment recognized long ago by Menken as driven by the overriding fear that somebody somewhere was having a good time."[28]

Outside the Ozarks, Memphis was the place where a lot of many early rock and roll and country music acts got their start. Much of that action found a home in Sun Records. There was also the King Biscuit Festival, which hosted many of the gospel, rhythm and blues, and country singers coming out of the Arkansas Delta. The Ozarks, on the other hand, had the Ozark Jubilee and a few radio stations out of Missouri. Folk music remained the popular genre in the region.

Much of the British Invasion and psychedelic rock did not make it to the Ozarks. One of the few rock acts that emerged out of Arkansas in the mid-1960s was Black Oak Arkansas.[29] Jim "Dandy" Mangrum, lead singer, told reporter Mary Campbell that most of the members "worked the fields" in the Arkansas Delta town of Black Oak. When they could, they practiced their songs in a cotton gin. Mangrum recalls, "We were loners when we got together. We were growing our hair out and the Beatles hadn't hit yet. Then we became a group of mavericks."[30] The band got into trouble stealing music equipment and soda machine money. When the police finally caught them, they were encouraged to leave town. No one was willing to hire them anyway because of their long hair.

Mangrum and the other band members moved from Arkansas to New Orleans, and then to California, before settling back in the Arkansas Ozarks.[31] Although the band had been around for some time, it wasn't until 1970 that they started performing for money. In the early 1970s, the band played in big and small towns throughout Missouri and Arkansas and toured all over the country.

Besides the return of BOA, another noteworthy event that took place in 1970 was the Ozark Rock Festival, one of the first rock festivals held in the Ozarks, from June 26 through 28. The festival led to be a series of events taking place between New Orleans and Atlanta, with the first being the Delta Fest in Greenville (October). July 1971 saw the Delta Fest (in Birmingham) and the Celebration of Life Fest (in McCrea, Louisiana).

The Ozark Rock Festival was billed as "Music, peace, and all the love that can be found in 48 hours." The festival was held near Fayetteville, on an eighty-acre farm and was expected to attract around 10,000 people. The actual number of participants was around 1,500 people. The bands that played over the two-day period included Moloch (out of Memphis), Heavy Water (from Tulsa), and Zig Zag (from Little Rock). One of the acts, the Cate Brothers (from Fayetteville), also enjoyed some regional success.[32]

The Ozark Rock Festival was sponsored by a communal group, A Family Called Us, led by Gorton D. Hitte, who also provided food and other support. Often, local citizens such as farmers, carpenters, ministers, would offer assistance. It is likely that the commune was accepted by the locals because it was Christian and professed to be "based on a blind faith in God and The Golden Rule."[33] The Family did good works throughout the city and even fed the concert goers for free. The Family was also instrumental in bringing other rock groups to the area such as Vanilla Fudge, Blue Cheer, and Space Opera.[34]

Local leaders were not happy about the Ozark Festival. Charles Cripps, the farm's owner, was arrested by the sheriff "after two of Cripps neighbors signed complaints of disturbing the peace."[35] The local media did not support the festival either.[36] Leaders and the local press in various southern states such as Alabama, Arkansas, Louisiana, and Mississippi feared the genre and sought to suppress rock festivals. Nevertheless, the festivals continued.

The next major musical event in the Ozarks was in May 1973, in Eureka Springs at the Ozark Mountain Folkfair. A number of bands performed such as Mason Proffit, Earl Scruggs, the Nitty Gritty Dirt Band, Lester Flatt, John Lee Hooker, and the Ozark Mountain Daredevils[37] It was in Eureka Springs that John Talbot, one of the members of Mason Proffitt had an epiphany and metanoia. According to April Griffith, "Concurrent with (and in some conflict with) the countercultural movement within Eureka Springs was the resurgence in popularity of Christian-based tourism driven largely by the Five Sacred Projects (including the *Great Passion Play* and the *Christ of the Ozarks* statue) undertaken in the city by Gerald L. K. Smith. Proselytizers from a local street ministry attended the festival to pass out copies of the New Testament, and John Michael Talbot, guitarist for Mason Proffit, is said to have been moved by what he saw during the festival to quit the band and purchase land nearby for his Little Portion Hermitage in Berryville (Carroll County)."[38] By the end of their run, Mason Proffit had five albums under their belt.[39]

Around the same time, BOA attracted much criticism. Reporter Mike Kelly asserted that fans of bands such as Grandfunk Railroad and BOA were shallow or "bubble gum" compared to fans of Bob Dylan.[40] Dave Thompson, author of *I Hate the New Music*, wrote, "Black Oak may well have been country boys at heart, but they were evil."[41] By "evil," he meant truly evil, and not just in the way of the schlocky Satan-rock routines that would become popular: "They were far worse than that. Most rock bands came to town and you had to lock up your daughters. A handful came to town and you'd lock up your sons as well. When Black Oak came to town, your lawn died, your cow stopped producing milk, and your records spontaneously warped."[42]

Famed rock critic Lester Bangs hated them so much he fantasized about someone shooting Mangrum.[43]

With all the naysayers and authorities, whom Mangrum referred to as the "system," "coming down" on the band, BOA sought refuge.[44] They found a 1300-acre site deep in the Ozarks, twenty miles from Mountain Home. In 1973, they established a commune that served as a farm, a business, and a studio.[45] The compound was encircled by a tall wooden fence. It boasted a lake, houses, a school, and even a post office. The band paid $55,000 for the property initially but sunk about $750,000 into the compound over the years.

Mangrum and his fellow commune members identified themselves as "naturalistic." People in the compound raised their own meat and vegetables. They were interested in solar power. Communal life was "wholesome" and members lived "humbly but tastefully."[46] BOA played country music at the compound; when out making money, they performed "hot and nasty" rock and roll.[47]

Mangrum's beliefs veered toward the libertarian. A bit at odds with more liberal communards, he agreed with Thomas Jefferson's belief that the best government is the least government.[48] He thought that people should rely more on family and friends than on government. "Just trying to hold our own," he explained, "not strain the system." Mangrum argued that rock and roll music worked well with his views about communal living. He pointed out that Carl Perkins' song "Blue Suede Shoes" was about simplicity and independence. He also told a Springfield reporter, "We've always stuck with the basic sounds that came from people like Jerry Lee Lewis and Elvis Presley."[49]

One way in which BOA did fit dominant southern culture was in its perpetuation of Confederate ideology and identity. However, the band existed within the margins of southern culture. Known as the "raunchiest critters to ever emerge from the Confederacy,"[50] BOA reveled in presenting themselves with symbols of the Confederacy, such as Dixie flags. They also liked to fight—something that W. J. Cash argued was favored by southern men. The band felt it represented the voice of the common man, with those "common men" consisting of young white southerners. Kirk Hutson observed: "In the eyes of Black Oak and its fans an ideal south was a place where southern youth could smoke marijuana and wear their hair long, yet remain a region where macho, violent, and Confederate flag-waving white men ruled. In an age when young southern white males felt that they were losing their unique privileges that message gained Black Oak Arkansas the respect of the good ol' boy element."[51]

The song "Jim Dandy to the Rescue" is one of the band's better-known tunes. This signature song highlights Jim "Dandy" Mangrum the singer and "Jim Dandy" the song's character, with both playing the trickster. The song was written by LaVern Baker in the late 1950s. In the early 1970s, Elvis told Mangrum that BOA needed to cover the tune. The band, up to that point, was unaware of the tune. Well, when the king of rock tells you to do something, you do it, and Jim "Dandy" Mangrum—like the song's name-sake—was always getting into trouble. He like other tricksters reminds us of the fallibility of elites and the corrupting influence of power, itself. Such a thin-boundary person "will often be seen as a bit unreliable—a critic, a rebel, 'not a team player.'"[52]

BOA's 1972 album *Keep the Faith* is lyrically one of their more substantive albums. The song "Revolutionary All-American Boys" informs the listener that BOA is there to help create a new and better place for people. "Revolutionary All American Boys" fits Jung's ambiguous savior-trickster figure Mercurius: "We're just what you need . . . We're your crowd pleasers, We're your body heaters, We're your human crutch." The song asserts that we shape our world and that all of us are "God's children." Another song, "Feet on Earth, Head in the Sky," promotes authenticity and staying true to one's dreams. Mangrum often let reporters know that authenticity was important to the band.[53]

Critics are a bit unfair to reduce BOA to little more than sex tunes. Mangrum and fellow members were socially conscious and famous for their charitable endeavors. As Mangrum told Campbell, "We still see things that need to be changed; you shouldn't ignore things that are wrong. America ain't good enough yet. But music took us to the top of the mountain."[54] The theme on their second album, *If an Angel Came to See You, Would You Make Her Feel at Home?*, was "Stay together with your ideals and have faith and trust."[55]

Still, BOA never shied away from sex. Mangrum told Campbell, "Sex is a big part of our success—magnetism, people can relate to. It's not the only thing we do. We know everybody has a spiritual and social side. But the kids relate to a sex excitement because of the taboos they've had on the subject."[56] Sorority member Billie Jean Johnson reported that when she and her sorority sisters attended a BOA concert, "the group's heavy sensual appeal had them dancing in their chairs."[57] Referring to the sexual nature of many BOA songs, reporter Dick Richmond wrote, "One [song] like 'Hot and Nasty' doesn't take much explanation, but some of the others do. Many of them concern sex apparently. However, there's really no way of knowing. A listener can't pick out the words. But then the songs obviously are not for lyrics freaks."[58]

Anthropologist Paul Radin regarded the trickster as having "unbridled sexuality." It isn't only BOA, much of rock and roll is sexualized. One interesting way in which sexuality is manifested in rock is by linking it to religion and spirituality. Such a link is a classic example of a cultural inversion, something sacred and pure turned into something base and dirty, especially to a traditionally minded person. On the other hand, BOA and others saw sex as an expression of the sacred world. Michael Gilmour, a literature and theology professor in Canada, noted that sexuality and religion are often interwoven in rock and roll songs.[59] For example, many BOA songs are devoted to romantic love and sacredness or lovers as saviors. In some cases, songs suggest the act of sex is spiritual. Even the word "Angel" can take on sexual connotations. On Black Oak Arkansas's self-titled debut album in 1971, there are quite a few songs about love and sex such as "The Hills of Arkansas," "I Could Love You," "Hot and Nasty," "Singing the Blues." Other songs on the album are religious like "Uncle Lijah," and "Lord Have Mercy on My Soul." On *Keep the Faith* (1972), again, most of the songs are either about sex or religion. The song "White Headed Woman" leaves nothing to the imagination with lyrics such as "I want you this afternoon. White headed woman please come soon. I can feel the vibes A humpin on through the room." The album *If an Angel Came to See You, Would You Make Her Feel at Home?* (1972) is again a collection of sexual and religious songs. In "Fertile Woman," the sex act is natural and spiritual. The same goes for "Spring Vacation." Mangrum sings, "Less clothes on women from the warm skies of heaven. The season of creation Comes with spring vacation." Other songs are more religious and focus on community, fighting evil, and immortality by being one with God.

The next major rock and roll event in the Ozarks was the July 1974 Ozark Music Festival in Sedalia, Missouri. Estimated as one of the best-attended concerts in American history, the festival's performers included Aerosmith, Lynyrd Skynyrd, the Eagles, and a band from Springfield called the Ozark Mountain Daredevils. Black Oak Arkansas, just out of CalJam in April, also participated. The Daredevils and BOA would go on to become two of the most famous bands to come out of the Ozarks.

Figure 8.1 Black Oak Arkansas, early 1970s. Courtesy of Jim Mayfield.

Most people who listen to rock and roll from the 1970s are aware of the OMD, who recorded such hits as "If You Wanna Get to Heaven" from their eponymous 1973 album and "Jackie Blue" from their sophomore album *It'll Shine When It Shines*. Compared to other southern rock bands, the Daredevils wrote substantive lyrics that dealt with a number of complex topics. Furthermore, they spent less time identifying with the South and expressed greater concern with social justice.

The Daredevils emerged in the early 1970s in Springfield, Missouri. Originally known as the Family Tree, the band became a fixture in Springfield and played with other local favorites, such as Granny's Bathwater. Music industry insiders, critics, and fans often struggled to categorize the band's music. According to one *Rolling Stone* article, the Daredevils were "a mixture of country, the South, Appalachia, and rock 'n' roll that always takes a fresh approach."[60] Another writer was far off the mark in writing that the band was something in between the Eagles and Black Oak Arkansas.[61] The fact was that the band was eclectic and played all sorts of music. Moreover, they were not part of the typical southern rock scene that consisted of Lynyrd Skynyrd,

Figure 8.2 Ozark Mountain Daredevils, Folk Fair 1973, Eureka Springs. Courtesy of Jim Mayfield.

Charlie Daniels, BOA, and similar bands. One of the band members told Campbell that the group members "aren't daredevils, don't ride motorcycles, play country music or act wild and sexy on stage like Black Oak Arkansas."[62]

In Springfield the band members shared a big house, transportation, and other expenses—a normal arrangement for emerging musicians during the 1970s. As they grew successful, they settled down with families on their own homesteads. Two of the members bought land in the Arkansas Ozarks—one bought 500 acres in the Yellville area, and another bought 279 acres in Ponca. OMD Bass player Michael "Supe" Granda compared his band's philosophy about resources with that of the Daredevils: "Unlike our neighbor Jim Dandy and his Black Oak Arkansas boys, what each us decided to do with our share of the money was our own business."[63]

The band had landed a generous recording contract with A & M that resulted in two of their most recognized songs climbing the charts in the summer of 1974. In 1975 "Jackie Blue" would reach number 3. Like other southern rock bands, OMD's popularity declined in the 1980s. By end of the 1970s, A & M had already chosen not to renew their contract.[64]

The records from the A & M years, especially the first ones, were filled with well-written songs that were socially relevant. Like Lynyrd Skynyrd in "Free Bird" and other songs, the Daredevils often wrote about wandering and coming home. Often, the lyrics describe seeking something or leaving something or someone behind. Alternatively, settling down, home, and community are the focus of songs such as "Standing on the Rock" (1973), "What's Happened Along My Life" (1974), "Backroads" (1977), and "Southbound" (1977). In "Following the Way That I Feel," the singer notes the irony of the fact that, while he knows he travels too much, his very nature is that of a wanderer.

Modernity was another major topic for the band, as can be seen in songs such as "Within/Without" (1973) and "Time Warp" (1975). The band vocalist and drummer writes about being disillusioned with society and the need to find a place to be one's true self. These two songs and other similar tunes were the closest that the band got to a back-to-the-land theme. Although not communal like BOA, the Daredevils shared the same network as more communally inspired Ozarkians who lived in Springfield. They cut demos for the album *Don't Look Down* at Dungeon Studio, the same studio used by the Hot Mulch Band to record "Ozark Mountain Mother Earth News Freak." Hot Mulch's signature tune became the anthem for many Ozark back-to-landers and even aired on *Dr. Demento*.

The band identified themselves "as rural . . . and their lyrics are full of references to nature."[65] Rivers and oceans are for wanderers and the mountains are home in "Breakaway." The Daredevils urge listeners to get out into nature before it is gone in "Mountain Range." The songs "Snowbound" and "Homemade Wine" are about chilling out at home and getting high on wine. "Homemade Wine" is one of the few songs that mentions the Ozarks. Many of the songs are set in dreams and mythic places that emphasize ambiguous or indeterminate facets of liminal space. Often, these fables focus on the wanderer, the homebody, modernity, and nostalgia.

"Jackie Blue" is one of the band's songs that deal with authenticity and persistence. Here the singer describes a character named Jackie Blue playing a game with herself and with other people's lives. In the words of the song, she "lives a dream that can never come true." Other songs urge the listener to be patient—more specifically, to live in the moment and take it easy.

Two songs by the Daredevils represent their feelings about social justice. The first is "It's How You Think," written by Larry Lee. Here Lee asks why we look away from deep social problems such as poverty in very personal ways and how we need to rethink fundamental social structures such as how we distribute wealth in society. Lee goes on to remind the listener that leaders of all kinds, including religious ones, direct our attention away from what truly matters. The other related song about social justice, also written by Lee, is "Giving It All to the Wind." This time, the message is subtler, urging listeners to not fritter away an opportunity to do good in their communities and society. In both songs, Lee encourages the listener to persist through darkness and realize that we are all in it together and should help each other.

Compared to BOA, the songs of the OMDs reveal little explicit sexuality or religion. Their songs tend to be more spiritual and often tied to nature and landscape. Part of the spirituality of OMD songs deals with the journey rather than an outcome.

Discussion

In the 1970s, BOA put out 10 albums. The last album, *10 Yr Overnight Success*, was released in 1976. By the end of the decade the first wave of southern rock was beginning to end. In 1977, Ronnie van Zandt of Lynyrd Skynyrd was killed in a plane crash. Meanwhile, the Carter administration—supported by BOA, Charlie Daniels, and Lynyrd Skynyrd—was being sabotaged by Washington politicians and press figures alike, who didn't like the peanut farmer from Georgia. Capricorn Records, the label for many southern rock bands such as BOA, folded in 1979.

In 1978, BOA left their compound as the band's popularity began to wane. Later, they dropped "Arkansas" from its name in an attempt to become more mainstream. Mangrum left the band but returned later with a heavier sound. Yet despite the tweaks, the band never reached its former glory. BOA remains popular mainly among biker crowds and performs at famous biker gatherings at Sturgis, South Dakota and other venues.[66]

Like the Grateful Dead, BOA advocated for communalism through its music. BOA lived communally like the Group, who were south in Hagarville, Arkansas. The Group, Also, in the early 1970s, during the formative years for the Daredevils, the members of that band loosely lived cooperatively, both in Springfield and on a rural ranch.

BOA and the Group started in the late 1960s. The Group left the music world just when they were about to realize major success. On the other hand, BOA remained in the music industry. Both groups lived on a compound rather than out in the community. Furthermore, BOA and the Group were not well received into their respective new communities. BOA lived communally in a house in Jonesboro and were constantly harassed by neighbors. The Group was run out of Greer's Ferry in 1973. Another point of commonality between the two groups is how they sought to do charitable projects or raise money for community issues and even political candidates that fit their ideals.

BOA challenged the dominant conservative sentiments in the area, with their rock music, long hair, drugs, and wild ways. On the other hand, they held southern identity in high esteem, particularly from a white vantage point. Many songs expressed nostalgia for the Confederacy and portrayed the perceived loss of power among young white men. BOA also wrote unfavorably about integrated school busing. Thus, their utopia was retreatist in orientation in that it mourned the loss of the imagined community of Dixie and southern identity. The Group, too, was retreatist, but it was more concerned with the inauthenticity and hurried nature of modern life.

Ozark rock music, like all other genres, reflects the social boundaries of race, gender, and class; at other times, the music highlights the connections between different groups. Class differences emerge within genres as well. Many people consider Yes and other progressive rock groups highbrow, but AC/DC and BOA catered to working-class people from humble backgrounds. According to Mangrum, BOA was "crude [but] authentic."[67] Furthermore, there is a long history of people seeing country, hillbilly, rockabilly, rock, and country rock as "low" culture. Indeed, much early southern rock was tinged with misogyny and racial pride. Bands such as the Daredevils, however, wrote songs in a spirit of social insight and inclusiveness.

One of the most important forgotten facts about BOA is its position at the forefront of southern rock. According to Hutson, "Black Oak was the first heavy metal rock group from the South, and it created a new 'hillbilly metal' rock sound."[68] Not only is BOA considered part of the first wave of southern rock, but it was among the first acts playing that style of music.

If ever there was a right time to sing about communalism, it was in the 1960s through the mid-1970s—when the back-to-the-land movement flourished. The role of music in the movement often is overlooked. In the song "Waterfall," the band 10 CC sang about leaving the city for a more rural life. Cat Stevens was even more straightforward, singing about living in an intentional community "I Want to Live in a Wigwam." The Moody Blues and Todd Rundgren both sang about utopias, and Joni Mitchell wrote about how "we've got to get back to the garden." Although not explicitly so, much of the spirit of early Grateful Dead is communal and they even stayed frequently at Rancho Olompali, a commune in California.

Most Arkansas rockabilly acts and the bands that influenced them, such as the Band and the Cate Brothers, did not sing much about the region and its mountains. BOA was the band that celebrated the region and sang about it. The Daredevils did have a few explicit songs about the Ozarks, but their lyrics were subtler and often focused on leaving and coming home to the mountains. It may be that the band shared the sentiments of author Willie Morris, that "when a writer knows home in his heart, his heart must remain subtly apart from it. He must always be a stranger to the place he loves, and its people."[69] Often, we carry home with us even we are away. The longer we are gone, the more we yearn to return, not realizing that home is always within us even if we aren't physically there.

Both bands did tap into the hedonist-puritanical dichotomy that Cash thought typified the South. For BOA, the song "Lord Have Mercy on My Soul" highlights that struggle. Mangrum sang about being caught between God and the devil, who are trying to figure out how to divvy him up. In the end God, gets his mind and Satan gets his body. The message from OMD was simpler: "If you want to get to heaven, you got to raise a little hell."

What is the future of rock? Over the decades, I endured a generally accepted notion that rock-and-roll is dead. Dave Thompson, author of *I Hate the New Music* even suggested that rock and roll died sometime in 1978. I found nothing compelling after reading his book for him choosing that particular date—maybe he was just being cheeky. I do recognize that the 1980s and more recent decades brought forth social trends and tastes that forced rock to change, but those changes did not kill rock.

I concede that musical tastes are subjective and find value in Thompson's truer answer to when rock died *for him*, which was when he "started hating new music."[70] For me, I do not want to be that older person who ridicules newer music just because it is new. And the same goes for the various flavors of rock such as rockabilly, hillbilly rock, and southern rock. Times and taste change, and so does the music, but it never really dies. Other bands such as the Cate Brothers continue to make good music and maintain a very loyal fanbase. In fact, one fan remarked, "I've told everybody that for my 70th birthday I want a walker so that I can go hear the Cate Brothers and still dance, 'cause they'll still be playing."[71] There will remain a place for rock if it gives voice to those people marginalized and alienated. On an even more basic level, as Duke Ellington once said: "If it sounds good, it is good."[72]

The Hot Mulch Band
and the Missouri
Back-to-the-Land Experience

To dare is to lose one's footing momentarily. To not dare is to lose oneself.
—Soren Kierkegaard

As a teenager, one of my favorite things to do was listen to Dr. Demento on my world radio that could pick up a Chicago station late in the evening. It was the early part of 1982 when Dr. Demento had a show devoted to lampooning President Ronald Reagan. Ever since moving to the Ozarks in the late 1970s, I tried to listen to the show. Fortunately for me, I remember the show, but not the Reagan songs. Other songs, such as "96 Beers" by J. J. and the WRIF Morning Crew, Rich Little and Walter Williams's "Mr. Bill," and "Take Off," by Bob and Doug McKenzie stuck with me.[1] There was another song that I heard, forgot, and then reconnected with serendipitously several times over the years. It was the Hot Mulch Band's *Ozark Mountain Mother Earth News Freak*. Ron Hughes, the band's leader, was a musician and songwriter who also is a long-time alternative energy expert.

Anthropologist Victor Turner wrote that "prophets and artists tend to be liminal and marginal people, 'edgemen,' who strive with a passionate sincerity to rid themselves of the clichés associated with status incumbency and role-playing and to enter into vital relations other men in fact or imagination."[2] In other words, these edgemen, another term for the trickster, wanted out of the rat race of achieving more education, prestigious jobs, and income. They wanted a more connected and human-centered life. They used religion, music, and social movements such as environmentalism to leave the city and move to more austere and isolated conditions. Many of these edgemen and women made their way to the Ozarks, persuading many of their family and friends to come along too. This chapter focuses on how these marginal, often trickster-like liminars founded a well-connected and effective network in the Missouri Ozarks using environmental sentiments and music.

In this chapter, I will briefly discuss material that Brian Campbell and Jared Phillips cover in greater detail (e.g., the New Life Farm and OACC). What makes this chapter different than previous work is how important liminars and music were to the back-to-land movement in the Missouri Ozarks. Often music conveys the essence of a movement and inspires people to action. I won't go as far as Carl Jung, who said "music should be an essential part of every analysis," but it is necessary in this case, where music and the back-to-land movement are so intertwined in the Missouri Ozarks.[3]

"Ozark Mountain Mother Earth News Freak" details the back-to-the-land movement of the 1960s and 70s. The genesis of the song and the various groups and people associated with it are the subject of this chapter. Although there were several intentional communities and associated organizations in the Missouri Ozarks, two contributed most to the Hot Mulch Band's emergence. Many of the bandmembers were from Seven Springs, and Ron Hughes, the leader, worked at New Life Farm and was active in various ecological projects there. Unlike the Dan Blocker Singers, Mason Proffit, OMD, and BOA, all of which began as musical acts, the Hot Mulch Band arose out of the region's communal efforts, and thus, it emerged as the musical expression of alternative living in the Ozarks. Indeed, the band epitomized the cultural and creative matrix of the region and showed people that there was a third way to life rather than left or right.[4] The band's reliance on portable instruments such a guitar, fiddle, and where part of the "toolkit" for liminars or "*communitas*-bearers."[5] Many back-to-landers in the Missouri Ozarks were focused on living harmoniously with nature, each other, and with their neighbors. Such living is a form of *communitas* that linked a reverence of nature and highlighted sustainable energy and food practices.[6]

I realized that few people in the Ozarks knew about the back-to-the-land movement, and even fewer knew about the Hot Mulch Band. Although newspaper articles helped provide some context, I had to be wary. Many of the articles mischaracterized, and in some cases sensationalized, the experiences of various people and groups linked to intentional communities. As

Figure 9.1 Hot Mulch Band in 1985. Courtesy of Arrow Ross.

luck would have it, in the fall of 2018, a number of members of Hot Mulch and other people pivotal in various communal endeavors in the Missouri Ozarks met with me in Springfield, Missouri. We spent an evening talking about all sorts of things; however, most of the discussion centered on sustainability and environmentalism. I also was blessed to hear Ron and Jon Tickner sing "Ozark Mountain Mother Earth News Freak" and "Hot Mulch Band." In addition to meeting everyone, they fielded my questions, offered opinions, provided documents and other materials, and gave me substantive comments that are peppered throughout this chapter.

Late in the 1960s and throughout much of the 1970s, many people and groups moved to the Ozarks to establish alternative forms of living and communities. As a part of the back-to-the-land movement in the Arkansas Ozarks, I have focused most of my scholarship later in my career on that region. However, a good deal of the story about the genesis of "Ozark Mountain Mother Earth News Freak" involves a number of communal groups in south-central Missouri associated closely—many of them near the Arkansas border. The Missouri Ozarks had a thriving communal history that was just as important and interesting as anything in Arkansas. Furthermore, that history intersects with popular culture that reveals networks within the back-to-the-land community through music. It also saw the emergence of organic, healthy living, especially in food production, which mainstream society now has embraced.

To *Living in the Ozarks* newsletter editor Joel Davidson, the Ozarks are a "state of mind" and "gives one a sense of place."[7] On the other hand, he also noted that "the Ozarks are an exploited colony, a part of the media's Third World underdeveloped regions." Ozark bioregionalist David Haenke argues that the Arkansas-Missouri border, itself, is an obstacle to recognizing that the Ozarks constitute a bioregion that even can be understood biologically and with respect to physical geography.

Like Vance Randolph, Charles Morrow Wilson, and others, Haenke believes that the region shapes the culture of those people who live there in unique ways. One way the land shapes the culture is the relative isolation it affords Ozarkians to live their lives as they wish and even "develop self-sustaining economy" and "living within the limits of the region's unique ecology."[8] Another way the land and culture work in an interesting way is the relative symbiosis between the old-time residents and the back-to-the-landers, both of whom recognized that many of the old ways of life had value. Certainly, in American popular culture, the *Foxfire* series, *Mother Earth News*, and similar literature indicate that there is a market that highlights the knowledge and experience of "the people of these mountains in the hope, that through it, some portion of their wisdom, ingenuity and individuality will remain after them to touch us all."[9] The same is true for the edgemen and women portrayed in this chapter, who continue to challenge the status quo and shape a better world for us all.

Missouri's Intentional Communities

The Missouri Ozarks was host to a number of socialist communities in the nineteenth century.[10] Among those known were Reunion (1868–1870), Friendship (1872–1877), Bennett Cooperative (1873–1877), and Home Employment Cooperative (1894–1906). Like many recent intentional communities, money was a major concern and probably contributed more than anything else to the quick demise of each.[11]

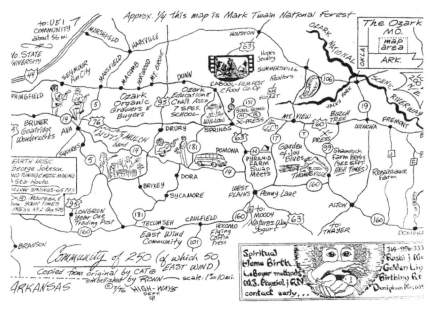

Figure 9.2 Map of Yronwode/Ross. Courtesy of Fellowship of Intentional Communities.

Much of the communal effort that occurred in the Missouri Ozarks, or the "MOzarks," took place from 1970 to 1975. David Haenke wrote about the increasing number of immigrants, "Instead of twenty homestead refugee[s] . . . in 1971, there are 250 to 300 in this area of Southern Missouri [in 1975]."[12] Many of these groups were located in rural areas of the Ozarks, and these immigrants created very close knit networks that provided some level of stability for their members and fostered the formation of various communities and organizations in the region.[13]

These rural communities were comprised of a couple of hundred people defined loosely as groups that had a niche in addition to their skills and interests, such as artists, crafts workers, and technical-types like those at New Life Farm. By comparison, Saint Louis, not usually thought of as part of the Ozarks, was home to several urban intentional communities in the late 1960s to early 1970s. Often these were communities, individuals, and families living cooperatively in one or several houses. These cooperatives were Basta Ya House, Contemporary Mission (1968), KDNA (1970), and Mississippi House.[14] Even a contingent of the Group, discussed in the previous chapter,

Name	Date	County	Source
Zion's Order	1953 to present	Wright	FIC* 72 (36), 74 (38), 75
Family Farm	1969-????	Wright	Hughes et al. 2018 FIC 75 (34)
Edge City	1971-early 1980s	Howell	FIC 75 (32); Hughes et al. 2018
Dragonwagon	1970-present	Douglas	Miller 99 (260)
Seven Springs	1972-1982	Texas	Miller 99 (279); 75 (36-38)
Yronwode/The Garden of Joy Blues	1972-1975	Shannon	FIC72 (36) /FIC 74 (32), 75 (34); Miller 99 (264)
New Life Farm/Ozarks Resource Center	1973-mid 1980s	Douglas/Ozark	FIC 81, 83; Miller 99 (274)
East Wind	1974-present	Ozark	Miller 99; FIC 75 (21), 78 (36), 81 (37), 83 (63), 85; Mercer 84
Valley of Peace	1974-????	Douglas	FIC 74; Miller 99 (284)
U & I	1975-1984?	Lacklede	Miller 99 (283); FIC 75 (25, 27), 78 (46), 81 (53), 83 (78); Mercer 84
Earth Wonder Farm	1975-????	Stone	FIC 75 (27); Miller 99 (261)

* FIC is Fellowship for Intentional Communities Directory followed by year of directory and page number in parentheses.

Table 9.1 List of Known Missouri Ozark Communal Groups

lived in St. Louis in the early 1970s. Table 1 below lists some of the communal groups known in the Missouri Ozarks.[15]

According to some members of Hot Mulch, the Family Farm might have been the earliest they remembered from 1969. The Family Farm was in Norwood, and its members lived in a pig shed. Another early group that formed in 1971 was Edge City, made up of immigrants from Ann Arbor, Michigan, who settled primarily near Caulfield in Howell County.[16] Edge City was formed to offer an ecological alternative to a mainstream society heavily dependent on fossil fuels. Like many other communal situations, life at Edge City was always in flux—at times the community included just a handful, while at others, there were 10 or more people living together.[17]

Located in Mansfield, Zion's Order was a farming-based Christian community. Founded in 1972, members advertised it as an "interracial colony of 40 people on a 1,720-acre ranch, connected with Bethesda Colony."

Historian Timothy Miller wrote that they were "rooted in the Latter Day Saints tradition [. . .] absorbed some of the many communal inquirers who dropped in to visit."[18] They emphasized a "simple lifestyle influenced by former Hutterian background."[19]

Established in 1972, the Garden of Joy Blues (also known as Yronwode) is one of the earliest back-to-the-land groups that formed in the Missouri Ozarks, where members lived on 40 acres near Birch Tree. Early on, members of Garden of Joy Blues lived in a lean-to made of hides and followed an "ecologically balanced, simple life style."[20] By 1974, several families were living on 80 acres. They advertised a "non-sexist, simple handmade life. Shared belief in the grace and glory of nature. Willing to work toward cooperative network especially on land trust."[21] The work of environmentalist Murray Bookchin, who advocated casting off the state, city, and the like, for a more decentralized economy and living, influenced many of its members.[22]

The Garden of Joy Blues's name came from an esoteric blues song. Many people came through Garden of Joy Blues, and it became a sort of gateway location for the Missouri communal experience. Nancy Spaeder, a friend of Hot Mulch, spent six months living in the Garden before moving on to Seven Springs, where she and her husband could focus on their children's education and not endure continued primitive conditions.[23]

The Garden of Joy Blues was led by Cat and Peter Yronwode. Peter was very practical and philosophical at the same time. He also expected incoming members to take a vow of poverty and to share whatever resources they had with other members.[24] Cat, originally Catherine Manfredi, was the archetypical flower child. Her father was a former jazz musician and Buddhist monk. Her mother, "Lilo Glozer, had been involved in intentional communities, at one time having had some association with Ralph Borsodi of the School of Living."[25] A true bohemian and edgewoman, Cat literally sat on Joan Baez's knee as a child.

Cat Yronwode's communal lineage began with Tolstoy Farm, which is thought to be one of the earliest examples of a rural commune that was founded in the 1960s.[26] A fan of folklorist Vance Randolph, Cat wanted to explore the culture of the Ozarks. She also fell in love with the Ozark scenery and decided to stay and help found Garden of Joy Blues.

Another draw to the Ozarks for Cat, as someone who appreciated unique culture, was Buck Nelson and Columba Krebs. Nelson, who claimed to have flown with bearded bib-overall-clad aliens to the moon, Venus, and Mars, organized an annual "Spaceship Conference" on his farm near Mountain View, during the 1950s and 1960s. The peripatetic and eccentric Krebs was a cartoonist-painter and author. She also had a long history of paranormal beliefs and was a frequent attendee of Nelson's conferences. However, when Cat got to the Ozarks, Buck had ended his Spaceship Conferences and moved to California. Cat did meet and become friends with Columba.[27]

Garden of Joy Blues, like many communes described by historian Jared Phillips, relied on the generosity of old-time locals in order to survive. Cat wrote: "As our commune grew, Virgil hired us to haul hay, and then taught us how to do it. He was a dairy farmer, a New Deal Democrat, and a World War II veteran." Virgil's wife, Mary Lou, was also quite a forward thinker, a trait not uncommon for older-generation Ozarkians as historian Blake Perkins documents so well in his book *Hillbilly Hell-Raisers*.[28] Cat, who refers to herself in lowercase, wrote of her time at Garden of Joy Blues,

> In 1971, Peter and i had another daughter, Altahea yronwode. We spent much of the 1970s raising goats and sheep in the Missouri Ozarks on an 80-acre commune called the Garden of Joy Blues, south of the tiny town of Birch Tree. We were subsistence farmers, using 19th and early 20th century technology and home-schooling our children. There was no running water, and the only electrical appliance we used was a battery-operated cassette tape recorder, to play our precious compilations of rural acoustic blues. To supplement our home-grown garden produce and meats, the group of us earned money by hauling hay, hand spinning, and making quilts. I started seriously pursuing a career as a freelance writer, beginning with articles on old-time crafts and farming techniques.[29]

Later, she and Peter divorced. Furthermore, historian Timothy Miller noted that Garden of Joy Blues lost its primary residence because of fire, and thus forced the group to disband.[30] Cat and her daughter left the Garden of Joy Blues and moved away to a four-room cabin in Howell County—"ten miles from the nearest town along Little Creek, near Mountain Grove." Life was hard for both of them. She wrote:

> We had no money, and I had no vehicle, no partner, and very little food, he [her exhusband] did visit us once and bring me a mix-tape he had made off a radio station in New Orleans where he was working, and the first song on side

one was Desmond Dekker and the Aces' "Israelites." Every morning I would put the tape on and drag myself up to get Althaea ready for school, and walk her up the hill to meet the school bus, and come back down the hill sobbing to myself . . . my life was in ruins, and this song helped pull me through. I started selling freelance magazine articles, we did not starve, and after a while we got welfare cheese, which also helped out a lot.[31]

Cat's dire circumstances mirrored that of some many other back-to-landers (e.g., my own family). Music was a refuge from the hardship and isolation experienced by many migrants to the region. Moreover, the welfare cheese became a common staple for many marginalized families.

Yronwode's four-room cabin was near Mountain Grove, where Ozark comic book fans met. Ron Hughes helped move an attic's worth of *Mary Worth* comic books to her cabin that had been gifted to Cat by a local woman in Cabool who had collected them since the beginning and was thrilled to give them to someone who appreciated them.[32] She even helped Will Eisner organize and catalog his life's work.[33] Kirk Chritton remembered when he met Cat: "The meeting was held in a log cabin at the end of a dirt trail in rural Howell County. At that meeting we met Chris [a friend who invited Kirk and others to the meeting], cat, and a number of other local fans, including Ronn Foss who was a pioneer of small press comics fanzines. I have to say that cat was the most dynamic personality of the evening, educating, entertaining, and challenging a trio of pimple-faced adolescents."[34]

Ronn Foss, a cartoonist, later became editor of the underground newspaper *Your Times X-Press*.[35] The newspaper served as a "proto-internet," to use Ozark historian Jared Phillips's phrase for many of the counterculture newspapers and other resources back-to-the-landers relied on in the late 1960s and 1970s. Foss became the go-to person for getting the word out. He drew maps, interviewed people, contributed to the fledgling cartoon community, and other activities. Like many of the other people described in this chapter and throughout the book, he was multitalented and a little eccentric.[36]

The Garden of Joy Blues, and Cat herself, became a focal point of communal activity in the region. Members of Hot Mulch admired Cat, and while she was in the Ozarks, they and other people formed deep connections with her. Ron's most vivid memory of Cat was a roadkill skunk she turned into a purse that she never failed to sling on her hip. According to Ron, it never lost its attraction or its pungent odor. Many of the Mulchers believe

din of Joy Blues , Ruthr. Lelaine, Nic, Tim, Viki, Mikael, Nancy, Althea, Cat

Figure 9.3 Garden of Joy Blues. Courtesy of Arrow Ross.

that Cat was on the vanguard of the rural communal movement. Later, Cat moved to California and coauthored a book with Trina Robbins, *Women and the Comics*, published by Eclipse Comics in 1985, a business cofounded by Yronwode and where she was the editor-in-chief.

Earthwonder Farm was located near Blue Eye. According to a FIC entry for 1975, the community had seven people living on 100 acres who sought to provide natural foods for the area through a co-op. They referred to themselves as vegetarians who led a "natural lifestyle."[37]

The intentional community of East Wind is located in Tecumseh, Missouri. Originally, founding members stayed on Elixir Farm with Ron Hughes and Vinnie McKinney, while searching for a suitable place. They found such a place in Techumseh on 130 acres to settle.[38] Now on 1,045 acres, East Wind is one of the longest-lived independent communities, as it formed in 1973 and still operates today. East Wind is modeled after Twin Oaks, another community in Virginia based loosely on B. F. Skinner's book *Walden Two*. By 1975, they had 40 adults but no children,[39] and hoped to increase to 750 people. About life at East Wind, they reported: "Our culture is egalitarian, nonsexist, & noncompetitive. We share financial resources and expenses in a communal fashion, altho [sic] members may keep some goods, such as clothes and books, in their private possession. Weaving and odd jobs in various local communities."

Like Twin Oaks, East Wind has managers of all facets of community life, and work is based on a labor credit system.[40] By 1978, East Wind had increased to 60 members. Members noted that the standard of living was sufficiently low to allow rapid growth. They were expected to work 45 hours per weeks largely to produce hammocks and other rope products. East Wind also planned a federation conference for 300 people for September 1–4, 1978.[41] By 1981, its membership was down to 45 members, which led to 47-hour work weeks.[42] Over the next two years, East Wind added several more members, and members reported that they produced 45 percent of their own food.[43]

Migrants from the East Coast founded Dragonwagon farm in Ava, Missouri. Crescent Dragonwagon, a founding member, became a well-known children's book author and a former innkeeper in the Eureka Springs community for many years. Crescent, then known as Ellen Zolotow, cofounded an intentional community in Brooklyn, where other members introduced her to eating healthy foods.[44] Later, she went on to write *The Commune Cookbook*, which helped fund her move to Ava, Missouri, in 1970, where she and her husband co-founded Dragonwagon.[45] Many of the folks in the area also began to gather at Dragonwagon for solstices and to play music. In fact, Hot Mulch found its saxophonist, Toby, there.[46]

Following anthropologist Arnold van Gennep's three phased-rites of passage model (separation, marginalization, and reincorporation), Crescent Dragonwagon, like Cat and Peter Yronwode and other back-to-landers, left the comfort of civilization, became marginalized in some fashion, and reemerged with a new identity.[47] What makes Crescent Dragonwagon and the Yronwodes unique is that they really broke with the past by changing their names. Crescent told a *Chicago Tribune* reporter about her time in Ava, Missouri, as an antistructuralist: "We were radicals not hippies. The difference has been lost, but we wanted to change society, not drop out. We were ecological activists."[48] When the couple divorced, Crescent moved to Eureka Springs.[49]

Sometime after Crescent's departure, the community lost its men and refocused as a place for women only. The women of Dragonwagon often spent time at a lesbian collective up in St. Louis, and the converse. One interviewee remarked about communal life at Dragon Wagon:

Down in Ava, at this farm, they lived very rustically. I think they did eventually have electricity, but it was very rough it was really, subsistence farming. It was raising goats, killing them, eating goat meat, eating goat cheese, drinking goat milk, farming their own crops, eating whatever they produced. Some women may go into Ava for jobs, but mostly they actually lived off the land, which was, pretty astounding [. . .] But it was certainly wonderful to have them come up to St. Louis, and also to have the opportunity to go down there, and to see it, and to see people who are actually doing that. And some of those women are still down there.[50]

In 1974, Valley of Peace formed in Squires. It was advertised as "a fully communal Christian colony made up mostly of younger people." One back-to-the-lander remembered that Valley of Peace operated a restaurant and that she didn't think that it was connected to the broader Missouri communal network.[51] The group last advertised in 1975.[52]

U & I Ranch was located in Lebanon but moved later Eldridge. The Ranch was composed of a "group of individuals, families, communal and semi communal groups" living on over 1,000 acres of land "held in a land trust." Members shared 400 acres, and "housing is mainly owner-built homes, teepees, tents and a few school buses. Variety of local employment. Neighbors are friendly and helpful." In 1978, they wrote, "Our neighbors are very friendly and helpful, and regularly come to us when they need an extra hand on their farms." It was governed by a board of stewards, but members voted on key decisions. U & I had a sister community in Leslie, Arkansas, called New Beginnings.[53]

Later, U & I advertised itself as the "gateway to alternative living [where] people are individually self-supporting, have varied diets and childcare and schooling arrangements. About 150 people passed through U & I and settled locally in our six-year history. Each year many of us attend the Rainbow Gathering."[54] They noted, "There is very little work outside of the community. So, we as [a] community are looking for people interested in the back to the land concept in hopes that we can attain and maintain a natural shared experience with the earth and the people around us."[55]

In a relatively short time, many of the back-to-the-land communities in the Missouri Ozarks established networks with each other. Music and other cultural activities offered an excuse for communards throughout the region to get together, and major gatherings of back-to-the-landers became a tradition beginning in 1972. There were back-to-the-land publications, such as *Life in the Ozarks* (*L.I.O.N.*) from Pettigrew Arkansas and *Your Times Express* out of Birch Tree, Missouri.[56] Moreover, food cooperatives like the

Ozark Organic Buyers and Growers Association (OOBGA) emerged. There also were people who focused on problems such as clear cutting, herbicides, and other issues. Anthropologist Joshua Lockyer pointed out the promise of environmentally oriented intentional communities: "Contemporary sustainability-oriented intentional communities are developing local-scale economic activities and networking in a wide variety of arenas: alternative energy production, appropriate scale technologies, organic farming and community supported agriculture, local and bioregional networking, alternative currencies and local exchange and trading systems (LETS), natural building, permaculture design, voluntary simplicity, decreased consumption, and concomitant construction of new culture identities rooted in particular places and communities."[57]

Many of the Missouri Ozark communes described above fit Lockyer's description, and both Seven Springs and New Life Farm seemed to serve as hubs for many of the activities he noted. Each will be described in detail below.

Seven Springs

Seven Springs, which was located deep in the south-central Missouri Ozarks, was one of the major intentional communities associated directly with the Hot Mulch Band. Immediately adjacent to the Mark Twain National Forest and the small town of Cabool, the area is remarkable for its many scenic views, creeks, and rural landscapes.

In 1972, a number of people from California, New York, the Midwest, and even Denmark, settled at Seven Springs on 120 acres of undeveloped land.[58] Like their back-to-the-land counterparts around the nation, they came from the middle-class, and according to reporter Margaret Norris, Seven Springers were "well-travelled and well educated."

They established a cooperative farm and community based on self-sufficiency and thin-boundary qualities,[59] an approach described in "Ozark Mountain Mother Earth News Freak." As leader Ron Hughes sang, "Self-sufficient, that's the name of the game/gonna get myself a system self-contained/a wind mill to give me my electricity/no phone in my dome, I'll use ESP."[60] Like communards across the country, they too read the *Whole Earth Catalog* and *Mother Earth News*. As Hughes noted in the song:

Well, I'm moving to the country where everything is fine
gonna live in a dome and drink dandelion wine
when the collapse comes I won't get the blues
I'll have all the back issues of the *Mother Earth News*.[61]

Seven Springers shared a love of " . . . education, music, art, herbs, massage, theater, and especially community."[62] Further, neighboring back-to-the-landers shared the same tastes as their Seven Springs friends.

Springs members found quickly that jobs were scarce and making money hard. "They tried various means of earning a living—cutting posts, raising worms, cultivating blackberries, making ginseng extract, selling mail-order puppets, and working at the cottage industries like stained glass and sandals." Generating income for individual families as well as the group became a constant concern.[63]

Some people were attracted to Seven Springs because of the prospects it offered for their children's alternative education. The intentional community established a school in 1974 and had 13 children at its peak. The school operated under the umbrella of Ozarks Education and Crafts Association, and parents shared in teaching. Seven Springs member Spaeder told Norris "We were looking for a place to raise our children where we wouldn't have to send them to public schools which we felt perpetuated society's problems." Spaeder also indicated that the parents wanted their children "to live in nature, to learn about the natural world in a less rigid way than the public school could offer."[64] At Headwaters, an alternative school in Arkansas, historian Jared Phillips wrote, "Initially reflecting the population, it served younger children and also became a hub of community action."[65] The same was true for the school at Seven Springs. Unfortunately, the school closed three years later in 1977.

New Life Farm

In 1972, Lavinia McKinney decided she wanted to move from Little Rock and live on a farm. Ron offered to help her move. They moved into an old abandoned house in Ozark County overlooking Bryant Creek. Ron decided to stay. They made the house hospitable, pulled water from the well, made a garden, and bought two horses. They began meeting other back-to-the-landers

Figure 9.4 Seven Springs. Courtesy of Arrow Ross.

at Dragonwagon in Ava and Ted and Rosemary Landers on Brush Creek near Drury. After a year, they bought a working livestock farm, which they came to call Elixir Farm. Like most other back-to-the-landers, Ron had a lot to learn about living off the land, while he was also working for the railroad at the time. He took an agricultural class offered at the Gainseville High School to learn more about farming such as welding and fertilizers.[66]

When Ron and "Vinnie" moved to Ozark County, the county had the least people and the most post offices of any county in Missouri. They found a new friend in Bessy Naugle at the Brixey Store and Post Office. Bessie was the post mistress and wrote a weekly stringer for the *Ozark County Times*.[67] Like many older folks in the Ozarks and Appalachias, Bessy and "Red" Leslie Naugle helped the back-to-the-landers. The old timers fit the cliché, with their attire and old ways, but they "got" what the back-to-the-landers were trying to do, and many of the immigrants regarded them with reverence. Seaton wrote about the relationship the two groups had: "Unlike their own children, these young people appreciated the elders' old ways and wanted to learn their skills. Furthermore, their friendships grew because the newcomers were very respectful of the mores and the traditions around them."[68]

In the next few years, the number of back-to-the-landers grew significantly. Michigan natives Ted and Rosemary Landers moved to Drury, Missouri, in 1973 and established New Life Farm on 130 acres. According to Ron, half of the back-to-the-land people in the country did not have running water. Thus, Ted built a sauna, which would become a popular Saturday night meeting place for many of the people who would later make up the Hot Mulch Band.

Springfield News Leader reporter Bill Maurer wrote, "Their long-range goal is to make their New Life Farm, a non-profit agricultural research farm, self-sufficient in energy."[69] In the years to come, Ted worked with his coordinator, Ron Hughes, and others on a number of demonstration projects. Both men, as well as other people at New Life, shared their expertise about alternative energy with those throughout the Missouri and Arkansas Ozarks, and in "Mother Earth News Freak," Hughes spread the word to a wider audience through his music. One part of the song in particular draws on his New Life Farm experience:

> I'll get a Solar Air Heater from New Life Farm
> in the winter time it will keep me warm
> my methane digester's a great big hit
> It makes methane gas out of Chicken manure.[70]

New Life Farm was registered as a research corporation in 1978. According to anthropologist Brian Campbell, "New Life Farm (NLF) served as the hub for bioregionalism through financial management, technological innovation, and a physical location for congregation and brainstorming tangibility."[71] An advertisement in *Communities* magazine said:

> Thirty active members maintain a forty-acre farm with working demonstrations of methane digesters, hydraulic rams, solar space and water heaters, waterless toilets, waste-water recycling systems, a solar greenhouse, and tree-crops. The center of farm activities is the large restored farmhouse which has offices, library, and conference facilities for up to twelve people. Members do not live on the farm. The main emphasis is on conservation, self-reliance, bioregionalism, and continuing education.[72]

The farm served research and outreach; members lived elsewhere and were available for lectures and workshops about sustainable practices, especially renewable energy and interconnectedness between society and nature, as developed at New Life. David Haenke explained that New Life Farm sought to be an appropriate technology research center, following the latest research and insights from organizations such as the New Alchemy Institute in Massachusetts, a premier pioneering group in alternative/ecological technology.

Around the mid-1970s, David Haenke cofounded the Ozark Area Community Congress (OACC). OACC and NLF had much in common, as anthropologist Brian Campbell noted: "New Life Farm's objectives meshed perfectly with the goals of the politically minded Ozark bioregionalists." In fact, many of the people who staffed the first meeting of OACC were NLFers.[73] OACC and other Ozark organizations' efforts laid the groundwork for many innovative ideas about sustainability in energy and food, as well as environmental protection.

Other ideas NLF championed were the composting toilet and systems to produce methane gas from anaerobic digestion. One such system, custom built on a trailer frame and towed to DC, was rigged for demonstration at the 1979 Appropriate Community Technology Fair in on the Capitol Mall in Washington DC. It included a small methane digester/toilet that produced truly "natural" gas to fuel a cooking range burner. Former NLFer Denise Henderson Vaughn[74] provided more detail about one successful demonstration: "A methane digester was mounted on a trailer; it had a public toilet on one side, and the contents of that toilet were fed to the digester, which produced gas that in turn was burned on the trailer's other side in a gas cook stove. Hot dogs were roasted to demonstrate how waste can be turned into cooking fuel."

At another event, the results were not so good. Vaughn recalled,

One of our members convinced someone to fund a demonstration showing the innards of a composting toilet. It was a large walk-through structure where stuffed burlap bags in the upper area represented uncomposted toilet contents. Lower down, tubs of peat moss with flowers growing in it represented these same contents after they were composted. Visitors who went through either did not understand it at all or if they did, they were grossed out. Most people in DC do not deal with groundwater pollution associated with karst geology and could not see the point about why flush toilets are sometimes a problem.[75]

Following this demonstration, in December 1979, Senator William Proxmire, a Democrat from Wisconsin, lampooned the Energy Department's paltry funding of the composting toilet plan by awarding the department the Golden Fleece Award.[76] Moreover, even though the Carter administration supported environmental projects such as what was going on at NLF, all of that changed with Reagan, who went line-by-line eliminating alternative energy efforts.

Undeterred by negative sentiments coming out of Washington, research continued to focus on perennial energy systems, and landfills have adopted some of the technology in the way to use methane New Life helped start. NLFers also had a hard time demonstrating the utility of methane extraction to farmers who chose fossil fuel over more renewable sources because—due to it being heavily subsidized—it was still cheaper than alternative technologies. Ron recalled accompanying Ted Landers to a dairy farm:

> After [the] first experience, went north U.S. to large dairy farm where the farm had a manure disposal problem in his barns where the cows spent a lot of time. Ted designed a system that included a methane digester that would turn the manure and straw bedding into methane that drove a generator that made electricity for the farmer. After digesting the manure, the bedding was removed from the digester, washed and recycled for bedding for the cows. The farmer got a three-year payback with the money saved on electricity and bedding.[77]

NLFers also did research on solar heaters and they toured Missouri doing workshops on that technology. Thus, they were the first people in the region to show homesteaders and farmers how to create and use solar power.

They also associated with the area food cooperatives, including the one in Fayetteville. Their efforts gave birth to the Ozarks Organic Growers and Buyers Association that set uniform standards for the use of organic labeling in marketing. Many of the Mulchers were involved in various aspects of New Life Farm, other communal endeavors and organizations, and other activities.

By the summer of 1983, Hughes left New Life Farms to establish Ozark Sun and Water in Mountain Home, Arkansas.[78] Several years later, NLF moved from Drury to Brixey, a less remote location.[79] Reporter Mike Penprase wrote, "It may no longer be a hands-on, back-to-the-earth experiment, but New Life Farm is still alive, according to the people who are aiming the organization in a new direction."[80]

By the mid-1980s, NLF was no longer able to fund its operations and sold the farm, moved to a different location with an office, and was renamed the Ozark Resource Center (ORC).[81] The move did not seem to dampen Hughes's activities with his colleagues in Missouri. Further, Hot Mulch continued to play gigs to support NLF/ORC and other groups and activities.

The Hot Mulch Band

Everything began with the school parties at Seven Springs in 1974. There also were the times in the sauna on Saturday nights, when it was so good to take a long soak in the winter. Haenke reminisced: "We would sit and get roasted then jump into an animal water trough to cool off, then back to the sauna. Music was always around either performed at the sauna or at the potluck." By summer, "Ron talking about starting up a traveling band. Can he do it? Can they do it?"[82] One evening on the way back to Elixir Farm from the Ava teen center, Ron wrote "Mother Earth News Freak." According to Haenke, the following year was the "year of Hot Mulch." He wrote:

> At one time known as Buster Clod and the Hot Mulch, the question asked at Summer Solstice '74—will Ron and friends put together a traveling band?—was answered when some of the musical and other energy of the South Missouri Farm Crazies went public as Hot Mulch in a summer gig at Ava Teen Town. The Hot Mulch review interfaced with the local young people in Ava as outrageous good fun and craziness, where time warps bumped together on the dance floor amid the pinball wizardry, with every teenage and hillbilly and rock and roll mythos from 1950 on bubbling together in stewpots of rock and blue grass. We work out some Dharma for the world. The Hot Mulch scene shifted to near Mountain Grove at the Hideaway Bar where we all continued to get together and boogie down into fall.[83]

In 1981, the band put out a 45 of "Mother Earth News Freak" that had Patty Van Weelden and Ron Hughes on vocals (also guitar). Other members were Jon Tickner on fiddle and banjo, and Jeff Dunshee on guitar. Besides the regulars, other area musicians played with the Mulchers on occasion such as bassist Jerry Heath, drummer Stan Smith, and even Ruell Chappell, formerly of the Ozark Mountain Daredevils.

Tickner came from Illinois originally. Before moving to the Ozarks, he was in another band out of St. Louis called Road Apples ("road apples" is another word for horse manure), and the band's name was a play on shit kicking. While in St. Louis, Jon met Haenke, who would show up at Road Apple gigs and dance like a whirling dervish.

The band emerged out of the Mozark communal milieu. In addition to Ron, Jon, Patty, and Jeff, many people came in and out of the band, such as guitarist Steve Markley, Jan and Danny Chisolm, Tom Engh, Jan Mandrus, Toby Masterson, and Nancy Spaeder. Jeff wrote that the band "consist[ed] of anyone who showed up. Often, we weren't well rehearsed, making public appearances [was] like an act of terror (just improvise, fool)."[84] Hot Mulchers often found themselves performing at all sorts of benefits in the area, such as one for Mau Blossom, a midwife. In David's words, the band often turned into a hippy convocation that raised funds for various purposes. In their song, "Hot Mulch," they describe such a scene:

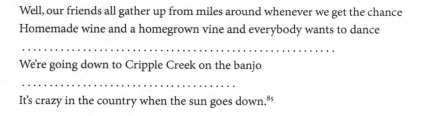

Well, our friends all gather up from miles around whenever we get the chance
Homemade wine and a homegrown vine and everybody wants to dance
. . . .
We're going down to Cripple Creek on the banjo
. . . .
It's crazy in the country when the sun goes down.[85]

The band grew from an informal jam session after a sauna soak or school planning meeting at Seven Springs into a tighter group that entertained larger crowds. However, for many back-to-the-landers, from the beginning, Hot Mulch meant a break from hard work. As they observe in the song:

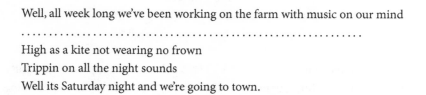

Well, all week long we've been working on the farm with music on our mind
. . . .
High as a kite not wearing no frown
Trippin on all the night sounds
Well its Saturday night and we're going to town.

According to Louise Wienkowski "Every dance, everybody. Danced our legs off," or, again, as Ron urged in the song:

Come on baby put your dancing shoes on
Hot Mulch is going to boogie woogie all night long
Lock your chickens in the house and the cows in the barn
It'll durn be daylight 'fore we get back to the farm.[86]

The band was the focal point for back-to-the-landers. They played in Dunn at the Hideaway, at solstice parties—really everywhere they could, and their music became the glue of the wider Mozark back-to-the-land movement. Through their music and other efforts, the Hot Mulch Band and associated intentional communities in the Missouri Ozarks were able to generate *communitas*—a sense of community that is spontaneous, and authentic.[87]

The Mulchers' musical influences were eclectic, but there is a southern tinge to their music. As Ron notes in *Hot Mulch*:

Well, some folks call it country music, others call it soul

. . . .

We call it rock and roll
well this music from the country cause that where we live
It's music from the soul cause that's what we give.[88]

In addition to their own songs, they played some by the Rolling Stones, Grateful Dead, and the Beatles. However, they really loved the Grateful Dead.

The OMD, with whom some of the Mulchers felt a certain musical kinship, visited Hot Mulch several times. I asked Ron and Jon if they ever wanted to pursue a music career like the Daredevils. They told me that they did not want to get caught up in the commercial music business and that they were more involved in trying to scratch out a living.

David told me that OMD had the feel of trance music, such as what the Dead were doing, and argued that the sound cannot be replicated. Later, when the Daredevils broke up, Patty hosted founding member John Dillon at her Ozarks House Concert several times in the 1980s. The OMD and Hot Mulch's music has inspired the current music scene in the Ozarks to some degree, especially country-punk.[89]

Figure 9.5 Ronn Foss' Drawing of Hot Mulch Band. Courtesy of Fellowship of Intentional Communities.

Planting the Seeds

Haenke reflected about the people marching in the streets and the counterculture of his generation. It was a very creative period during which all sorts of ideas were being hatched and tested, and the back-to-the-land movement was one of those counterculture ideas that captured significant public attention. The essence of counterculture was about escaping the cities to more rural environments, rethinking everything, and focusing on ecology. It was not frivolous but involved a great deal of deep thinking about our economical and environmental practices. David leaves the cultural aspect of the back-to-the-land movement for people like me to study. However, for him, it is all about ecology. He argues that modernity, particularly mindless consumption, violates ecological sense. He pointed out that one of the major reasons New Life Farm was established was to rethink the human relation with the environment systematically. Even more basic, he argues, is that the back-to-the-land movement seeks to offer people a chance to live well. Such a vision defies both conservative and liberal ideologies; nonetheless, it is very meaningful and transformative. Religion professor A. Whitney Sanford's view complements Haenke's, and after analyzing four intentional communities, he stated: "From the outside, intentional communities might appear exotic and so far beyond the mainstream that they are irrelevant to most of us. However, these experiments help us imagine and think through alternatives, and these small, cohesive communities provide a lens into the performance of social change. Further, their deliberations and practices demonstrate the trade-offs, negotiations, and compromises that are necessary to translate abstract values into specific practices, including governance, food, structures, and communication."[90]

Louise Wienkowski saw the movement in more personal terms. To her, the entire point of back-to-the-land was to reconnect herself with the natural world. She remarked: "Gee, there's woods here . . . a forest. We got to Missouri, riding on the hilly roads. Sensed a difference. A sense of peace. All you saw were the trees and forests. The land, this hill, this rock . . . [referring to Haenke] no water. How can we rig up a shower? Solar showers. Inspiration you figure things out."[91] Like the Mulchers, David and others involved in the back-to-the-land activities in Missouri, Louise tied the aesthetics of rural life with the practical aspects of living in it.

David pressed on about getting back to nature. He noted that people have a great deal to learn from observing nature for ideas or biomimicry. Much of the work of ecologically sound development requires a long-term, patient approach that is oriented to nature. Much of the process New Life Farm and other vanguards in ecological endeavors created has become mainstream. As an example, David pointed out that some pig farmers are employing progressive farming techniques now, including anaerobic digestion of manure and the production of methane gas for farm use because it makes both economic and ecological sense.

One might wonder whether many of the back-to-the-landers feel that people who are more interested in making money than sustainability have coopted their ideas and efforts in recent decades. Many of the people I talked with had no issue with the mainstreaming of formerly sustainable and environmental practices that they and others pioneered. David, Ron, Jon, and others felt that they and others had planted the "seeds" for such current mainstream endeavors as neighborhood food coops and natural food stores. Ron talked about the hippies who moved to Mountain Grove and opened a farmer's market. Everyone wanted to farm organically, but there was no baseline to determine what actually was organic. Standards were set for organic produce in the Ozarks only when entities such as Elixir Farms, OOBGA, and Roedale Press emerged. Now, many consumers expect organic produce.

Communal activity slumped in the 1980s and 1990s. Many of the back-to-the-landers' children turned out well but did not remain in the Ozarks, and fewer people migrated into the region. Further, many of the intentional communities of the 1970s disbanded during the period. However, many of the people I talked with reported that there has been a resurgence in communal activity in recent years.

Much as Murray Bookchin argued, some back-to-the-landers believe that politics is inadequate to affect progressive change, particularly that in environmental issues. Action takes place at the grassroots level and remains antistructural. Change occurs individually and through organizations such as OACC, NLF/ORC, and any others that truly share a collective ethos. It also helps to have a band spread the gospel of sustainability across the Ozarks, and effective organizations embodied both praxis and wisdom. They also became *communitas*-bearers but such collective action is ephemeral. More solid approaches that involve collective land use and other practical, grounded approaches also persist. Even if intentional communities are fleeting, people of like mind can live near each other and share and live environmentally conscious lives. Or, as Jon called it, "proximity without communalism," which may be where the future lies, as in the term known better, "eco-villages."

One final "seed" that came from the efforts of all these people, organizations, and communities is that the Ozarks gained recognition as a place of change and experimentation. As a liminal or "thin" region, the Ozarks defies boundaries of all sorts—it is a work in progress. As OACC co-founder David Haenke argues, efforts should continue to blur the line between Missouri and Arkansas and unite Ozarks as a region. The bioregion, not arbitrary boundaries, shapes the Ozark culture. As David, noted "mores, culture come from the hills, like is the case for hill people all over the world." Such a place offers something unique for its inhabitants and even American culture at large. Truly, *Ozark Mountain Mother Earth News* does epitomize the back-to-the-land movement in Missouri quite well.

Back-to-Landers
in the Arkansas Ozarks

"How do you know I'm mad?" said Alice. "You must be," said the Cat, "or you wouldn't have come here."
—**Lewis Carroll,** Alice in Wonderland

"Hippies," as we've come to call them, took issue with some major characteristics of American society in their time. These activists' targets included consumerist culture, passive participation, and the culture's general lack of concern for the future.[1] In response, another group of people, known as "back-to-landers" simplified their lives and became more self-reliant and practiced, as Louise Meijering and colleagues termed it, "progressive ruralism."[2] Those back-to-landers or as historian Jared Phillips, called them, "Hipbillies," found their way to Arkansas.[3] Like their back-to-lander counterparts elsewhere, the Hipbillies were among the first Americans to seriously think about sustainable living.[4] They sought more agency in their own lives by leaving cities and towns in pursuit of a rural life.[5] They valued living in the present rather than living for a distant future. One writer relates their journey: "In the 1970s, exiles from cities often took refuge in the Ozarks. Lured by relatively inexpensive acreage and simple living conditions, young city dwellers, many of them burned out by urban demands, removed themselves to the hills. Their plan was to set up communes and homesteads and live off the land. Usually, the back-to-landers came and went. The reality of extracting a living from a stubborn land undid them. Yet in most counties a few stayed."[6]

Communes, formally known as "intentional communities," emerged from this movement. Timothy Miller defines intentional communities as groups where members share their money, time, and other resources.[7] Members live together; they share an ideology and an identity. In order to work, communes must have a "critical mass" in terms of membership. This usually means "five or more adults," according to Aidala and Zablocki.[8]

While the communal movement that emerged in the early 1960s was not started by back-to-landers, the movement did contribute to people becoming back-to-landers.[9] The movement is more than a regional affair, as historian Jared Phillips has argued; "a study of the back to the landers, of country hippies, in the Ozarks, necessarily becomes a study of America the same time."[10] It involved a lot of people, families, and groups from around the country, and sometimes other countries, converging into one spot—the Ozarks.

A number of these communes were established in and around the Boston Mountains, which sit along the Little Mulberry River, in the early 1970s. These early communities included Mulberry Farm, settled by families such as the Strubels, near the Mulberry River. There were other communities located near small towns such as New Beginnings in Dutton, Red Star in Boxley, and Sassafras in Ponca. Most communities disbanded in a year or two.

For many back-to-landers, the mountains are important. Reporter Frank Fellone noted that "Much of the back-to-land movement was to mountainous places around the country." [11] Back-to-lander Ruth Weinstein McShane told Fellone that the Ozarks were . . . wild and beautiful."[12] Speaking more towards the wilderness aspect of the Ozarks, author Ken Carey asserted, "It counts for nothing to head off into the wilderness and leave behind only the trappings of civilization. To experience the transformative energy of the wild places you have to be willing to leave more than externals behind."[13] For many of these in-migrants, moving to the Ozarks was a transformative experience, which allowed them to restart at all sorts of levels.

In spite of all the flux in communal longevity, communal activity was strong in the Ozarks. Land was cheap, there was a lot of privacy, and beautiful views attracted many in-migrants. For some, the area bordered on the mythical. One Ozark back-to-lander told Denelle Campbell, "Having traveled to a lot of places, I felt like northeast Arkansas was Hobbitland. It was an area to be treasured."[14] The lure led to huge numbers of people migrating into the region which even led to the creation of the Ozark In-Migration Conference in Eureka Springs.[15] Arriving at the tail end of the "invasion," the extended Driver family would settle on the Little Mulberry River. About 25 miles to the east of my family's intentional community, who established themselves on the border of Johnson and Newton Counties, near Highway 21. To the south, Dan Blocker's Singers, also known as the Group, had already left their ranch near Lamar, later Greers Ferry, for a less hostile environment in Little Rock.

To the east, in Searcy County, the communities known as Dry Creek Farm, Indian Camp, Leslie, and Snowball had formed and disbanded by the end of the decade.[16] Only the Nahziryah, also known as the Purple People, who moved from New Orleans in the 1980s to a secluded area outside of St. Joe in Marion County continue to exist in some fashion. Regarding the number of in-migrants into the county, back-to-lander and writer Ruth Weinstein McShane cited Maurice Tudor, who characterized the movement into Searcy County as the "Marshall Mountain Wave." Tudor, as reported by McShane, wrote, "Back in 1973 the first serious waves of "hippies" were converging on Searcy County from all points of the compass and setting up "communes" of one kind or another. Some of them were real outlaws, into drugs of all kinds, and their presence was nothing but trouble."[17] It is true that some groups operated outside the law in various ways, but many other communities caused little trouble to their neighbors and larger communities.

Ruth Weinstein McShane and her husband, Joe McShane, were part of the "wave" of back-to-landers coming to Searcy County.[18] Driving a decrepit 1954 Chevrolet pickup truck from Pennsylvania, the couple settled in a very small house on 40 acres. When their house burned down, communal folks from Chimes helped rebuild their house in two days. Chimes and another community in Alread were located in Van Buren County, south of Searcy County. Both communities existed for a few years, but not much is known about Alread and Chimes besides the few anecdotes provided by McShane.[19]

To provide a little more context about communal life in the Arkansas Ozarks, I referred to published directories put out by the Fellowship of Intentional Communities (FIC) for all its member communities since 1972. Entries usually provide contact information and brief information about each group. A number of Arkansas communities mentioned in this chapter had entries in the FIC directories over the years. Some of them are listed below.

In 1974, Indian Camp formed in Leslie, Arkansas. According to their FIC entry, they were a "simple down-home tribe sharing 60-acre homestead. Looking for sincere people who flow with nature."[20] Another community formed in Leslie in 1975 called Leslie Community. They described themselves as a "Spiritual, survival-oriented commune into yoga, astrology, ESP, Cayce, teachings of Christ, organic living and survival." They also were looking to grow their numbers.[21]

Around 1975, the group Sassafras formed in Ponca, Arkansas. According to their FIC advertisement, Sassafras "is a just a bud . . . seeds of a community have been sown. Need more folks to help build community on 520 acres of fine Ozark hill land. Forming land trust to take land out of private ownership. Gardening, crafts, pottery & woodworking all possible trips."[22] By 1978, Sassafras did form a land trust and expanded to include "weekly meetings individual homes and shared buildings. Organic gardening. A legally recognized school but need students."[23] Members were diverse and supported egalitarian ideals but did not endorse any ideology. Not shy about having fun, Sassafras members reported, "Music and dancing are favorites at celebrations."[24] Later, as detailed by Phillips, Sassafras became a woman-centered community.

New Beginnings, later part of the Ozark Regional Land Trust, was located in Dutton. Like its sister community, United and Individual Community in Eldridge, Missouri, New Beginnings was formed by people whose central concern was living and creating ecologically sustainable economies. Moreover, both groups sought to set aside land from development through land trusts. According to their FIC advertisement from 1975, "New Beginnings has their land paid for and requires a substantial cash investment. About ten families with some openings. All families pay a share of the cost of the land and have 99-year renewable leases on their individual homesteads. The community association is open democracy."[25]

Two organizations noteworthy because they were resources for back-to-landers in the Ozarks as well nationally were the New Schools Exchange and the Meadow Creek Project. Although New Schools Exchange in Pettigrew was not an intentional community, the enterprise was established in 1969 to help back-to-landers and others navigate alternative schooling for their children.[26] Meadow Creek Project was founded by internationally known David Orr and his brother Will Orr, near Fox in Stone County. Much of their work revolved around sustainability, environmental topics, and healthy eating and food.[27]

The cheap land and scenic views offered by the Ozarks back-to-land experiment was promoted by *Mother Earth News*, the *Fox Fire* series, *Communitas* (later known as *Communities*), underground papers and magazines that shared information about land and communal opportunities and taught readers how to live off the land. Timothy Miller has noted that

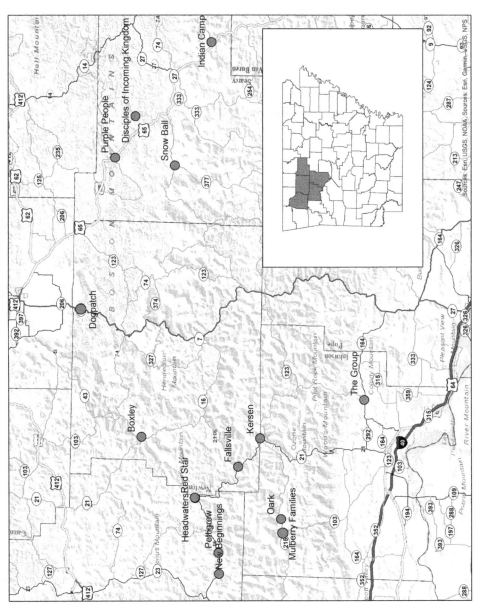

Figure 10.1 Map of Select Ozark Intentional Communities. Courtesy of Billy Higgins.

the ongoing presence of utopian and visionary literature in America also promoted a communal vision. In 1948 B. F. Skinner published *Walden Two*, which became a perennial best seller and eventually directly inspired several intentional communities including Twin Oaks in Virginia and East Wind in Missouri. Robert Heinlein's *Stranger in a Strange Land* became a hip literary favorite, and in due course communes devoted to its ideas emerged, including Sunrise Hill in western Massachusetts. The communal vision certainly received a boost from the dozens of utopian fantasy novels appearing annually.[28]

Not only did various media provide a way for back-to-landers to share information, but a counterculture ethos was conveyed through popular culture, according to sociologist Michael Brown. He wrote that a countersystem ethos was "carried by underground media (hundreds of newspapers claiming hundreds of thousands of readers), rock music, and collective activities, artistic and political, which deliver and duplicated the message; and it is processed through a generational flow."[29] It is important to note that countercultural ethos spread around the country, but that worldview was permeable enough to take in practical information and traditional culture to help back-to-landers succeed.

But the media attention was just the tip of the iceberg. Joel Davidson also describes "folks starting local newsletters, information points, local bulletins, and exchanges."[30] Some of the better-known Ozark media resources were *Life in the Ozarks Newsletter* (*LION*), published in Pettigrew by Joel Davidson; Ed Jeffords' *Ozark Access Catalog*, a bulletin printed out of Leslie by Jerry Friedberg; and Ronn Foss's *Your Times X-Press*, out of Missouri. Thus, multiple sources got the word out about the BTL life in the Ozarks.[31]

Urban to rural migration changed the Arkansas Ozarks more than many other regions of the country. Population increased for all regions of Arkansas between 1970 and 1980, but especially so in the Ozarks.[32] In fact, the population in 1970 (392,040) increased to 445,087 by 1980, resulting in a 39.7 percent increase in a single decade. This increase was larger than for the state (18.9 percent) and even for even the nation (11.5 percent). Over the same period of time, two Ozark counties in particular grew: Johnson County had a 27.8 percent increase and its neighbor to the north, Newton County, had a 32.7 percent increase.

These numbers can be attributed to economic and educational expansion as well as the influx of retirees into the area.[33] Many of the migrants had some previous experience in the state.[34] Historian Jared Phillips wrote, "While perhaps the most visibly obvious, the country hippies, according to the estimates of attendees at the Ozarks-In-Migration Conference in 1975, constituted only a small part of the influx."[35] However, communal activity did leave a demographic footprint across the nation, one noted not only by population scholars such as Michael Nolan and colleagues, Thomas Graff and Earl Neel, and Fred Shelley, but by students of the communal movement such as Rosabeth Moss Kanter, Hugh Gardner, Timothy Miller, and Benjamin Zablocki.

This newest wave of migrants to the Ozarks, like communitarians elsewhere, tended to be younger, more educated, and have more money than earlier Ozarkian settlers.[36] They had little experience or knowledge about living in rural and austere conditions.[37] Thus, in a demographic sense, the shift in the Ozarks population is really a story about large numbers of out-of-staters deciding to make the Ozarks their home. In the pages below, three back-to-lander stories will flesh out this demographic change.

The Strubels

Doug and Cathy Strubel live in northwestern Johnson County, in a beautiful grid-tied solar-powered house they built themselves. The town of Oark sits to the east of the Strubels and is where their two daughters attended a small public school. The family arrived in 1970 to practice sustainable and communitarian ideals. The couple stayed in the Friley area until 1979 and then moved to their current location on the Little Mulberry River, closer to Oark. The couple still practices sustainable living by growing food in a permaculture fashion, recycling building materials, preparing meals on a wood cook stove, and line-drying their laundry.

In the late 1960s, Doug and Cathy were living in Chicago, where they shared a two-story house with another family. Each family had its own floor but shared common areas for doing laundry and for the children to play. The Strubels became interested in communal living and read all the books that communal-minded folks enjoyed, such as *Walden Two* and *Stranger in a Strange Land*. They were serious about their studies, as Doug recalled: "During our community meetings in Chicago we studied the history of communities, the utopian communities of early America and Europe." They

Figure 10.2 Mulberry Group with Karen and Bill Driver right of the dog and Kathy and Doug Strubel on the far right. Picture courtesy of Billy Higgins.

also kept up with the latest sociological research. In 1969, Doug attended a conference in Indiana dealing with communal practices; the couple also visited Twin Oaks, a famous intentional community in Virginia.

The Strubels joined two couples who were already at Mulberry Farm. Doug remembers his first impression of his new homestead: "We were astounded that there was a place so remote and natural and beautiful, where people lived and didn't camp out. There was electricity and a little school." The three couples and their five children made up the little community.

Like many other migrants, the Strubels were attracted to Arkansas because the land was cheap. Mulberry Farm sold them 370 acres for $100 dollars an acre in 1970—a good deal at the time. Along with the land, the farm had many buildings, including a "barn, a red farmhouse, and two house trailers."[38] Later, a dorm, a dome, and a greenhouse were built by Mulberry Farm folk. The community also had a large building, called the "Dorm," and an old Chinquapin schoolhouse.

One of the early missions of Mulberry Farm was to educate "troubled children" who used drugs and had other parent-identified problems. Mulberry was advertising in many of the major communal publications of the period, such as *Communitas*, later known as *Community*. Many of the troubled children came from a school in Florida that was affiliated with Mulberry Farm. Apparently, Mulberry Farm answered a real educational need, given that the school filled quickly once parents realized there was an alternative to private and reform schools.

The students ranged from 13 to 17 years of age. Movies and other events gave the children some supervised time outside Mulberry Farm School. Not only were the school's academic and behavioral standards high, but the standards for even the facilities and equipment was higher than those of the local public school.

Despite the isolation of the school and its zero-tolerance policy for bad behavior, some students still managed to get drugs into the school. Cathy remembers "a meeting that all of us had after a couple of kids had gone into Oark and tried to buy tobacco and Frank just hit the roof." Dealing with these and other serious issues was a source of many meetings between members.

One of the founding members passed away, but the Mulberry School remained and was doing well. Later, according to Cathy, the school folded "after a couple of students obtained drugs in Fayetteville."[39] A few miles to the northeast in Red Star, another alternative school called Headwaters was formed by back-to-landers from New York.[40] Around the same time, Seven Springs School in Mountain Grove, Missouri (three hours north of Pettigrew), opened to provide "a creative alternative to the fluorescent lights and crowded classrooms of public school."[41]

Although alternative schooling was a major draw, Cathy mentioned that people also were attracted to Mulberry Farm because of its back-to-the-land practices and communal living. Each member was expected to share chores and resources. Furthermore, each member was able to pursue her or his own spiritual path—some members were atheists, while others practiced various Christian traditions. Meditation was popular for a while, along with many other activities. The children found friends with whom they could learn and play.

The Mulberry Farm members got along well with their mainstream neighbors. Doug told *National Geographic* reporter Thomas O'Neill, "The local people were instrumental in keeping us here."[42] Neighbors offered carpentry tips and advice on raising cattle. These Ozark values of individualism and hard work appealed to the Strubels. Unlike earlier communes, by the early 1970s, Mulberry Farm and other "rural communes [. . .] were busy consolidating and building bridges of communication with their neighbors."[43] One of the Strubels' neighbors, a cattle man, helped them network with other locals and even did informal public relations for them. In return, Mulberry members helped haul hay for neighbors, and Cathy even taught fellow farmers about artificial insemination techniques for milk cows. Doug notes, "We probably had 40 to 50 people come down from surrounding counties and three or four professors from University of Arkansas and they did an AI, artificial demonstration . . . so projects like that got us known in the community."

At some point, Mulberry Farm folded. Cathy notes that "the divvying up of assets was difficult." The commercial kitchen equipment was given to Oark School. The cattle, as part of the liquidated assets, were highly desired by people even far outside the area. Other than Doug, Cathy, and their children, few communal members decided to remain in the area. In the end, Doug and Cathy stayed in that location until 1979.

Moving farther down the valley, closer to Oark, the Strubels met other back-to-landers who established homesteads in the area. Doug said, "After Mulberry Farm went its way, other families, individual families, in one case a whole group of families, the Drivers moved in, and that was not an intentional community, like a commune all living together but it was a wider community of people that had similar interests and ideas and I call that the Golden Age of the Little Mulberry Valley. Ten or 12 families. We had a softball team and we had a 10k run every year." Parties were common as well as sports tournaments, barn raisings, and other activities. For a few years, Little Mulberry Valley flourished as a tight-knit community of hardworking families.

In the 1990s, Doug and Cathy sought some type of communal experience either where they were or some place they might relocate, looking and visiting such places as Sandhill, Earthhaven, Lama, Eastwind, and the Farm. In the end, the couple remained in the valley. Sustainability is integral to who the Strubels are, and they remain inspired by and continue follow the environmental movement by reading such authors as Bill McKibben. They believe the communal spirit will one day reemerge. Cathy said, "The way the world's going I think there some great numbers of people [who desire community connection] . . . [T]he only way they can make it is by getting together." To this day, Cathy and Doug have a positive impact in their community and search for opportunities rekindle the communal spirit.

The Drivers

Karen Driver lives in western Johnson County, in the Boston Mountains. She and her family migrated into the area in the mid-1970s. Alice Driver, who is Karen's niece, wrote that the Driver brothers "bought eighty acres of land bordering the Ozark National Forest in northwest Arkansas, along the Little Mulberry. They moved there from Michigan, bringing their wives, girlfriends, and children—ten people in all."[44] Many of the Drivers were talented in arts and crafts. Karen's husband, Bill, created wonderful works of stained glass. Steve Driver was a potter, and his wife, Louise, was a weaver. Rocky made silver and turquoise jewelry. Although Karen and Bill realized that communal living was not viable for them, they kept abreast of communal trends in the area. The Drivers would become neighbors to the Strubels, the couple interviewed above.

In the fall of 1975, the Drivers sold everything and "bought a big old truck and left our home in Michigan and we ended up getting here April 3, [1976]." The land was bare except for an old workshop and barn. The Drivers lived an austere life, with no running water, and used an outhouse. The family camped down by the river under "two tents" and "[Bill] actually made a platform to keep it up off the ground and we put the two tents on either end of this platform. Kids had one tent and Bill and I had the other tent." Karen remembered further that "we had a campfire and cooked and everything in it and it was fun." Later, the weather spurred the family to move temporarily into one of the buildings, her brother-in-law's future pottery workshop, when the river overflowed and flooded the campgrounds.

Arriving in April meant the weather was still cold. Karen told me, "We'd wake up and there would be frost." It was also time to enroll their children Erin and Jason into Oark, the local public school. According to Karen, "the bus would stop by here, and they would go off to school and walk up from the river up to the road here, and we had no clue really what the school was like or what we were getting into. We just thought, 'Hey, we bought a pretty nice area. There is a school. Our kids can go.' And as it turns out that little school is a good little school."

As things dried out, the family moved back down to the river to live. It was difficult to site their eventual homestead because the Driver brothers wanted the land for pasture and other uses. Eventually, Bill began building a wonderful stone and wood house on land formerly used to feed pigs. The family of four finally moved from the campground to a 16'x20' cabin with a loft. Bill and Karen received help from local people in building the house, "even though the locals were skeptical about an architectural style that incorporated asymmetrical rooflines, stained-glass windows, and a cathedral ceiling."[45] As for the Driver brothers, who lived in tents, "everybody was trying to decide what they were going to do and where they were going to live." One thing was for sure—no one wanted to live in a tent down by the river anymore.

The Drivers, according to Karen, were not accepted by the local townspeople because they were considered hippies. Furthermore, the family "swam naked, and we were a little different and everybody wondered about us, and I think no one expected that we would stay." As it turned out, most of the brothers and their families moved away. Karen was trying to find work in the town of Clarksville but some people thought she should change her appearance: "I had long hair and sometimes would wear a feather in my braid or whatever, and one day when [a hardware store owner] knew I had an education, he said, 'You know if you just change your image a little bit, you could probably get a job.'" Sometime would pass the community would accept her, but she finally landed a job teaching at Oark.

Finances were tight. Karen reported that at one point they were down to $5 and really worried about where to get more money. Bill's stained glass saved the day and even allowed Karen to go back to school to get her teacher's certification. Karen joined Larry, her brother-in-law, at Oark in 1983 as a fifth-grade teacher. Larry, some years earlier, was a fourth-grade teacher.

Nonetheless, the Drivers still lived a rather austere life. With the birth of her third child, Karen had had enough. She reflected:

Had a wood cook stove for a long time and then I finally got where when I started teaching and then I got pregnant and had a baby. It was like wait a minute, I want modern facilities. I want a flush toilet. I want a shower. I want hot water and we did that and I learned, I think, it was a wonderful experience because I learned to appreciate all the things I had as a young married person in my 20s before I moved here and went through this experience. Once you learn to get it and you can learn to appreciate it. Oh man! A gas stove that I just turned the dial on. I don't have to wait for 45 minutes for the stove to heat up to get my coffee.

The family still would practice a simple life in some ways but would not suffer needlessly either. Bill and Karen did not have lofty goals but just wanted to live as close to the land as possible. Later on, the kids worried about the small size of the school, so Karen and Bill gave them the chance to go to school elsewhere, and Erin did so for a semester.

Many of the brothers moved away to live and pursue other things. Whatever their paths, all of the Drivers followed their dreams and talents. Karen spent many years teaching students at Oark. Bill left his own mark with a beautiful house and other structures of stone, stained glass, and wood.

The Kersens

In the late 1970s, my father, twenty-nine-year-old Michael Kersen, who was living in El Paso with his family, made plans to create a commune. Working as the manager of a fast-food restaurant, Dad was tired of the rat race. The same was true for my mom, Debra, who was a supervisor at Sears. Dad knew that his father, Walter, had 80 acres of land deep in the Arkansas Ozarks. Some of Dad's friends, many of whom stayed in our house, also started believing that moving to Arkansas to live on the commune would be good. They and Dad wanted to try living off the land in a sustainable way. So, in 1979, our family, several couples, and a few single people left El Paso in a caravan of old pickup trucks and headed for a dilapidated cabin in the middle of the Arkansas Ozarks, along the Johnson-Newton County line. The group had no idea what it was getting into. I was bewildered at leaving the relative comfort of El Paso—where there was a 7–11 at the end of the block—to a geographically and socially isolated place. There was absolutely nothing to do there except go to school, work, or walk in the woods.

The winter of 1978–1979 was bitter. The snow piled so high that the group was often stuck in the cabin. The cabin did not offer much protection from the cold weather either. It was made in the 1920s and 1930s, with rough-hewn slats covered in newspaper on the inside and tarpaper or shingles on the outside. Crowded into the cabin were my parents, me and my two sisters Bridget and Vicci, along with all the other people who came with them. To create more space, Dad made one loft for Bridget and me; each of us had our own side. Because we could see through the roof in spots, Bridget and I would fill the holes with newspaper and other material that fell apart in the rain. As for the other buildings, there was a barn and something like an outhouse with no walls or roof—just a bench to sit on. There was no running water either—just a hand-dug well. Life for all of us was difficult.

Like the Drivers, our family had a rough start. Although no one went hungry, it was difficult to get food into the commune during the winter months. Some of the members of our commune hiked 12 miles for the entire trip to get a few bags of food and other items from Fallsville in Newton County. The family always was in danger of running low on provisions and money.

Other modern conveniences were scarce. The only source of heat was a potbelly stove. My parents and I spent lot of time hunting for firewood. We used a little hacksaw, hiking around to find sticks to cut to a certain length to fit into the stove. Pine and cedar knots were highly sought after. Since there was no running water, I was always embarrassed about my hygiene and clothes. Yet although I was an outsider at the local school for many years, I was never picked on like other children.

Unsurprisingly, our commune disbanded as soon as the thaw came in the late spring of 1980. Not far from the homestead, however, lived some back-to-landers in Fallsville. An interviewee told Ruth McShane, "There was a time when there was a sort of a crafts guild together in Fallsville."[46] Indeed, I remember the folks at Fallsville were involved with a health food store and various arts and crafts. They were the only communards we were aware of in the area. It wouldn't be till many years would pass before I knew that the Drivers and Strubels were out-of-state back-to-landers like us.

The group in Fallsville had hippie hoedowns in which the Kersen family participated on occasion. Being extremely shy, I hated that everyone was expected to get into a circle and dance. Behind the old tomato cannery where the dancing took place sat a muddy pond in which people would skinny dip during the summer months. I got in the pond too, but I would not part with my shorts. In spite of my shyness, I looked forward to the rare visit to Fallsville because hardly anyone visited our place, and I found the people in Fallsville rather interesting. There was even a guy who often walked on his hands from one place to another.

Unlike the Strubels, we had a hard time assimilating into the area. Dad could not find good paying work because he would not cut his hair. His political views and general perspective were at odds with almost everyone in the area as well. In one of the lean years, he even certified as a cosmetologist, hoping that this could open up some opportunities. There were several

years where the family was living well below the poverty line. Much barter-
ing took place—the family members would offer their labor to neighbors in
exchange for food, gas, and other provisions. Often there was no money for
me to participate in field trips and other school activities. Yet I still had to
go because the whole class was going. I often said that I was sick or needed
to study, so I could stay on the bus while the other kids had fun.

Mom worked at the hippie health food store in Fallsville, where she was
usually paid for her services in food. Soybean products became one of the
mainstays of the family menu. We even learned how to make tofu from soy-
beans. To supplement the food earned from Fallsville, the family gardened.
Dad got some horticultural ideas from his army service in Vietnam, such as
fertilizing the garden with a honey bucket. We would rotate outhouses—when
the hole filled up, we would make a new hole and clear out the old one. To
Dad, the whole communal experience centered on self-sustainment, a concept
he admired. His life in the Southwest even inspired him to build with adobe.
However, Arkansas red mud would not stick together. The family tried adding
straw but that did not work. We also tried our hand at other novel practices,
many inspired from *Mother Earth News*, and most did not work either.

The family also gathered a lot of wild plants and fruits from the land. We
picked all sorts of different wild things, such as red clover and mint for tea
and berries for fritters and pancakes. Dad and I tried to hunt one time, but
neither of us knew what we were doing, and it is doubtful that we would have
had the heart to kill a deer. We relied a great deal on *Fox Fire*, the *Whole Earth
Catalog*, and *Mother Earth News* to figure out what to eat and what not to eat.

Historian Jared Phillip and other scholars found that there were few alter-
cations between the back-to-landers in Arkansas and elsewhere where the
new in-migrants settled.[47] The same was true even in the case of the Driver
and Strubel families. We had no issues with older homesteaders and Ozarkers.
I remember learning some interesting things from an old logger who used a
mule to drag logs out of the woods. On the other hand, my family frequently
ran into problems when newer natives from outside the Ozarks (e.g., Little
Rock) moved up on the hill. Some newer neighbors moved in midway from
where the dirt road fed out onto Highway 21 and the end of the road, where
our property was located. Prior to this, our only neighbors were an old couple
who had a couple of chicken houses at the end of the road. Our new neighbors were Arkansans who moved up from somewhere south who tried to
take some of our 80-acres for themselves. Later, when my grandfather, Walter,

moved onto the property, these new homesteaders armed themselves and tried to force us to accept a shady survey line that cut substantially into our land. They did not know that Dad served two tours in Vietnam with Special Forces. Grandpa, for his part, was a merchant marine veteran in World War II and also served in the Korean War. Once Dad, Grandpa, and I actually fought them in an altercation and won, property issues disappeared. Our experiences highlighted the occasional case where "rural areas can be less of a place of escape than a place of conflict in which power struggles are played out between different lifestyle groups."[48] Often, if there was conflict, it was between retiree in-migrants and the back-to-landers, much like what was detailed in the chapter about Eureka Springs, who were at opposites even in the fundamental notion that traditional practices were worthy to learn and perpetuate (BTL) and the Ozarks as a mythic refuge away from a modern, more diverse America (retirees).[49]

Fitting into school was not easy for the Kersen children. When one of my teachers asked what we read for the summer, I mentioned that I read Dante's *Inferno* and other classics, she was doubtful and asked if I was a smart alec. But other teachers, such as Larry Driver, would spark my imagination and encourage me to explore different things. Over time, I learned that using humor was a way to get around my shyness.

Even though Strubel and Driver kids were my classmates, I didn't really understand that in many ways their background was so similar to that of our family. Indeed, I didn't know that those two families were back-to-landers like us until I was in my late 30s. Later I came to realize how special they were; if not for them and their communally minded parents, I probably would not be where I am now in life. It is extraordinary that, from of a class of 12 kids, a girl—and a back-to-land transplant to boot—would earn a PhD in psychology from Harvard. I would get a PhD in sociology from Mississippi State University. The Strubel girls, who also lived in the commune, became quite successful in their own lives. As a matter of fact, many of the students who graduated from Oark during the mid-1980s did well.

One reason Oark students did as well as we did is that we had amazing faculty during those years. Each of these teachers in his or her own way showed students how to think critically and be imaginative. The former students' success also demonstrates what can happen when teachers can exercise greater autonomy and apply fewer standardized tests. In some ways, the ideals of Mulberry Farm and the other alternative schools that emerged

Figure 10.3 The Author in the early 1980s, in the Ozarks.

in the Ozarks in the early 1970s were realized at a small public school near the Little Mulberry River in the Boston Mountains.

Concluding Thoughts

Throughout the 1980s and 1990s, migration into the Ozarks showed signs of slowing down.[50] Between 1980 and 1990 the region saw a 10.2 percent increase compared to a 39.7 percent increase during the 1970s. Johnson County grew at 4.6 percent between 1980 and 1990, a rate far lower than the 27.8 percent reached in the previous decades. Newton County experienced a 1.2 percent decline. The decline was partly attributable to the fact that fewer people wanted to move to rural areas and endure the hardships that the back-to-landers did. Many elderly communitarians were returning to urban settings in search of the amenities they had done without for so long. However, a few of the back-to-landers decided to stay and make a life in the Ozarks.

Some of people mentioned in this chapter stayed where they settled in the Boston Mountains region. Perhaps the ideals that originally brought them to the Ozarks served as a touchstone through the years. After Mulberry Farm disbanded, the Strubels worked hard to establish themselves in Oark and Clarksville. I consider them to be a lighthouse, to borrow Timothy Miller's metaphor, benefitting the wider community with their presence. To some extent, the same was true for the Drivers even though they were not, strictly speaking, communal. The Kersen commune, in contrast, was more socially and geographically isolated, a place to retreat from mainstream society.

Regarding the children of the hippies and communitarians, as the rock band the Who sang: "the kids are alright." A widely published 1976 newspaper article by Delores Barclay stated that children of communal parents turned out just fine—a finding supported by major researchers on the topic.[51] Her reporting fits well with the stories of these three families. Jared Phillips came to the same conclusion in his book *Hipbillies*.[52] Moreover, Barclay reported that "social scientists say that commune youngsters developing well. They believe these children often are more self-sufficient, realistic, and better behaved than children raised in traditional ways." However, many of the children eventually decided to move to towns and cities across the United States. That is to say, most did not follow the communalistic paths of their parents.

Arkansas Democrat Gazette reporter Frank Fellone interviewed me and a woman who was born in a log cabin to back-to-land parents.[53] Her parents moved to Marshall in Searcy County in the early 1990s. Her father was a Vietnam veteran who operated a natural food store. She talked about the hard work but also that her childhood years was wonderful living in the Ozarks. She also told Fellone that compared to her two other sisters, she is more closely aligned the ideology her back-to-land parents. All three girls would go on to become successful in their own right.

The mainstream population typically associates free drugs and sex with communal life. In reality, the prevailing activities for communities in the Boston Mountains, and probably in communes everywhere, was eking out a living and trying to get along with neighbors. Communal living is hard work, and a passion for the lifestyle is essential. Nowadays, older members of intentional communities wonder how much longer they can continue living as they did in the 1970s.

Although most communitarians are well established in their respective communities, there remains a clear distinction between being a "foreigner" and a "native" for some back-to-landers. My father, Michael Kersen, relishes the relative seclusion of his homestead; he finds his neighbors and the forces of modernity itself closing in on him. Thus, in some ways, he remains an outsider, especially in terms of his politics, where he finds himself on the far left of almost everyone around him. National Geographic reporter Thomas O'Neill wrote, "The in-migrants realize that they will always be considered outsiders. But what they have also come to learn is that Ozarkers' traditional wariness of strangers can give way to an even more fundamental trait: Ozarkers look after their neighbors."[54] O'Neill's observation has become even truer over time.

The story for many back-to-landers, however, was of one of serendipitous opportunity for them to gain the trust and support of the locals, especially the older generations.[55] For the old timers, they were able to pass on cherished crafts and trades to someone. The brain drain from the Ozarks, much like that from Appalachia, left a gap in maintaining and perpetuating any cultural heritage. Newcomers filled that gap to some extent. Those back-to-landers who learned a craft or trade were better able to navigate a difficult job market in these regions. Over time, many of those in-migrants became established in their respective communities and have offered much to their fellow Ozarkians.

The communal movement is nothing like it was in the late 1960s through the mid-1970s. Rarely do communes last more than a couple of years. Religious ideology, or for that matter any deeply held ideology, seems to keep these groups together more than other communal arrangements. Of special concern in the Ozarks are those communes established on the basis of white racial identity in the 1980s and later, although I was not aware of such communities during my time there. It is ironic that the area that once hosted intentional communities whose mission involved doing good works in some form (e.g., sustaining the environment, maintaining LGBT rights, combating inequality) also is the home of a number of race-based communes. The Ozarks also has attracted a few groups in which members were exploited by charismatic leaders, as we will saw in the recent case of the Nahziryah, discussed in chapter 6.

Conclusions

Ever since the Ozarks was settled by pioneers from the East, there always has been talk about the way the region was changing. Prior to the Civil War, the region was "in the vanguard of the Great American Frontier."[1] As was the case in much of the South, life in the Ozarks was in flux after the Civil War and Reconstruction. By the early twentieth century, newspapers began to report about some of those changes that, more often than not, accompanied increased migration into the region.

In 1925, the *Neosho Times*, a paper in the Missouri Ozarks, predicted that the population in the region would increase and spur a variety of changes thereby.[2] The writer encouraged readers to be open and try new and different things that benefitted the Ozarks in the end. Sociologist Walter Cralle argued that the "Ozarks is an area in transition," in that isolation is giving way to modernity. Cralle continued: "Largely within the life time of those now living, this protective isolation [in the Ozarks] has been broken down, and only in the interior and isolated counties does the uniqueness remain. The agencies of transportation and communication are playing the most important part; far more important than density of population, the economic factor, or ethnic stock."[3] Cralle's view seems at odds with that of most observers who viewed change as a result of in-migration.

By 1957, some Ozarkians' income was higher than the national average—a direct result of increased in-migration.[4] A.C. Meigs, author of the report, wrote: "The once-popular image of the Ozarks as a country of simple mountaineers leading a picturesque but stark life may have had roots in fact, but it is no longer a true one. The few isolated hollows which fit the description are now sought out by balladeers and graduate students who hope to record something of a vanishing way of life. The Ozarks are changing, and anyone who tours Northwest Arkansas and Southern Missouri cannot help but see the change."[5] The issues implicit throughout Meigs' article are in-migration and development's effects on a region known for its isolation. This same issue is one that continues to characterize life in the Ozarks today.

According to historian Robert Flanders, there have been several waves of population influx over the course of the Ozarks's history, beginning with the pioneers when the region was a frontier.[6] After the Civil War and through the Progressive era, many people came to the region to create or improve its social and physical infrastructure. The next wave came during the New Deal era, when expanded government programs and opportunities attracted people to the Ozarks. The last wave arrived during the late 1960s-1970s and consisted of back-to-the-landers, urban refugees, retirees, and others. It is this last wave that really worried Flanders. He continued, "The Ozarks is undergoing the most powerful and extreme change it could experience—next to war or a natural disaster." He pointed out that the population increased four times more than anywhere else in the country. He stated further, "We don't want the Ozarks 'steamrolled' or 'Californicated.'" I am not sure what Flanders meant by "Californicated," but his use of the word made the popular press well before the Red Hot Chili Peppers wrote a song about it. His notion is not new, as Vance Randolph worried that all the wild characters would leave the Ozarks as more people migrated into the region.[7]

However, Flanders overlooked a major point in his polemic against increased population. To some extent, the region retained its unique culture despite the influx of migrants. As Jared Phillips documented, many of the back-to-the-landers kept older traditions and lifestyles alive. In the case of many Ozarkian tourist towns, attracting people to the area was, and remains, essential. This was the main concern Otto Ernest Rayburn expressed about Eureka Springs's future, but it could be applied to the whole region, as he looked at it in the 1950s.[8] Although he was referring to tourists, towns need stable or growing populations for economic development, taxation, and other purposes. One of the region's persistent paradoxes is finding "the best of both worlds—rurality and industrialization."[9]

Today, such technological innovations as the Internet and social networking sites as Facebook may change some aspects of Ozark culture, but they are changing all cultures. Thus, for the Ozarks, what comes out on the other end likely still will retain an Ozarkian flavor. The same is true of popular culture too.

However, there may be some truly transformational changes in store for the Ozarks. While the Ozark label seems to be becoming a variant of the term "southerner" in Arkansas and to some degree in Missouri, I think more mobility, anywhere, will dilute any one particular region's sense of identity. Nevertheless, it will be interesting to see the way the Ozark identity changes as racial and ethnic diversity increases in the region.

Didi Tang reported about the Hmong, a group of people originally from the mountains of Indo-China that at first, many settled in states like Minnesota and Wisconsin.[10] However, as they learned that the Ozarks was more like what they were used to in their native countries, many moved to Missouri and Arkansas. One Hmong told Tang, "It feels like home again . . . [The Ozarks] looks pretty close to [Laos]: nice hills, up and down; streams running; nice weather; a lot of farming, and a lot of types of animals."[11] According to Tang, in just a few years, more than 1,000 Hmong had settled in the Ozarks, and many of them decided to make a living running poultry farms for companies such as Tyson. Tang also noted that the locals like them because they are hardworking and have diversified the culture (e.g., food).

The presence of Hispanics in the Ozarks is an even greater cultural change I did not see coming when I moved up into the mountains in the late 1970s, even during my years in the little school I attended. I began to notice changes when I worked in a chicken plant in the River Valley of Arkansas and met people who were African American, Hispanic, and even from the Marshall Islands. It is remarkable to see so much more diversity in people and choices in the area, and perhaps is even more ironic to hear a person speaking Ozark-Hispanic- or Ozark-Hmong-accented English. Thus, I think the archetype of the mountaineer/hillbilly probably will be ever less characteristic of the Ozarks' residents. I also believe the gap between the mountaineer/hillbilly and "Ozark" and "Ozarker" will grow, and it will be interesting to see what replaces it.

One of the unexplored facets beyond the scope of this book is the need to address Ozark identity and gender. Popular culture has focused for too long on some version of Daisy Mae/Mammy Yokum. The world of literature is far ahead of the social sciences in trying to create a better narrative space for the Ozarks women in the form of such strong characters as Ree in Daniel Woodrell's *Winter's Bone*. As I followed the various stories about the back-to-the-land people, I was struck by how many women were at the forefront of that movement.

I am concerned about the acceptance of radical conservativism and of the very tenuous notion that the Ozarks was monolithic in its support of the Confederacy. Of course, such sentiments play right into stereotypes of the southerner/mountaineer/Ozarker (e.g., intolerant and bigoted) that the culture at large has created. For some reason, like much of the South, the Ozarks cannot, or will not, escape its past, and popular culture has accentuated a past that often is more nostalgic than "real." Not only has it led to a muddled collective identity in the Ozarks, but Brexit and Make America Great Again also are reflected in this hyperreality. Perhaps Willie Morris was right in saying that "one's past was inside of a man anyway; it would remain there forever."[12] It may be the case that demographic shifts in the region change that fact. On the other hand, more in-migrants, particularly more diverse ones, may exacerbate extreme white nationalist and neo-Confederate sympathies.

It is important to return to Woodward's question: "When will a southerner stop referring to himself as a southerner?" and extend it to Ozarkers too. As I reviewed a number of books, I noticed two interesting things: outsiders, much like in a religious conversion process, came in and accepted the region and the South's culture, and may be even more southern/Ozarkian now than their native counterparts. That is not to say that most natives would not refer to themselves readily as southerners/Ozarkers. On the other hand, there are some southern/Ozarkian expatriates who shuck their former identity to avoid ridicule or for many other reasons. None of this is unusual. Often, I hear people refer to themselves as non-Mississippians, although they spent most of their lives in the state. I also am guilty of that practice—I have spent the majority of my life in a number of southern states, but still consider myself a Colorado native because I was born in that state. Perhaps Woodward's question is unanswerable.

Over the past several decades, Li'l Abner and Dogpatch have become a distant memory for most Ozarkers, and more so for most people around the country. Sadie Hawkins Day is rarely observed and is even more anachronistic given the increased awareness of gender relations. Literally and figuratively, it would appear that Dogpatch is a ghost town. Moreover, it would seem that examples within popular culture of the mountaineer/hillbilly are increasingly difficult to find. Using IDMb, I found that the keywords that came up most frequently for the phrase "Ozark Mountains" indeed were hillbilly, singer/song, deception and scheming, murder and other forms of violence/guns, and unconventional relationships of all sorts. Using the term "hillbilly," the keywords associated with the term most were "singer," "murder," "violence," and "redneck." Except for a few really foul examples, movies about the Ozarks in recent decades are remarkably less stereotypical than the bulk of movies made about the region from the 1930s through the 1950s.[13]

Dogpatch was the mythic place where the trickster Li'l Abner exposed readers to the ironies and contradictions of American society. Because of the rise of conformity and McCarthyism from the late 1930s to the 1950s, social critics had to be clever and employ satire and metaphor. Al Capp found that freedom to critique society through Dogpatch and its inhabitants. In a similar vein, *The Simpsons* in Springfield, *Family Guy* in Quahog, and *South Park* in South Park function the same way, although those shows certainly are not subtle or metaphorical in their critiques. Like Dogpatch, the towns serve as a character in each of the shows as well.

Ozark Area Congress founder David Haenke argues that the Ozarks form a distinct bioregion that he believes shapes the people's culture too. As I reviewed newspaper articles about the Ozarks from all over the United States, I noticed that many reporters would agree with his assertion. In some ways, they are more like their Appalachian neighbors than other cultures. The region is poised perpetually on the verge between America's pastoralist ideal and modernity. The hyperreal experiences in the Ozarks offered formerly in Dogpatch, Branson/Silver Dollar City, and to some extent, Eureka Springs, constitute a mythical world for tourists who want them, while those who want authenticity don't have to look far to find it in the Ozarks.

When I first visited Eureka Springs, I fell in love with it. I should have realized I was not the only one. Most people describe the town as quaint or eccentric, and there is something to that assessment. I don't think it is metaphysical either. The magic of Eureka Springs is that the town is a mass of contradictions and microconflicts that breed creativity. It is at once inclusive and exclusive. It is fundamentalist, pagan, atheistic, and every other thing, and is a town unafraid to have as its motto "Where Misfits Fit." Given that Eureka Springs offers everything one can think of, the town has a true liminal quality. I felt the same way when I visited Sedona, except I believe Eureka Springs is more authentic in accepting paranormal beliefs.

The town is a crossroads for all sorts of people. In more sociological terms, it reminds me of Elijah Anderson's cosmopolitan canopy concept. Anderson notes that a cosmopolitan canopy "is peculiar in that people of diverse backgrounds feel they have an equal right to be there."[14] It is a safe place to express oneself in whatever way one wants to. And the town is a generator of *communitas*.

Eureka Springs and other areas of the Ozarks have a long history of superstition and folklore traditions that Charles Morrow Wilson and Vance Randolph documented. That rich folkloric structure already present in the Ozarks may be one way to explain the rapid transition from ghosts, swamp gas, and other older traditions to more modern ones such as aliens and fly-ing saucers. A few months after Oregonian Kenneth Arnold made one of the first UFO claims, reports of UFOs emerged from the Ozarks. Over time, more UFO reports came from the Ozarks than other regions in Arkansas. The same is true for the Missouri Ozarks and other regions in that state. I follow the tradition of other scholars who treat UFO narratives as a modern form of folklore. What I mean by that is that folklore of any form usually functions as a way to explain unexplainable things with familiar concepts.

It is likely that unforeseen, emergent issues will require a new folkloric framework. It is likely, too, that UFO devotees, like other devoted followers, will be hard-pressed to change their views. Paranormal manifestations, such as UFOs and aliens, are common in popular culture, particularly in television shows such as *The X Files* and the like, and tourists flock to Roswell, New Mexico, to buy all sorts of alien trinkets. On the other hand, serious UFO believers have found Eureka Springs and the Ozarks amenable places to share their experiences and research. Having visited Sedona, Roswell, and Eureka Springs, I am impressed with the earnest efforts of organizers, vendors, and attendees who meet in northwestern Arkansas. Moreover, I have not sensed any reduction in the UFO community's commitment, although the ubiquity of cellphones with cameras and instantaneous communication has failed to provide the public with a flood of evidence. Regardless, as Leon Festinger suggested in *When Prophecy Fails*, UFO enthusiasts likely will remain com-mitted. What will interest social scientists like me is exploring what is the next explanatory transition to emerge when UFOs and aliens no longer serve to explain issues associated with modernity.

In addition to being a magnet for reported paranormal phenomena and believers, as mentioned, the Ozarks is home to a number of cultic movements and also is a region in which militia and white race-based groups have had a long sordid history. A number of charismatic figures found the Ozarks attrac-tive. Searcy County came to be the home to two groups that I explored in chapter 6, the Disciples of Incoming Kingdom and the Nahziryah, otherwise known as the Purple People, both of which were led by charismatic men who dictated all aspects of members' lives, and to some extent, their afterlives as well. Further, both groups found Searcy County attractive because it is isolated geographically.

I first learned about the Purple People when I saw them selling items in the vendor booths at a UFO conference in Eureka Springs. This group is unique in that it is one of the few predominantly African American cults in American history. In many ways, the Nahziryah share a great deal with other cults in that members are segregated from the mainstream and suffer all forms of abuse at their leaders' hands.

Seeds of Change

When I met with members of the Hot Mulch and their fellow back-to-the-landers, I asked if they felt that mainstream society, and particularly those who may not have the same values as theirs, had co-opted their endeavors. They told me without hesitation that they did not feel that way. Instead, they believed that they had planted the seeds to initiate change. What were those seeds, and did they grow and thrive?

The first thing to consider is the back-to-the-land movement itself, which was one of many waves based on a long-held preference in the United States for rural areas or country over the city. Leo Marx argued that "this impulse gives rise to a symbolic motion away from centers of civilization toward their opposite, nature, away from sophistication toward simplicity, or, to introduce the cardinal metaphor of the literary mode, away from the city toward the country."[15] Marx continues to note that much of popular culture is steeped in pastoralist ideals. Indeed, it seems that *Mother Earth News*, *Whole Earth Catalog*, *Walden Two*, and *Stranger in a Strange Land* are omnipresent. He also noted Aldo Leopold's 1949 *A Sand County Almanac* and Wendell Berry's *The Unsettling of America*.[16] Thus, it is not a surprise that such an impulse drove a small portion of the counterculture to leave the city and try their hand at living as closely off the land as they could. Most were white, educated, and middle class, and many who came to the Ozarks were refugees from urban America. By most accounts, almost none of the intentional communities survived longer than a few years. Many of the back-to-the-landers of the 1970s had little experience or skills to accomplish what they set out to do, and most did not stay long. However, those who did had a greater effect than their numbers should have warranted.[17] Those back-to-the-landers who stayed helped sustain old folk traditions. In *Hippie Homesteaders*, Carter Taylor Seaton wrote about the people who moved to the Appalachian Mountains in West Virginia: "Unlike their own children, these young people [in-migrants] appreciated the elders' old ways and wanted to learn their skills. Furthermore, their friendships grew because the newcomers were very respectful of the mores and the traditions around them."[18] In many cases, back-to-the-landers became very successful artisans and craftspeople who often contributed significantly to their communities and the region.

The hipbillies were fond of creating all sorts of groups.[19] Some were communal in nature. Others focused on specific things, such as farmer-to-consumer distribution of produce that cooperatives offered. Still others were based on entertainment, such as music and movies. Many of these organizations in the Ozarks, particularly in Missouri, formed in the 1970s and revolved in one way or another around sustainability and ecological principles. It is difficult to keep track of all of the myriad organizations, and thus Brian Campbell's chapter "Growing an Oak: An Ethnography of Ozark Bioregionalism," in *Environmental Anthropology Engaging Ecotopia*, published in 2013, is an excellent resource to guide a reader through many of the Ozark organizations that emerged in the 1970s and 1980s.[20]

Another important factor that likely would not have been considered had it not been for the back-to-the-landers' efforts was a concern for the environment and sustainable practices that centered on farming and energy activities. They also engaged in activism related to herbicide use as well as clear-cutting of old-growth forests. In some cases, the newcomers were in step with the elders of the region, who saw little they liked in modern, corporate agricultural practices. Often both natives and such people as Ron Hughes, David Haenke, Louise Vaughn, Doug and Cathy Strubble, and others worked with each other and shared information about ways to improve their farming practices, which was the explicit goal of New Life Farm.

Early efforts in solar energy technology in the Ozarks have reaped many benefits in the past several decades, while other technologies, such as methane capture, have yet to become popular. The plan for composting toilets stalled because Ozarkers were unwilling to give up their flushing toilets.

However, organic food and food cooperatives truly have become main-stream. Both locals and back-to-the-landers cooperated to make organic farming work, and the Ozark Organic Growers Association is one of the oldest organizations in the country today.

Music played a large part in exposing the Ozarks to mainstream popular culture and the converse. The back-to-the-land movement captured many people's imaginations through *Mother Earth News*, various books such as *Walden Two*, and often, music. With respect to music's power to spread the communal spirit, Hugh Gardner wrote: "Through the magic of electronics and the purchasing power of middle-class youth, music created by the young for the young carried the message more persuasively and with more feeling than television ever did, especially when the communal living arrangements of many of the rock groups carrying the message, such as the Grateful Dead or the Jefferson Airplane, became commonly known."[21]

BOA, OMD, and Hot Mulch did the same for the Ozark region. These groups left a lasting impression on more recent Ozarkian musician/activ-ists such as singer/multi-instrumentalist Erik Tumminia and bassist Amelia LaMair of Creek Stink.[22] Creek Stink is a popular band that plays throughout the Missouri Ozarks. Erik is a second-generation back-to-the-lander whose parents moved from St. Louis to Texas County in the mid-1970s, where he was born several years later. Other members of his family were part of the U & I communal experience in Lebanon, Missouri.

Growing up, OMD was played all the time in Erik's home. He found it dif-ficult to separate his consciousness from OMD's song "Standing on a Rock." He told me he was indoctrinated into their music, and it became a large part of the soundtrack of his youth. Later, as an adult, his friend David Haenke, who distributed Hot Mulch's 45 rpm with "Ozark Mountain Mother Earth News Freak" on it, introduced him to Hot Mulch while the two men were working at Elixir Farm.

Erik sees Black Oak Arkansas and OMD at opposite ends of the Ozark spectrum. On one end is OMD, whose lyrics are peppered with communal-ism and hippy sentiments, while BOA, gun-toting, long-haired Southerners, are on the other. Creek Stink tries to strike a balance between those two extremes. I think they do that well, and they really are more consistent with Hot Mulch in perspective, sound, and lyrics. For example, in the song "Hardwood Hop," Erik tells the listener:

> Let's sweep the floors let's kill a goat/build a bonfire and rosin up the bow. Get on the phone call everyone you know tonight/there will be a rock n roll show. The crazy kids are down from Como town, guitar, tub, and banjo man, I like that sound. It's two, three, four, and away we go; to be good music ain't got to be slow.

However, they are their own band and bring other interesting influences into the mix, such as punk. Erik refers to the style as "Punks with banjoes." I think it is a blend of Meat Puppets, OMD, and something unique and new that defies classification. In addition to the music, Erik and Amelia are active in environmental, health food, and other issues that long have been concerns of back-to-the-landers in the Ozarks.

People and issues have changed since the 1970s for socially aware musicians. Now, gender is a large focus for many artists. Erik noted that one Springfield record label, Push-n-Pull Records, has bands that females lead, such as Suzy Trash and the Slugs, a group of women who grew up in the Missouri Ozarks. Another Springfield label, WeeRock Records, represents Creek Stink.

Like much else produced in modern life, music and other forms of popular culture are delivered efficiently, predictable, quantifiable in terms of money or units consumed, and controlled easily by technology.[23] We expect the same in solving social problems and even our private troubles. However, what I've learned about the Ozarks, and I suspect is true anywhere in America, is that true movements, great music and art, and transformative ideas arise organically in the right place and time. They can't be recreated—Woodstock and its various incarnations thereafter are cases in point.

The Ozarks' strength is that it accepts people who are willing to make the mountains their home. Hot Mulcher Ron Hughes sees the economy as a major issue for the region. He believes that leaders in the region should tie the economy with the land by remaining on the forefront of sustainable technology, organic farming, and permaculture. The land and the people are related closely, and understanding that fact may be the way forward. As Ken Carey, author of *The Flat Rock Journal* wrote, "Our Ozark economy is rooted in the land—a reality that will endure long after those flashy economies whose survival depends on the daily fix of fossil fuels have faded into the footnotes of history."[24] We can only hope that, with even more worrisome social and environmental challenges looming before us, younger generations in the Ozarks, the nation, and even the world will follow in the footsteps of all those environmentalists, back-to-the-landers, and others who tried alternative ways of living.

Notes

Chapter 1. The Ozarks

1. Docia Karell, "Ozarks 'Culture Preserve' Is Suggested by Teacher," *Springfield Leader and Press*, October 29, 1930, 1–2.

2. Karell.

3. Milton Rafferty, *The Ozarks: Land and Life* (Fayetteville: University of Arkansas Press, 2001), 1–3.

4. Frederick Jackson Turner, *The Frontier in American History* (New York: Henry Holt and Company, 1920), 14.

5. This process is usually associated with rites of passage and focuses on liminality or transitions between phases. See Arnold van Gennep, *The Rites of Passage* (London: Routledge and Kegan Paul, 1909).

6. Turner, *The Ritual Process*, 94–130.

7. Sharon Zukin, *Landscapes of Power: From Detroit to Disney World* (Berkeley and Los Angeles: University of California Press, 1993).

8. Turner, *The Ritual Process*, 127.

9. Charles Morrow Wilson, *The Bodacious Ozarks: True Tales of the Backhills* (Gretna, LA: Pelican Publishing Company, 2002), 12.

10. Ernest Hartman, *Boundaries in the Mind: A New Psychology of Personality* (New York: Basic Books, 1991).

11. Hartman, *Boundaries*, 143.

12. Wilson, *The Bodacious Ozarks*, 75.

13. Max Weber, Hans Gerth, and C. W. Mills, *From Max Weber: Essays in Sociology* (New York: Oxford University Press, 1958).

14. Victor Turner, *The Ritual Process: Structure and Anti-Structure* (New Brunswick, NJ: Aldine Transaction, 2009), 126–28.

15. Turner, *Ritual Process*, 111, 132–85.

16. Flannery O'Connor, in *Mystery and Manners: Occasional Prose*, ed. by Sally and Robert Fitzgerald (New York: Farrar, Straus, and Giroux, 1969), 192.

17. Ken Carey, *Flat Rock Journal: A Day in the Ozark Mountains* (San Francisco: Harper, 1994), 32–33.

18. Anthony DeCurtis, "The Eighties," in *Present Tense: Rock & Roll and Culture*, ed. Anthony DeCurtis (Durham, NC: Duke University Press, 1992), 11–12.

19. Often, a story has a turning point or epiphany when characters are faced with a major change or issue that alters their worldview or life in lasting ways. In *Interpretive Interactionism*, sociologist Norman Denzin argues that it is important to recognize and study epiphanies in narratives at all levels (e.g., individual, institutional, and communities). Norman Denzin, *Interpretive Interactionism* (Thousand Oaks, CA: Sage Publications, 1989), 40, 129–31.

20. Howard Becker, *Sociological Work: Method and Substance* (Chicago, IL: Aldine Publishing Company, 1970); Ken Plummer, *Documents of Life: An Introduction to the Problems and Literature of a Humanistic Method* (Boston, MA: George Allen and Unwin, 1983); John Creswell, *Qualitative Inquiry and Research Design: Choosing among Five Traditions* (Thousand Oaks, CA: Sage Publications, 1998).

21. Denzin, *Interpretive Interactionism*, 66–82.

22. Becker, *Sociological Work*, iBook Location 66.

23. Becker, iBook Location 131.

24. Georg Simmel, *On Individuality and Social Forms*, ed. Donald Levine (Chicago, IL: University of Chicago Press, 1971), 145.

25. Robert Park, "Human Migration and the Marginal Man," in *Classic Essays on the Culture of Cities*, ed. Richard Sennett (New York: Appleton-Century-Crofts, [1928] 1969), 141.

26. E. Joan Miller, "The Naming of the Land in the Ozarks: A Study in Cultural Arkansas," *Annals of American Geographers* 58.1 (1968): 51–77; Charles Morrow Wilson, *The Bodacious Ozarks: True Tales of the Backhills* (Gretna, LA: Pelican Publishing Company, 2002), 231.

27. *The Mountain Echo*, Yellville, AR. April 23, 1909, 2.

28. J. C. Tillman, "Nobody Seems to Know Just Where 'The Ozarks' Lie," *Northwest Arkansas Times*, Fayetteville, AR. June 13, 1964, 2.

29. George Hansen, *The Trickster and the Paranormal* (Xlibris Corp.: Kindle Edition, 2001), location 242.

30. Turner, *The Ritual Process*, 111.

31. Turner, 127.

32. Jared Phillips, *Hipbillies: Deep Revolution in the Arkansas Ozarks* (Fayetteville: University of Arkansas Press, 2019).

Chapter 2. Exploring Regional Identity in Arkansas: The Salience of the Term "Ozark"

1. Published originally with Candis Pizzetta in 2017. See Thomas Kersen and Candis Pizzetta, "Exploring Regional Identity in Arkansas: The Salience of the Ozark Term," *Elder Mountain: A Journal of Ozark Studies* 7 (2017): 66–83.

2. Used by permission of Phillip Howerton and Golden Antelope Press. Phillip Howerton, *The History of Tree Roots: Poems* (Kirksville, MO: Golden Antelope Press, 2015), 3.

3. Joel Garreau, *The Nine Nations of North America* (New York: Avon Books, 1981).

4. C. Vann Woodward, *The Burden of Southern History* (Baton Rouge: Louisiana State University Press, 1970), 3.

5. John Reed, "The Heart of Dixie: An Essay in Folk Geography," *Social Forces* 69 (1976): 221–33; Derek Alderman and Robert Beavers, "Heart of Dixie Revisited: An Update on the Geography of Naming in the American South," *Southeastern Geographer* 36 (1999): 190–205;

Christopher Cooper and H. Gibbs Knotts, "Declining Dixie: Regional Identification in the Modern American South," *Social Forces* 88 (2010): 1083–1101; John Egerton, *The Americanization of Dixie* (New York: Harper's Magazine Press, 1974).

6. The percentage by race of self-identified southerners is 44.0 percent for whites, 44.7 for African Americans, and 25.6 for Hispanics. White self-identified southerners differ from their African American and Hispanic counterparts by being more fundamentalist/literalist, conservative, climate denying, or republican. Angie Maxwell, "Southern Political Attitudes: Geography versus Identity, Results from the 2012 Blair Center of Southern Politics and Society," Accessed https://blaircenter.uark.edu/polling-data-reports/2012-poll/geography -versus-identity on December 13, 2019.

7. The idea of the South as a region goes back even further—to the turn of the nineteenth century. Howard Odum of the University of North Carolina at Chapel Hill was the main force in the emergent field of regional sociology in the 1920s and 1930s. In addition to stressing a more applied and socially active research agenda, he introduced regional sociology as a theoretical orientation. This approach focused on geographic regions' "cultural landscape," particularly that of the South. The theory was organic, in that it stressed the importance of institutions and equilibrium. However, other studies did focus on social and demographic changes within certain regions.

Frederick Jackson Turner, *The Frontier in American History* (New York: Henry Holt and Company, 1920); Samuel Wallace, "Regional Sociology: The South," *Sociological Spectrum* 1 (1981): 431; cf. William Hesseltine and David Smiley, *The South in American History* (New York: Prentice-Hall, 1943); Rupert Vance, "The Concept of the Region," *Social Forces* 8 (1929): 216; Howard Odum, "A Sociological Approach to the Study and Practice of American Regionalism: A Factorial Syllabus," *Social Forces* 20 (1942): 431–32; Odum, "A Sociological Approach," 432.

8. Alvin Bertrand, "Regional Sociology as a Special Discipline," *Social Forces* 31 (1952): 132–36.

9. Bertrand, 133.

10. Howard Odum, "From Community Studies to Regionalism," *Social Forces* 23.3 (1945), 246.

11. Odum, "A Sociological Approach," 427.

12. Brooks Blevins, *Hill Folks: A History of Arkansas Ozarkers and Their Image* (Chapel Hills: University of North Carolina Press, 2002); Charles Morrow Wilson, *The Bodacious Ozarks: True Tales of the Backhills* (Gretna, LA: Pelican Publishing Company, 2002).

13. Immanuel Wallerstein, "The West, Capitalism, and the Modern World-System," *Review* 15.4 (1992): 561–619.

14. Pitirim Sorokin, *Contemporary Sociological Theories: Through the First Quarter of the Twentieth Century* (New York: Harper Torchbooks, 1956). For the interested reader, Sorokin, an important early twentieth-century applied sociologist, admired Le Play. He devotes a whole chapter to his work. Specifically, refer to Sorokin's review of Le Play's *Place, Work, and People* (his term for family) and its influence within sociological theory on page 68. Cf. Vance, "Concept of Region."

15. Vance, "Concept of Region," 925. Cf. H. C. Brearly, "Homicides in South Carolina: A Regional Study," *Social Forces* 8 (1929): 222.

16. David Haenke, personal communication with the author, November 18, 2018.

17. Robert David Sack, *Homo Geographicus* (Baltimore, MD: Johns Hopkins University Press, 1997), 132 and 135.

18. Dewey Grantham, "The Regional Imagination: Social Scientists and the American South," *Journal of Southern History* 34 (1968): 3–32; Larry Griffin, "The Promise of a Sociology of the South," *Southern Cultures* 7.1 (2001): 50–71.

19. Reed, "The Heart of Dixie," 925; John Reed, "The Dissolution of Dixie and the Changing Shape of the South," *Social Forces* 69 (1990): 222.

20. Odum, "A Sociological Approach," 430; Rudolf Herberle, "Regionalism: Some Critical Observations," *Social Forces* 21.3 (1943): 280–86.

21. Thomas Gieryn, "A Space for Place in Sociology," *Annual Review of Sociology* 26 (2000): 463–96.

22. Reed, "The Heart of Dixie," 925.

23. John Reed, *One South: An Ethnic Approach to Regional Culture* (Baton Rouge: Louisiana State University Press, 1982), 79.

24. Howerton, *The History of Tree Roots: Poems*, 3.

25. Sack, *Homo Geographicus*, 246.

26. Victor Turner, *The Ritual Process: Structure and Anti-Structure* (New Brunswick, NJ: Aldine Transaction, 2009), 112.

27. Karen Cox, "Branding Dixie: The Selling of the American South, 1890–1910" in *Dixie Emporium: Tourism, Foodways, and Consumer Culture in the American South*, ed. Anthony J. Stanonis (Athens: University of Georgia Press, 2008), 51.

28. James Cobb, *Redefining Southern Culture: Mind and Identity in the Modern South* (Athens: University of Georgia Press, 1999).

29. Rupert Vance, "The Sociological Implications of Southern Regionalism," *Journal of Southern History* 26.1(1960): 49–50.

30. Walter Cralle, "Social Change and Isolation in the Ozark Mountain Region of Missouri," *American Journal of Sociology* 41.4 (1936): 435–46.

31. Bob Franson, "The Changing Ozarks," *Springfield Leader and Press*, July 3, 1977, F1.

32. Wallace, "Regional Sociology."

33. Reed, "The Heart of Dixie."

34. Center for the Study of the American South. Odum Institute for Research in Social Science, University of North Carolina at Chapel Hill, 2007, "Southern Focus Poll, Fall 1992," https://hdl.handle.net/1902.29/D-20174, UNC Dataverse, V1; Center for the Study of the American South, 2001, "Southern Focus Poll, Spring 2001," https://hdl.handle.net/1902.29/D-31552, UNC Dataverse, V1.

35. Howard Campbell, "Escaping Identity: Border Zones as Places of Evasion and Cultural Reinvention," *Journal of the Royal Anthropological Institute* 21 (2015): 307.

36. Cora Pinkley-Call, "Stair-Step-Town" (Eureka Springs, AR: Times-Echo Press, 1952), 5.

37. Reed, "The Dissolution of Dixie."

38. Cooper and Knotts, "Declining Dixie"; see also Alderman and Beavers, "Heart of Dixie Revisited."

39. Brooks Blevins, *Arkansas/Arkansaw: How Bear Hunters, Hillbillies, and Good Ol' Boys Defined a State* (Fayetteville: University of Arkansas Press, 2009).

40. E. Joan Wilson Miller, "The Naming of the Land in the Ozarks: A Study in Cultural Processes," *Annals of the Association of American Geographers* 9.2 (1969): 240–51.

41. Larry Griffin, "The American South and Self," *Southern Cultures* 12.3 (2006): 8–9.

42. Miller, "The Naming of the Land," 247.

43. Brooks Blevins, "Wretched and Innocent: Two Mountain Regions in the National Consciousness," *Journal of Appalachian Studies* 7.2 (2001): 257–71.

44. Damien Francaviglia, "Branson, Missouri: Regional Identity and the Emergence of a Popular Culture Community," *Journal of American Culture* 18 (1995): 57; c.f., discussion about the "Outlanders" in Baxter Hall and Cecil Wood, *The South* (New York: Scribner, 1995).

45. Blevins, *Arkansas/Arkansaw*, 164.

46. Francaviglia, "Branson, Missouri," 58; Charles Morrow Wilson, *The Bodacious Ozarks: True Tales of the Backhills* (Gretna, LA: Pelican Publishing Company, 2002), 127.

47. Patrick Huber, "The Riddle of the Horny Hillbilly," in *Dixie Emporium: Tourism, Foodways, and Consumer Culture in the American South*, ed. Anthony J. Stanonis (Athens: University of Georgia Press, 2008), 69–86.

48. Huber, "The Riddle,". 71.

49. Cox, "Branding Dixie," 54.

50. Huber, "The Riddle," 73–75.

51. John Williams Graves, *Town and Country: Race Relations in an Urban-Rural Context, Arkansas, 1865–1965* (Fayetteville: University of Arkansas Press, 1990); Blevins, *Arkansas/Arkansaw*, 65–79.

52. J. Blake Perkins, *Hillbilly Hell-Raisers: Federal Power and Populist Defiance in the Ozarks* (Urbana: University of Illinois Press, 2017) Kindle edition.

53. Patrick Huber and Kathleen Drowne, "Hill Billy: The Earliest Known African American Usuages," *American Speech* 83.2 (2008): 214–18.

54. Huber and Drowne, 218.

55. Blevins, *Arkansas/Arkansaw*, 137–38.

56. Blevins, 119–27.

57. Blevins, 6.

58. Mary Grinstead-Schneider and Bernal Green, "Adjustment Stresses on Rural Laborers in the Mississippi Delta and the Ozarks," *Growth & Change* 9.3 (1978): 37–43.

59. United States Department of Agriculture data, "County Level Data Sets." Accessed http://www.ers.usda.gov/data-products/county-level-data-sets.aspx on February 23, 2105.

60. John Kuehn, and Lloyd Bender, "A Dissent: Migration, Growth Centers, and the Ozarks," *Growth & Change* 6.2 (1975): 46.

61. Grinstead-Schnieder and Green, "Adjustment Stresses," 39–40; Kathleen Morrison, "The Ties that Bind: The Impact of Isolation on Income in Rural America," *Journal of Public Affairs* 7.1 (2004): 18–19.

62. Robert Sandmeyer and Larkin Warner, "A Note on the Discouragement Effect," *Industrial and Labor Relations Review* 23.3 (1970): 406–13; Grinstead-Schneider and Green, "Adjustment Stresses," 42.

63. Grinstead-Schnieder and Green, "Adjustment Stresses," 40.

64. Kenneth Johnson, "The Continuing Incidence of Natural Decrease in American Counties," *Rural Sociology* 76.1 (2011): 83.

65. Grinstead-Schneider and Green, "Adjustment Stresses," 38.

66. Brooks Blevins, "Retreating to the Hill: Population Replacement in the Arkansas Ozarks," *Agricultural History* 74.2 (2000): 479–80.

67. Nina Glasgow and David L. Brown, "Social Integration among Older In-migrants in Nonmetropolitan Retirement Destination Counties," in *Population Change and Rural Society*, ed. William A. Kandel and David L. Brown (Netherlands: Springer, 2006), 193.

68. Anthony Petto and Lloyd Bender, "Responsiveness to Local Economic Conditions in the Ozarks," *Growth & Change* 5.2 (1974): 11.

69. Jared Phillips, *Hipbillies: Deep Revolution in the Arkansas Ozarks* (Fayetteville: University of Arkansas Press, 2019), 11.

70. Phillips, *Hipbillies*, 9.

71. Hendrix, "Kinship, Social Networks," 103.

72. Griffin, "The Promise of a Sociology," 10.

73. Egerton, *The Americanization of Dixie*.

74. James C. Cobb, *Away Down South: A History of Southern Identity* (Oxford; New York: Oxford University Press, 2005).

75. Cobb, *Away Down South*; Joshua I. Newman and Michael D. Giardina, "NASCAR and the 'Southernization' of America: Spectatorship, Subjectivity, and the Confederation of Identity," *Cultural Studies Critical Methodologies* 8.4: 479–506.

76. Blevins, *Arkansas/Arkansaw*, 161.

77. Blevins, 147.

78. Cobb, *Away Down South*, 81–91.

79. James C. Cobb, *Redefining Southern Culture: Mind and Identity in the Modern South* (Athens: University of Georgia Press, 1999), 89.

80. Blevins, "Retreating to the Hill," 478.

81. Data were gathered from Arkansas Secretary of State Reports to determine the prevalence of the use of the terms "Ozark," "Southern," "Dixie," and "American" in names of corporations, cooperatives, banks, and insurance companies. See Arkansas Secretary of State, "Search Incorporations, Cooperatives, Banks and Insurance Companies." Accessed at https://www.sos.arkansas.gov/corps/search_all.php on June 24, 2014. Numbers refer to entities that were coded by the Secretary of State's office as being in good standing, revoked, and dissolved. Duplications were removed (e.g., counselors listed individually who also were affiliated with an entity). Data from IRS's exempt organizations database were also analyzed. See Internal Revenue Service, "Exempt Organizations Select Check." Accessed at https://apps.irs.gov/app/eos/ on May 24, 2014. Cities or places were aggregated by county and larger internal geographic groupings in Arkansas based on Polidata's ISRs. Polidata, "Region Maps: County-Based Regions and Markets for Arkansas." Accessed http://www.polidata.us/pub/maps/rg2000/ar_reg.pdf on October 9, 2018.

82. Regions for Missouri followed Milton Rafferty's designation for the Ozarks region. The remaining regions are based on Missouri Department of Conservation data. Name data for Missouri was gathered from the Internal Revenue Service's tax-exempt organization search page. All data were included except for redundancies in names and erroneous entries. American Legion and American Legion Auxiliary were counted together, and multiple instances of such an entry were counted only once for each place. The counts for "Ozark" by region were: Central 2, Kansas City 1, Northeast 0, Northwest 6, Ozarks 300, Southeast 6, Saint Louis 15. The counts for "American" by region were: Central 89, Kansas City 235, Northeast 61, Northwest 98, Ozarks 217, Southeast 29, and Saint Louis 198.

83. Brooks Blevins, "When an Ozark Boyhood Really Isn't: Reconsidering Wayman Hogue's *Back Yonder*," Ozark Symposium, West Plains, Missouri. September 18, 2015.

84. Blevins, "Retreating to the Hill."

85. Cooper and Knotts, "Declining Dixie," 73.

86. Garreau, *The Nine Nations*, 136.

87. Cobb, *Redefining Southern Culture*, 89; Howard Zinn, *The Southern Mystique* (New York: Knopf, 1964).

88. Jean Baudrillard, *Simulations* (New York: Semiotext, 1983), 4; George Ritzer, *Enchanting a Disenchanting World: Revolutionizing the Means of Consumption* (Thousand Oaks, CA: Pine Forge Press), 114.

89. B. C. Hall and C. T. Wood, *The South* (New York: Scribner, 1995), 55.

90. Sack, *Homo Geographicus*, 9–10.

91. Willie Morris, *Terrains of the Heart and Other Essays on Home* (Oxford, MS: Yoknapatawpha Press, 1985), 77.

Chapter 3. Li'l Abner the Trickster: Mythical Identity in the Ozarks

1. John Shelton Reed, *One South: An Ethnic Approach to Regional Culture* (Baton Rouge: Louisiana State University Press, 1982), 78–87; cf. Angie Maxwell, "The Duality of the Southern Thing," *Southern Cultures* 20.4 (1982): 97; Benedict Anderson, *Imagined Communities: Reflections on the Origin and Spread of Nationalism* (New York: Verso, 1991), 5–7.

2. Baxter C. Hall and Cecil T. Wood, *The South* (New York: Scribner, 1995), 14.

3. M. Thomas Inge, "Li'l Abner, Snuffy, Pogo, and Friends: The South in the American Comic Strip," *Southern Quarterly* 48.2 (2011): 6–74, 13.

4. Brooks Blevins, "When an Ozark Boyhood Isn't: Reconsidering Wayman Hogue's *Back Yonder*. Ozark Symposium. West Plains, Missouri. September 18, 2015.

5. Alternatively, James Black noted that British readers were not so enamored with *Li'l Abner*.

6. Inge, "Li'l Abner," 6.

7. Inge, 36.

8. Inge; Elliott Caplin, *Al Capp Remembered* (Bowling Green, Ohio: Bowling Green State University Popular Press, 1994), 30–31.

9. Caplin, *Al Capp Remembered*, 61–63.

10. Caplin, 10.

11. James Black, "'Amoozin' but 'Confoozin': Comic Strips as a Voice of Dissent in the 1950s," *ETC: A Review of General Semantics* 66.4 (2009): 461.

12. Leo Bogart, "Adult Talk about Newspaper Cartoons," *American Journal of Sociology* 61.1 (1955): 26.

13. Inge, "Li'l Abner."

14. Alan Dundes, "Folklore as a Mirror of Culture," In *Meaning of Folklore*, ed. Simon Bronner (University Press of Colorado, Utah State University, 2007), 55.

15. E. Joan Miller, "The Ozark Culture Region as Revealed by Traditional Materials." *Annals of the Association of American Geographers* 58.1 (1968): 57–58.

16. Wilbur Zelinsky, *The Cultural Geography of the United States*. Revised edition (Englewood Cliffs, NJ: Prentice Hall, [1973] 1992), 114.

17. Zelinsky, 166.

18. Michael Fazio, "Architectural Preservation in Natchez, Mississippi: A Conception of Time and Place," (edits.) in *Order and Image in the American Small Town*, ed. Michael Fazio and Peggy Prenshaw (Jackson: University Press of Mississippi, 1981), 142.

19. Karen Cox, "The South and Mass Culture," *Journal of Southern History* 75.3 (2009): 677–90, 681. Craig Thompson and Kelly Tian, "Reconstructing the South: How Commercial Myths Compete for Identity Value through the Ideological Shaping of Popular Memories and Countermemories," *Journal of Consumer Research* 34.5 (2008): 609–11.

21. Cox, "The South and Mass Culture," 681.

22. *Bridgeport Post*, "Arkansas to Get 'Dogpatch' as New Tourist Attraction," Bridgeport, CT, January 6, 1967, 44; Allan Gilbert Jr., "Dogpatch U.S.A.," *Northwest Arkansas Times*, Fayetteville, AR, October 10, 1967, 7; Alex Washburn, "Jones Returns: APA Delegation Scatters to Dog Patch, Hot Springs," *Hope Star*. Hope, AR. June 14, 1971, 1.

23. *El Dorado Times.* "Vacation Trip to Harrison an Answer to Fuel Savers." El Dorado, AR. March 25, 1974, 7; *Hope Star,* "Dogpatch Opens 7th Season Today," May 3 1975, 1.

24. Gilbert. "Dogpatch U.S.A."

25. Jean Speer, "Hillbilly Sold Here," in *Parkways: Past, Present, and Future* by International Linear Parks Conference (Appalachian State University, 1987), 15–25.

26. Thomas Bender, *Community and Social Change in America* (Baltimore, MD: Johns Hopkins University Press, [1978] 1991).

27. Hall and Wood, *The South*, 37.

28. Zelinsky, *The Cultural Geography*, 124.

29. Michael Carroll, "The Trickster as Selfish-Buffoon and Cultural Hero," *Ethos* 12.2 (1984): 105–31.

30. Dundes, "Folklore as a Mirror," 56.

31. Hall and Wood, *The South*, 127.

32. Steve Wiegenstein, "The Lure of the Ozarks: What's the Bait and Who's the Fish?" Ozark Symposium. West Plains, Missouri. September 19, 2015.

33. Hall and Wood, *The South*, 66–67, 110.

34. Hall and Wood, 162–64.

35. Hall and Wood, 161.

36. Robert Morris, "The Arkansan in American Folklore," *Arkansas Historical Quarterly* 9.2 (1950): 104.

37. Thompson and Tian, "Reconstructing the South," 213–14.

38. *Hannibal Journal,* "Phrenological Democracy—A Lecture on Heads," Hannibal, MO. October 7, 1852, 2.

39. *Springfield Leader and Press.* "The Wastebasket," April 19, 1929, 20.

40. Morris, "The Arkansan," 106.

41. Walter Blair, "Laughter in Wartime America," *The English Journal* 34.4 (1945): 180.

42. Fred Starr, "Hillside Adventures," *Northwest Arkansas Times*, Fayetteville, AR, July 12, 1952, 2.

43. Speer, "Hillbilly Sold Here," 213; Speer cited Percy Mackaye (1924) as one who offered a romanticized notion of mountain people, 213.

44. Morris, "The Arkansan," 102.

45. Blair, "Laughter in Wartime America," 181.

46. Richard Chase, *The Jack Tales* (Cambridge, MA: Houghton Mifflin Co., 1943 [1971], 188; S. C. Fredericks, "Roger Zelazny and the Trickster Myth: An Analysis of Jack of Shadows," *Journal of American Culture* 2.1 (1979): 273.

47. Chase, *The Jack Tales*; Karl Kerenyi, "The Trickster in Relation to Greek Mythology," in *The Trickster: A Study in American Mythology,* Paul Radin (New York: Schocken Books, [1956] 1972), 167; Arthur Berger, *Li'l Abner: A Study in American Satire* (Jackson: University Press of Mississippi, [1969] 1994), 63.

48. Radin, *The Trickster*, 167–68.

49. Radin, *The Trickster*; Fredericks, "Roger Zelazney," 275.

50. Berger, *Li'l Abner*, 92.

51. Inge, "Li'l Abner," 33.

52. Kerenyi, "The Trickster in Relation," 175; Carl Jung, "On the Psychology of the Trickster Figure," in Paul Radin, *The Trickster*, [1956] 1972, 200; Carroll, "The Trickster as Selfish-Buffoon," 106; Jeff House, "Sweeny among the Archetypes: The Literary Hero in American Culture," *Journal of American Culture* 16.4 (1993): 66; Berger, *Li'l Abner*; Natalie Kononenko

and Svitlana Kukharenko, "Borat the Trickster: Folklore and the Media, Folklore in the Media," *Slavic Review* 67.1 (2008): 10.

53. Morris "The Arkansan," 104; House "Sweeny among Stereotypes," 66; Kononenko and Kukharenko, "Borat the Trickster," 10.

54. Kerenyi, "The Trickster in Relation," 185.

55. Radin, *The Trickster*; Fredericks, "Roger Zelazney," 273.

56. Inge, "Li'l Abner," 13; Black, "'Amoozin' but 'Confoozin,'" 466.

57. Berger, *Li'l Abner*, 90.

58. Blair, "Laughter in Wartime America," 182; Thompson and Tian, "Reconstructing the South"; House, "Sweeny among the Archetypes," 598.

59. Berger, *Li'l Abner*, 91.

60. As Inge noted, "There is a clearly a world of spirits and powerful supernatural forces which inform the beliefs of the people of Dogpatch, and they are not out of accord with traditional Southern folk belief" (2011:28). See also Howard Peckham, "Flying Saucers as Folklore" *Hoosier Folklore* 9.4 (1950): 103–7.

61. Simp-Li-Me, "An Open Letter to the Hill-Billies of Arkansas," *Madison County Record*. Letter to the editor, April 27, 1950, 1.

62. Black, "'Amoozin' but 'Confoozin,'" 462; *Alley Oop* Cartoonist V. T. Hamlin would use aliens in ways similar to that of Capp.

63. For comics from July 7–8, 10–12, 1950, see Dean Mullaney and Bruce Canwell, eds., *Al Capp's: Li'l Abner: Complete Daily and Sunday Comics, 1949–1950* (San Diego: IDW Publishers, 2016), 170.

64. Inge "Li'l Abner," 66.

65. Inge; Black, "'Amoozin' but 'Confoozin.'"

66. Al Segal, "Plain Talk: Smart Mammy Yokum," *Wisconsin Jewish Chronicle*, October 12, 1956, 8.

67. Berger, *Li'l Abner*, 151; Mullaney and Canwell, *Al Capp's*, 170.

68. Mullaney and Canwell, *Al Capp's*, 170.

69. Berger.

70. *Wheaton Journal*, "Sadie Hawkins Day November 4." Wheaton, Missouri. October 26, 1939. 1.

71. Saenger, Gerhart. "Male and Female Relations in the American Comic Strip." *Public Opinion Quarterly* 19.2 (1955): 204–5.

72. John Rose. *Barney Google and Snuffy Smith*. *Baxter Bulletin*. Mountain Home, May 3, 2005, 8; John Rose. *Barney Google and Snuffy Smith*. *Baxter Bulletin*. Mountain Home, February 20, 2010, 12.

73. I asked people on two Facebook groups, one for Arkansas cosplayers and one for cosplayers in general, about dressing up as Dogpatch characters. Only one person responded that he saw such characters a few times in "not just in Arkansas. Seen it in Kentucky, Alabama, Georgia, and Texas a few times." Nathan Jones. Correspondence with the author. Arkansas Cosplay Network. Facebook Group page. Accessed November 1, 2018; *Pampa Daily News*. "Nominations for H.J. [Hairless Joe] Wanted." Pampa, TX. October 19, 1939, 1; Martha Williams, "Dogpatch Drag Brings Out the Hillbillies," *Bridgeport Post*, Bridgeport, CT: May 22, 1960, 50.

74. The *Daily Herald* out of Provo, Utah, quoted *Life Magazine* about Sadie Hawkins Day that it was a "new minor national holiday." Indeed, it was for many decades and across the country. *Daily Herald*, "Better Practice on Your Runnin' Fellers, It's Sadie Hawkins Day," Provo, Utah. October 29, 1939, 5.

75. Jack Guenther, "Sport Parade," Tucson, *Daily Citizen*, April 30, 1942, 10; *Cumberland Evening Times*, "Air Outfit Creates Li'l Abner Settlement in Fighting Area," Cumberland, MD, January 18, 1951, 15.

76. *Mount Pleasant News*, "Major Accomplishments and Activities of 1953," Mount Pleasant, IA, December 30, 1953, 3.

77. Barbara Schmidt, "Hillbilly Characters a Hit in 'Li'l Abner' Production," *Chilliwack Progress*, Chilliwack, British Columbia, Canada. February 16, 1977, 6; *Santa Cruz Sentinel*, "Things are 'Hummin' Down in Dogpatch," Santa Cruz, CA, August 1, 1965, 24; *Feather River Bulletin*, "Rehearsals in Full Swing for 'Li'l Abner,'" Quincy, CA, October 7, 1992, 22.

78. The winner of the national Miss Dogpatch looked forward to winning $2,500 in cash, a Buick Electra, and over a thousand dollars in wardrobe. *Daily Reporter*, "Miss Dogpatch Pageant at Phila. July 25, 26," July 16, 1975, 13; *Hope Star*, "Charlene Gilbert is Miss Dogpatch," Hope, AR. May 25, 1975, 1.

79. *Daily Intelligencer*, "Li'l Abner: Goodbye, Dogpatch . . . Farewell Mammy Yokum," Doylestown, PA, October 8, 1977, 13; John Faddoul, "'Li'l Abner' Comes to an End," *Daily Leader*, Pontiac, IL, November 5, 1977, 8.

80. Berger, *Li'l Abner*, 63.

81. Werner Hoffman in Berger *Li'l Abner*, 50.

82. Radin, *The Trickster*, 168.

83. Thompson and Tian, "Reconstructing the South," 596.

84. Jung, "On the Psychology."

85. W. J. Cash. *The Mind of the South* (New York: Vintage Books, 1941 [1969]).

86. Berger, *Li'l Abner*, 130.

87. Kononenko and Kukharenko, "Borat the Trickster," 15.

88. Carl Jung, "On the Psychology," 206.

89. Jung, 202.

90. Jung.

91. Hall and Wood, *The South*, 287–92; Speer, "Hillbilly Sold Here," 218.

92. Blair "Laughter in Wartime America," 182.

93. *Boston Globe*, "Latest Books," November 28, 1936, 15; *Oneonta Star*, "Psychic Artist for Lecture in Area Town," September 12, 1951, 9; *Springfield Leader and Press*, "Cosmic Art Shrine Planned Adjoining Buck's Space Farm," June 30, 1971, 32; Cat Yronwode, personal communication, January 8, 2020.

94. "Catherine Yronwode." Yronwode. Accessed on February 5, 2019, http://www.luckymojo.com/cat.html.

95. "Ron Foss." *Lambiek Comiclopedia*. Accessed on February 5, 2019. https://www.lambiek.net/artists/f/foss_ronn.htm.

96. Ronn Foss, "The Local Scene: *Your Times-X-Press*," *Communities: A Journal of Cooperative Living* 22 (1975): 28–31.

Chapter 4. Eureka Springs, Where Misfits Fit

1. James Yenckel, "Arkansas Sampler: Footstompin Fun with an Old-World Twist," *Washington Post*, June 10, 1990, E1.

2. Douglas Burton-Christie, "Place-making as Contemplative Practice," *Anglican Theological Review* 91.3 (2009): 352.

3. Douglas Powell, *Critical Regionalism: Connecting Politics and Culture in the American Landscape* (Chapel Hill: University of North Carolina Press, 2007).

4. Howard Campbell, "Escaping Identity: Border Zones as Places of Evasion and Cultural Reinvention," *Journal of the Royal Anthropological Institute* 21 (2015): 308.

5. Edward Casey, "Between Geography and Philosophy: What Does It Mean to Be in the Place-World?" *Annals of the Association of American Geographers* 91.4 (2001): 687.

6. Peter Suedfeld and John Geiger, "The Sensed Presence as a Coping Resource in Extreme Environments," in *Miracles: God, Science, and Psychology in the Paranormal, Volume 3: Parapsychological Perspectives*, ed. J. Harold Ellers (Westport, CT: Praeger, 2008), 2.

7. Elizaveta Solomonova, Elena Frantova, Tore Nielsen, "Felt Presence: The Uncanny Encounters with the Numinous Other," *AI and Society* 26 (2011):171–78; Elena Frantova, Elizaveta Solomonova, Timothy Sutton, "Extra-Personal Awareness through the Media-Rich Environment," *AI and Society* 26 (2011):179–86.

8. Sean Wilsey, *More Curious* (San Francisco: McSweeney's, 2014), 37.

9. Cora Pinkley-Call, "Stair-Step-Town," 15–17.

10. *Springfield Leader and Press*, "Eureka Springs: A Beautiful Health Resort in North Arkansas," October 9, 1897, 16.

11. W. O. Hardeman, "Eureka Springs: A Grand Description," *Arkansas Democrat*, Little Rock, March 10, 1880, 1.

12. E. B. Moore and W. B. Moore, "Eureka Springs," *Fayetteville Weekly Democrat*, April 17, 1880, 4.

13. *Fayetteville Weekly Democrat*, "Eureka Springs Items," April 3, 1880, 1.

14. *Fayetteville Weekly Democrat*, "Eureka Springs: A Pen Picture of the Place," May 15, 1880, 2.

15. *Wichita Star*, "As a Kansan Sees It: How Eureka Springs, Ark., Looks to a Wichita Man with a Glass Eye," August 31, 1900, 4.

16. T. E. Murrell, "Letter to Dr. P. O. Hooper," *Arkansas Democrat*, Little Rock, August 17, 1880, 3–4.

17. Murrell.

18. *Fayetteville Weekly Democrat*, May 15, 1880, 2; Murrell "Letter to Dr P. O. Hooper," 3–4.

19. *Chetopa Advance*, "Eureka Springs," Chetopa, KS. January 18, 1883, 1.

20. *Daily Arkansas Gazette*, "Local Paragraphs," May 19, 1880, 8.

21. *Osceola Times*, "Eureka Springs," Reprint from St. Louis, Osceola, AR. May 7, 1881, 1.

22. *Fayetteville Weekly Democrat*, May 15, 1880, 2.

23. Murrell, "Letter to Dr P. O. Hooper," 4.

24. "All lines of general merchandise here, but no mills or machine shops. It is strictly a health resort, with about twenty springs in common use . . ." *Arkansas Democrat*, "A Trip to Eureka," Little Rock, AR, June 19, 1900, 4.

25. *Arkansas Democrat*, "Basin Park Hotel Advertisement," Little Rock, AR. June 23, 1913, 10.

26. *Batesville Daily Guard*, Advertisement for Eureka Springs, Batesville, AR. August 4, 1914, 2.

27. Alex Washburn, "Eureka Springs Ozark Resort Stages Comeback," *Hope Star*, Hope, AR, November 19, 1946, 6. Washburn quoted from a newsletter from the Arkansas Resources and Development Commission.

28. Otto Rayburn, "The Eureka Springs Story," *Times-Echo Press*, Eureka Springs, Arkansas, 1982, 72.

29. *Northwest Arkansas Times*, "Writers and Artists Guild Convention June 20–22 at Eureka," Fayetteville, AR. June 15, 1940, 1.

30. *Camden News*, "Artists Named to University," Camden, AR. April 14, 1948, 2; *Northwest Arkansas Times*, "Art School to Open at Eureka Springs June 7," Fayetteville, AR. June 7, 1948, 3.

31. Historian Jared Phillips provides a detailed account of the back-to-the-land movement, particularly in Eureka Springs. See Jared Philips, "Hipbillies and Hillbillies: Back-to-the-Landers in the Arkansas Ozarks during the 1970s," *Arkansas Historical Quarterly* 75.2 (2016): 89–110.

32. Todd Frankel, "Ozark City a Haven Divided," *St. Louis Post-Dispatch*, July 2, 2007, A1.

33. Alan Sverdlik, "In Arkansas, a Passion for Drama," *Washington Post*, September 6, 1998, E02.

34. *Times and Transcript*, "Town's Divisions Clear in Vote to Ban Discrimination of Gays," May 11, 2015, B6.

35. Yenckel, "Arkansas Sampler."

36. William Robbins, "Where a Good Squabble Mellows the Ozark Chill," *New York Times*, November 1, 1987, 42; Edward Harper and Mary Townsend, "Eccentricity at an Old Spa in the Ozarks," *New York Times*, May 28, 1989, 5.8.

37. Jared Phillips, *HipBillies: Deep Revolution in the Arkansas Ozarks* (Fayetteville: University of Arkansas Press, 2019), chapter 3.

38. Leroy Donald, "Speaks Out against Town Benefactor," *Kansas City Times*, November 29, 1969, 44.

39. Federal Elections Commission, "Campaign finance data, Advanced data, Filings." Accessed October 30, 2018, https://www.fec.gov/data/filings/?data_type=processed.

40. Richard Florida, *The Rise of the Creative Class and How It's Transforming Work, Leisure, Community and Everyday Life* (New York: Basic Books, 2002).

41. Charles Morrow Wilson, *The Bodacious Ozarks: True Tales of the Backhills* (Gretna, LA: Pelican Publishing Company, 2002), 10.

42. Southern author Willie Morris would find the same tragedy of the failure to recognize the shared fate that African Americans and whites have in the South. He wrote, "From my reading of our history, I have always believed the central thread that runs through us as a people is the relationship between the white man and the black man in America." See Willie Morris, *Terrains of the Heart and Other Essays on Home* (Oxford, MS: Yoknapatawpha Press, 1985), 123.

43. James Loewen, *Sundown Towns: A Hidden Dimension of American Racism* (New York: Simon & Schuster, 2006), chapter 1.

44. W. J. Cash, *The Mind of the South* (New York: Vintage Books, 1969), 219.

45. Much like other terrorist groups, the KKK endeared itself to various communities in the early twentieth century by providing charity and patriotic demonstrations. Harrison highlights a great deal of KKK activity, but many racist groups and communities have decided to make the Arkansas and Missouri Ozarks home according to a search on the Southern Poverty Law Center. Research on the rise of right-wing and racial-identity-based communal activity is needed. Communal scholar Timothy Miller mentions the rise of such groups. See Timothy Miller, *The 60s Communes: Hippies and Beyond* (New York: Syracuse Press, 1999), 244.

46. There are many sources the reader can use to learn more about the James Brothers and Carry Nation. See Rayburn, "The Eureka Springs Story"; Pinkley-Call, "Stair-Step-Town." As for Tim Curry, he fell in love with the town when he stayed in Eureka Springs for

some time to film the movie *Pass the Ammo*. See *Santa Cruz Sentinel*, "Curry Favors Arkansas as a 'jolly-good' Spot," April 10, 1988, 103.

47. Adam Romero, Amanda Baumle, M. V. Lee Badgett, Gary Gates, "Arkansas-Census Snapshot: 2000." Williams Institute, University of California, Los Angeles School of Law, 2007. Accessed August 7, 2018, from https://williamsinstitute.law.ucla.edu/demographics /arkansas/arkansas-census-snapshot-2000/; Gary Gates and Abigail Cooke, "Arkansas Census Snapshot: 2010." Williams Institute. University of California, Los Angeles School of Law. Accessed August 8, 2018, from https://williamsinstitute.law.ucla.edu/wp-content/uploads /Census2010Snapshot_Arkansas_v2.pdf.

48. Sara Evans and Harry Boyte, *Free Spaces: The Sources of Democratic Change in America* (New York: Harper and Row Publishers, 1986); Francesca Polletta, "Free Spaces in Collective Action," *Theory and Society* 28 (1999): 1–38; Elijah Anderson, *The Cosmopolitan Canopy: Race and Civility in Everyday Life* (New York: Norton & Company, 2011).

49. Paul Tillich quoted in Jane Jacobs, *The Death and Life of Great American Cities* (New York: Vintage Books, 1961), 238. For the full piece by Tillich, refer to pp. 347–48 in *Metropolis in Modern Life*, ed. Robert Moore.

50. *Pantagraph*, "Eureka Springs, Arkansas: A Born-Again Ozarks Town," Bloomington, IL, September 22, 1985, 12.

51. Evans and Boyte, *Free Spaces*, 20.

52. Wilsey, *More Curious*, 36, 38.

53. Victor Turner, *The Ritual Process: Structure and Anti-Structure* (New Brunswick, NJ: Aldine Transaction 1969 [2009]), 128, 133.

54. Jacobs, *The Death and Life*, 68.

55. Robbins, "Where a Good Squabble," 42.

56. Rayburn, "The Eureka Springs Story."

57. Gail Pennington, "Eureka! Found: A Spot in Northern Arkansas Where Whole Grains Reign Supreme," *St. Louis Post-Dispatch*, February 27, 1989, 1F; Frankel, "Ozark City."

58. Frankel, "Ozark City."

59. Richard Fausset, "Two Faces of Tourism Are Clashing in Arkansas," *New York Times*, April 20, 2015, 10.

60. Robbins, "Where a Good Squabble," 42.

61. Frankel, "Ozark City"; Dianne Keaggy, "Artistic Arkansas Sprawling Museum in Bentonville, Built with Wal-Mart Fortune, Has Emerged as a Must-See Destination for Art Lovers," *St. Louis Post-Dispatch*, April 29, 2012, H1. Although a number of reports note the over-representation of ministers and artists in the same town, the numbers differ between reporters. As for the ministers, Melissa Nelson observed in her article in 2000 that the marriage and wedding business is lucrative in the town and draws many Eurekans to consider ordination, some even by mail order.

62. Rayburn, "The Eureka Springs Story," 43.

63. Rayburn, 43–47; Jacobs, *The Death and Life*, 150.

64. Yenkel, "Arkansas Sampler," E1.

65. Robbins, "Where a Good Squabble," 42.

66. Keith McCanse, "Seeing the Ozarks First: A Weekend Trip to Eureka Springs," *Joplin Globe*, August 19, 1923, 7.

67. Jacobs, *The Death and Life*, 57.

68. Anita Manning, "Fast Getaways: Ozark Retreat Is Balm for the South," *USA Today*, May 24, 1990, 5.

69. Robert Harbison, *Eccentric Spaces* (New York: Avon Books, 1977).

70. Mircea Eliade, *The Quest: History and Meaning in Religion* (Chicago, IL: University of Chicago Press, 1971), 128–35; Thomas Kersen, "The Power of the Quest Narrative: Metaphors, Modernity, and Transformation," in *The Power of the Word: The Sacred and the Profane*, ed. Patsy J. Daniels (Newcastle, UK: Cambridge Scholars Publishing, 2015), 189–90.

71. Eric Weiner, *The Geography of Genius* (New York: Simon & Schuster, 2016), 254–55, 324.

72. Robert David Sack uses the term "thin places" to mean something similar to Ferdinand Toennis's term *gesellschaft* or a place with little history and communal linkages but does offer greater personal freedom. It is a place where strangers are more likely to interact. See Robert David Sack, *Homo Geographicus* (Baltimore, MD: Johns Hopkins University Press, 1997), 9–10; Lyn Lofland, *A World of Strangers: Order and Action in Urban Public Space* (Prospect Heights, IL: Waveland Press, Inc., 1985), 173.

73. Fred Schroeder, "Types of American Small Towns and How to Read Them," in *Order and Image in the American Small Town*, ed. Michael Fazio and Peggy Prenshaw (Jackson: University Press of Mississippi, 1981).

74. Wilsey, *More Curious*, 46.

75. Diane Mehta, "In the Ozarks, Mountain Greenery and Gingerbread," *New York Times*, July 6, 2007, 8.

76. Rayburn, "The Eureka Springs Story," 69.

77. Louis Freund, personal communication with Ruth McShane. Little Rock, May 1995. See Ruth Weinstein McShane, "A Force for Social Change: Ozark Back-to-the-Land Settlements, 1970–1995," Report to the Arkansas Humanities Council, Marshall, Arkansas. July 1996, 73.

78. Tom Uhlenbrock, "Saving Grace," *St. Louis Post Dispatch*, February 4, 2001, T1.

79. Dianne Keaggy, "Artistic Arkansas: Sprawling Museum in Bentonville, Built with Wal-Mart Fortune, Has Emerged as a Must-See Destination for Art Lovers," *St. Louis Post-Dispatch*, April 29, 2012, H1.

80. Janet Abe, "Sacred Place: An Interdisciplinary Approach for Social Science," in *Communities, Neighborhoods, and Health*, ed. Linda M. Burton (New York: Springer, 2001), 145–62; Beldon Lane, *Landscapes of the Sacred* (Baltimore, MD: Johns Hopkins Press, 2008).

81. Manning, "Fast Getaways," 5D; See also Melissa Nelson, "Ozarks Town Welcomes Eccentrics," *Toronto Star*, October 28, 2000; Pennington, "Eureka!," 1F.

82. Sylvia Anderson, "Little Switzerland: Discover the Magic of Eureka Springs," *St. Joseph News Press*, March 7, 2010.

83. Mehta, "In the Ozarks," 8.

84. Pennington, "Eureka!"; Robbins, "Where a Good Squabble," 1F.

85. Mehta, "In the Ozarks," 8.

86. Nelson, "Ozarks Town Welcomes Eccentrics," T1.

87. Oakley Talbott, "Out and About: Epiphanies in Eureka Springs, Ark.," *Santa Fe New Mexican*, June 3, 2007, RE-75.

88. Weiner, *The Geography of Genius*, 61–62.

89. Wallace Immen, "Beauty and the Bizarre: Red Cliffs and Rocky Spires Have Become Magnets for Mystics, Healers and Flying-Saucer Buffs," *Globe and Mail*, Canada. January 22, 1992, T1; Dick Sutphen, *Sedona: Psychic Energy Vortexes* (New York: Crown Publishers, 1994).

90. Immen.

91. Rob Lindsay and Wendy Lindsay, "A Warm Welcome to Sunny Sedona: New Age Mystics Claim the Arizona Town Is Situated on One of Earth's Energy Vortexes, Which Energizes Visitors and Draws Them Back," *Vancouver Sun*, British Columbia. November 7, 2000, D19.

92. Prior Smith, "Seeing Stunning Sedona," *Toronto Star*, November 25, 2000, T-1.

93. Anderson, "Little Switzerland"; Fausset, "Two Faces of Tourism"; Eric Hand, "In a Town Full of B and Bs, the Candlestick Has Its Own Allure," *St. Louis Post-Dispatch*, October 23, 2005, 5; Herb Hiller, "Only a Day Away," *St. Petersburg Times*, May 3, 1992, 1-E; Manning, "Fast Getaways," 50; Mehta, "In the Ozarks"; Nelson, "Ozarks Town Welcomes Eccentrics"; Sverdlik, "In Arkansas, a Passion," T-1; Tom Uhlenbrock, "Eureka Springs' Serene Setting Has a Healing Touch," *St. Louis Post Dispatch*, October 26, 2008, T1; Yenckel, "Arkansas Sampler," E-1.

94. Tom Uhlenbrock, "Tour Reveals Town's Quirks and History," *St. Louis Post Dispatch*, February 4, 2001, T5.

95. Oswald Spengler, "The Soul of the City," in *Classic Essays in the Culture of the City*, ed. Richard Sennett (New York: Meredith Corporation, 1969), 66.

96. *Pantagraph*, "Eureka Springs, Arkansas," 12.

97. Brooks Blevins, *Arkansas/Arkansaw: How Bear Hunters, Hillbillies, and Good Ol' Boys Defined a State* (Fayetteville: University of Arkansas Press, 2009), 26.

98. B. C. Hall and C. T. Wood, *The South* (New York: Scribner, 1995), 34.

99. Woodward, C. Van, "The Southern Ethic in a Puritan World," *William and Mary Quarterly* 25 (1968), 363.

100. Paul Tillich, "The Metropolis: Centralizing and Inclusive," in, *The Metropolis in Modern Life*, ed. Robert Fisher (New York: Russell and Russell, 1955), 347; see also Jacobs, *The Death and Life*, 238.

Chapter 5. Close Encounters of the Ozark Kind

1. Peter Shiras, "County Beat," *Baxter Bulletin*, Mountain Home, AR, July 11, 1947, 2.

2. The Ozarks are named after the mountains that form a region that makes up roughly the top third of the counties in Arkansas and half of those counties in southern Missouri. For a more detailed discussion of the geography of the Ozarks, see Milton Rafferty, *The Ozarks: Land and Life* (Fayetteville: University of Arkansas Press, 2001), 1–3.

3. George P. Hansen, *The Trickster and the Paranormal* (Xlibris Corporation, Kindle edition), Location 242. I should note that although with much of what Hansen wrote and his central premise that paranormal activity fits within the domain of the trickster, he approaches the topic as a believer.

4. Thompson noted that thousands of people from the western United States reported seeing "dirigible-type cylindrical airships" in the late 1890s. Keith Thompson, *Angels and Aliens* (New York: Fawcett Columbine, 1991).

5. National UFO Reporting Center, "State Report Index for MO," 2016. Accessed http://www.nuforc.org/webreports/ndxlMO.html on August 21, 2016.

6. *St. Louis Post-Dispatch*, "St. Louisan Reports Seeing 'Flying Saucers'; Silver Discs 'Sighted' at Many Points," July 5, 1947, 1.

7. David Jacobs found that UFO reports came in waves beginning in 1947, and then in 1950, 1952, 1957, 1965–67, and 1973–74. See David Jacobs, *The UFO Controversy in America* (Bloomington: Indiana University Press, 1975), 32–33, 66, 71.

8. William Dewan, "A Saucerful of Secrets: An Interdisciplinary Analysis of UFO Experiences," *Journal of American Folklore* 119.472 (2006): 186–88; Thompson, *Angels and Aliens*, 36–47; Jacques Vallee, *Passport to Magonia* (Chicago: Henry Regnery. Co., 1969);

Thomas Bullard, "Folklore Scholarship and UFO Reality," *International UFO Report* (July/August 1988): 9–13.

9. John Saliba, "UFO Contactee Phenomena from a Sociopsychological Perspective: A Review," in *The Gods Have Landed: New Religions from Other Worlds*, ed. James R. Lewis (New York: State University of New York Press, 1995), 212.

10. Howard Peckham, "Flying Saucers as Folklore," *Hoosier Folklore* 9.4 (1950): 107; Linda Degh, "UFOs and How Folklorists Should Look at Them," *Fabula* 18 (1977): 242–48; Carl Jung, *Flying Saucers: A Modern Myth of Things Seen in the Skies* (Princeton: Princeton University Press, 1978), 16; Valerii Sanarov, "On the Nature and Origins of Flying Saucers and Little Green Men," *Current Anthropology* 22 (1981): 165–66; Bertrand Meheust, "UFO Abductions as Religious Folklore," in *UFOs, 1947–1987: The 40-year Search for an Explanation*, ed. Hilary Evans and John Spencer (London, Forten Press, 1987), 352–58; Bullard, "Folklore Scholarship; John Whitmore, "Religious Dimensions of the UFO Abductee Experience," in *The Gods Have Landed: New Religions from Other Worlds*, ed. James Lewis (Albany: State University of New York Press, 1995), 65–84.

11. Peckham, "Flying Saucers as Folklore," 106; Stith Thompson, *Motif-Index of Folk Literature*, volume 2 D-E (Bloomington: Indiana University Press, 1966), 257.

12. Thompson, *Angels and Aliens*, 40.

13. Michael Kinsella, *Legend-Tripping Online: Supernatural Folklore and the Search for Ong's Hat* (Jackson: University Press of Mississippi, 2011), 8.

14. See chapter 16 about Carl Sydow in Alan Dundes, *International Folkloristics: Classic Contributions by the Founders of Folklore* (New York: Rowman and Littlefield Publishers, Inc., 1999), 137–51.

15. E. Joan Miller, "The Ozark Cultural Region as Revealed by Traditional Materials," *Annals of the Association of American Geography* 58.1 (1968): 57–61.

16. Hansen, *The Trickster and the Paranormal*, Location 242.

17. David Robertson, *UFOs, Conspiracy Theories, and the New Age: Millennial Conspiracism* (New York: Bloomsbury Academic, 2015), 9–10; Kinsella, *Legend-Tripping Online*, 8–11.

18. Brooks Blevins, *Arkansas/Arkansaw: How Bear Hunters, Hillbillies, and Good Ol' Boys Defined a State* (Fayetteville: University of Arkansas Press, 2009), 26; Saliba, "UFO Contactee Phenomena," 213–14; Thompson, *Angels and Aliens*, 40.

19. *Rolla Herald*, "The Ozarks," Rolla, MO, September 9, 1897, 7. Originally published in the *Fayetteville Sentinel*.

20. I extend my gratitude to Brian Irby, who has lectured on the parallels between 1897 airship sightings and UFO sightings in 1967 in Arkansas. *Southern Standard*, "Swear They Saw It: Two Reputable Citizens of Hot Springs Maintain that They Saw an Airship," Arkadelphia, Arkansas, May 14, 1897, 2; *Daily Arkansas Gazette*, "The Airships Are Coming," Little Rock, Arkansas, May 14, 1897, 4; *Daily Arkansas Gazette*, Little Rock, Arkansas, May 9, 1897, 4; *Daily Arkansas Gazette*, "Versicles," Little Rock, Arkansas, May 14, 1897, 4; Brian Irby, personal conversation December 23, 2019.

21. Edward Underwood and Karen Underwood, *Forgotten Tales of Arkansas* (Charleston: History Press, 2012), 17.

22. Gary Steward, Thomas Shrivers, and Amy Chasteen, "Participant Narratives and Collective Identity in a Metaphysical Movement," *Sociological Spectrum* 22 (2002): 111.

23. James William Buel, *Legends of the Ozarks* (St. Louis: W.S. Bryan, Publisher, 1880).

24. Buel, 5.

25. Buel, 6.

26. Charles Wilson, *Backwoods America* (Chapel Hill: University of North Carolina Press, 1935), 49.

27. Vance Randolph, *Ozark Magic and Folklore* (New York: Dover Publications, Inc., 2016), 301–27.

28. Library of Congress, "Conversations with 23 year old White Male, Arkansas (Transcription)," 1986d. Accessed http://www.loc.gov/resource/afc/986022.afc1986022_ms4403.

29. Underwood and Underwood, *Forgotten Tales of Arkansas*, 135–36.

30. Underwood and Underwood, 146–47.

31. Library of Congress, "Conversations with 16 year old white female, Arkansas (Transcription)," 1986b. Accessed at http://www.loc.gov/resource/afc/986022.afc1986022 _ms4402.;

Library of Congress, "Conversations with 77 year old White Male, Pettigrew, AR (Transcription)," 1986c. Accessed http://www.loc.gov/resource/afc/986022.afc1986022_ms4505.

32. Underwood and Underwood, *Forgotten Tales of Arkansas*, 137–42.

33. Wilson, *Backwoods America*, 58.

34. National UFO Reporting Center, "State Report Index for MO."

35. National UFO Reporting Center.

36. Vallee, *Passport to Magonia*; Thompson, *Angels and Aliens*; Randolph, *Ozark Magic and Folklore*, 234–35.

37. Jack Henderson, "Arkansas Mystery Lights," *Fate Magazine* 8.8 (1955): 68–72.

38. *St. Louis Star and Times*, "More 'Flying Saucers' (Or Beer Discs) Seen," June 30, 1947, 6.

39. *Moberly Monitor Index*, "Spiderwebs-New Theory in Mystery of Flying Saucers," Moberly, Missouri, July 8, 1947, 2.

40. Underwood and Underwood, *Forgotten Tales of Arkansas*, 75.

41. Library of Congress, "Conversations with 59 year old White Male (Transcription)," 1986a. Accessed http://www.loc.gov/resource/afc/986022.afc1986022_ms4501.

42. Particularly, refer to #24 The Mystic and #26 Peace Dude. Denelle Campbell, *Aquarian Revolution: Back to the Land: 32 Personal Stories* (Create Space Independent Publishing Platform, 2013).

43. Lee Prosser, *UFOs in Missouri: True Tales of Extraterrestrial and Related Phenomena* (Arglen, PA: Schiffer Publishing Ltd., 2011), 84.

44. Prosser, *UFOs in Missouri*, 31.

45. Jess Stearn, "Blonde Venus in a Saucer: Some Dish," *Daily News*, New York, July 14, 1959, 24; John M. McGuire, "Well, Come Down!," *St. Louis Post-Dispatch*, July 20, 1997, C-1.

46. Terry Dickson, "With Flying Saucers, Can Spring Be Far Behind?," *St. Louis Post-Dispatch*, March 17, 1974, 10G.

47. Bob Koonce, "The Strange World of an Ozarks 'Saucerman,'" *Kansas City Times*, April 8, 1961; Russ Leadabrand, "As I See It," *Pasadena Independent*, September 19, 1958, 10; *Kansas City Times*, "Can't Tell the Whole Story," September 22, 1959, J4 (54).

48. *Spokesman-Review*, "Trip to Venus Talk Packs Sunday School," Spokane, Washington, March 23, 1956, 5.

49. Sue Hubbell, "Buck Nelson and the Little Men," *St. Louis Post-Dispatch*, June 29, 1977, 2F (58).

50. *Springfield Leader and Press*, "'Cosmic Art Shrine' Planned Adjoining Buck's Space Farm," June 30, 1971, 32.

51. Bill Vaughn, "The Nicest People See Strange Things," *St. Louis Post-Dispatch*, April 4, 1966, 3D.

52. *Springfield Leader and Press*, "'Cosmic Art Shrine'" June 30, 1971, 32.

53. *Asheville Citizen-Times*, "Spacecraft Meeting Draws Few Members, June 28, 1964, 11 (57).

54. Terry Dickson, "Space Ships Welcome," *St. Louis Post-Dispatch,* July 10, 1966, 1, 7.

55. *Springfield News-Leader*, "Fire Information Reward by Nelson," February 21, 1966, 46.

56. John M. McGuire, "Just Say Cheese: How to Photograph an Extraterrestrial," *St. Louis Post-Dispatch*, August 12, 1997, 38.

57. Hubbell, "Buck Nelson," June 29, 2F (58).

58. Catherine Yronwode, personal conversation, January 12, 2020.

59. Baylor University, The Baylor Religion Survey, Wave II. Waco, TX: Baylor Institute for Studies of Religion [producer], 2007. David Childress, *Antigravity and the World Grid* (Kempton, IL: Adventures Unlimited Press, [1987] 2013).

60. Tom W. Smith, Michael Hout, and Peter V. Marsden, General Social Survey, 1972–2012 [Cumulative File]. ICPSR34802-v1. Storrs, CT: Roper Center for Public Opinion Research, University of Connecticut/Ann Arbor, MI: Inter-university Consortium for Political and Social Research [distributors], 2013–09–11. http://doi.org/10.3886/ ICPSR34802.v1.

61. Christopher Bader, F. Carson Mencken, and Joseph Baker, *Paranormal America: Ghost Encounters, UFO Sightings, Big Foot Hunts, and Other Curiosities in Religion and Culture* (New York: New York University Press, 2010).

62. Christopher Bader, F. Carson Mencken, and Joseph Baker, "Survey of Attenders: Texas Bigfoot Research Conservancy Annual Meeting 2009" (Waco, TX: Baylor University Department of Sociology [producer], 2009); Christopher Bader, J. Gordon Melton, and Joseph Baker, "Survey of Attenders: International UFO Congress Convention and Film Festival, 2010" (Waco, TX.: Baylor University Department of Sociology [producer], 2010).

63. Edward Tiryakian, "Toward the Sociology of Esoteric Culture," *American Journal of Sociology* 78.3 (1972): 496.

64. Eric Weiner, *The Geography of Genius* (New York: Simon & Schuster, 2016), 167–68; Richard Florida, *The Rise of the Creative Class* (New York: Basic Books, 2002), 267–73.

65. Weiner, 167–68.

66. National UFO Reporting Center, "State Report Index for AR." Accessed http://www .nuforc.org/webreports/ndxlAR.html on April 29, 2016.

67. *Blytheville Courier News,* "Farmer near Fayetteville Reports Saucers Flying Low on 2 Different Days," July 7, 1947, 1.

68. "Haunted Places." Accessed http://www.hauntedplaces.org/state on April 29, 2016.

69. David Deming, "The Hum: An Anomalous Sound Heard around the World," *Journal of Scientific Exploration* 18.4 (2004): 571–95.

70. Franz Frosch, "Hum and Otoacoustic Emissions May Arise out of the Same Mechanism," *Journal of Scientific Exploration* 27.4 (2013): 621–22.

71. *Week*, "Hearing the Hum," June 3, 2016, 15:36–37.

72. National Oceanic and Atmospheric Administration, "Earthquake Intensity Database 1638—1985." Accessed https://www.ngdc.noaa.gov/nndc/struts/form?t=101650&s=35&d=35 on April 29, 2016.

73. Glen MacPherson, "Who is behind this project?" Accessed https://hummap.wordpress .com/about/ on April 29, 2016.

74. National UFO Reporting Center, "State Report Index for AR,"; the Shadowlands, "Haunted Places in Arkansas." Accessed http://www.theshadowlands.net/places/Arkansas on April 29, 2016; "Haunted Places." Accessed http://www.hauntedplaces.org/state/Arkansas on April 29, 2016.

75. Heaven's Gate, the cult where members committed mass suicide in 1997, visited the Eureka Springs UFO Conference in 1994. They were given minimal access to attendees because they were deemed too weird by conference leadership. See Paisley Dodds, "Cultists Just 'too weird' for UFO enthusiasts," *Calgary Herald*, April 13, 1997, A8.

76. Viren Swami, Adrian Furnham, Janja Haubner, Stefan Stieger, and Martin Voracek, "The Truth Is Out There: The Structure of Beliefs about Extraterrestrial Life among Austrian and British Respondents," *Journal of Social Psychology* 149.1 (2009): 31; Robertson, *UFOs*, 19.

77. Swami et al., "The Truth Is Out There," 40.

78. Charles Emmons, and Jeff Sobal, "Paranormal Beliefs: Testing the Marginality Hypothesis," *Sociological Focus* 14.1 (1981): 54–55.

79. Saliba, "UFO Contactee Phenomena," 52–53.

80. Leon Festinger, Henry Riecken, and Stanley Schacter, *When Prophecy Fails: A Social and Psychological Study of a Modern Group that Predicted the Destruction of the World* (New York: Harper Torchbooks, 1956), 193–215.

81. Festinger, Riecken, and Schacter, 3.

82. James McGarry, and Benjamin Newberry, "Beliefs in Paranormal Phenomena and Locus of Control: A Field Study," *Journal of Personality and Social Psychology* 41.4 (1981): 734.

83. Thompson, *Angels and Aliens*, 145–54; Bullard, "Folklore Scholarship."

84. Robert Ellwood, "UFO Religious Movements" in *America's Alternative Religions*, ed. Timothy Miller (Albany: State University of New York Press, 1995), ebook; James Lewis, *Legitimating New Religions* (New Brunswick, NJ: Rutgers University Press, 2003), xii.

85. Diana Tumminia, "In the Dreamtime of the Saucer People: Sense-making and Interpretive Boundaries in a Contactee Group," *Journal of Contemporary Ethnography* 3.6 (2002): 692–94.

86. For an in-depth account of von Daniken, please refer to Ted Peters, *UFOs-God's Chariots? Flying Saucers in Politics, Science, and Religion* (Atlanta: John Knox Press, 1977).

87. McGarry and Newberry, "Beliefs in Paranormal Phenomena," 735; Robertson, *UFOs*.

88. Thompson, *Angels and Aliens*, 145–54.

89. Robertson, *UFOs*, 14–17.

90. Thompson, *Angels and Aliens*, 43.

91. Saliba, "UFO Contactee Phenomena," 48.

92. Thompson, *Angels and Aliens*, 227.

93. Robertson, *UFOs*, 38.

94. Thompson, *Angels and Aliens*, 246.

95. Kinsella, *Legend-Tripping Online*, 16.

96. Library of Congress, "Conversations with 59-year-old White Male."

97. Phillip Jenkins, "Sideways into Sociology," *American Sociologist* 29.3 (1998): 5–8.; Louis Menand, "Thinking Sideways: The One-Dot Theory of History," *New Yorker*. Accessed http://www.newyorker.com/magazine/2015/03/30/thinking-sideways on March 2015.

98. Robert Persig, *Zen and the Art of Motorcycle Maintenance* (New York: Bantam Books, Inc., 1985), 106.

Chapter 6. The Cults of Searcy County, Arkansas

1. Elizabeth Gleick, "The Strangers among Us," in *Religious Cults in America*, edited by Robert Long (New York: H. W. Wilson Company, 1994), 99.

2. Max Weber, *From Max Weber: Essays in Sociology*. H. H. Gerth and C. Wright Mills, ed. and trans. (New York: Oxford University Press, 1980), 246.

3. Max Weber, *The Sociology of Religion*, trans.Ephraim Fischoff (Boston: Beacon Press, 1969), 28–29, 46–47, 52–53, 58.

4. Rodney Stark and William Banbridge, "Of Churches, Sects, and Cults: Preliminary Concepts for a Theory of Religious Movements," *Journal for the Scientific Study of Religion* 18.2 (1979): 125.

5. The ARDA, "County Membership Report: Searcy County, Arkansas, 2010." Accessed at http://www.thearda.com/ on February 5, 2020.

6. John Adam Battenfield and Philip Y. Pendleton, *The Great Demonstration: A Harmony of all the Prophetic Visions of the Holy Bible* (Cincinnati, Ohio: Standard Publishing Company, 1914), 13.

7. Battenfield and Pendleton, *The Great Demonstration*, 13.

8. A. M. Morris, *The Prophecies Unveiled or Prophecy a Divine System* (Winfield, KS: Courier Press, 1914), 451–53.

9. Doris Thompson, "History of an Ozark Utopia," *Arkansas Historical Quarterly* 14 (Winter 1955): 363, 368.

10. *Mountain Echo*, Advertisement for "Primary Lessons in the Science of Prophecy," Yellville, AR. March 19, 1921, 3; *Arkansas Democrat*, "Cult Declares Strikes Are the Beginning of the End," July 17, 1922, 3. For a detailed story of one of the IKMU migrants who stayed after the cult dissolved, see Brooks Blevins, "Life on the Margins: The Diaries of Minnie Atteberry," *Arkansas Historical Quarterly* 64.4 (Winter 2016).

11. *Arkansas Democrat*, "Cult Declares," 3; Thompson, "History of an Ozark Utopia," 367.

12. *Baxter Bulletin*, "New Religious Cult," January 28, 1921, 1.

13. Thompson, "History of an Ozark Utopia," 365.

14. *Mountain Echo*, "Primary Lessons," 3.

15. *Neosho Daily News*, "Incoming Kingdom-Missionary Unit," Neosho, MO, August 7, 1925, 4.

16. *Arkansas Democrat*, "Twelve Spinning Wheels Are Ordered by Members of Cult," February 6, 1922, 2.

17. *Springfield Leader and Press*, "Split in Cult of the Kingdom: Views on Bobbed Hair and Whiskers Drive Out Barber," Springfield, MO, April 12, 1928, 5.

18. *Neosho Daily News*, "Incoming Kingdom-Missionary Unit," 4; Thompson, "History of an Ozark Utopia," 371.

19. *Springfield Leader and Press*, "Split in Cult of the Kingdom," 5.

20. *Springfield Leader and Press*, "A Colony Breaks Up," Springfield, MO, September 6, 1927, 2.

21. *Pantagraph*, "Hunted Chief Held in Arkansas," Bloomington, IL. September 20, 1964, 1; Ron Grossman, "Civil War," *Chicago Tribune*, March 31, 1988, 63.

22. *North West Arkansas Times*, "Near Walnut Ridge: Body of Boy, 6, Found Buried at Missing Cult Leader's Home," Fayetteville, AR, September 21, 1964, 3.

23. Ronald Gordon, "The Alamo Christian Foundation," The Arkansas Historical Foundation," *Arkansas Historical Quarterly* 76.3 (2017): 230.

24. For a more detailed account of the Alamo Christian Foundation, readers will want to read Ronald Gordon's 2017 article "The Alamo Christian Foundation," in the journal *Arkansas Historical Quarterly*.

25. Janet Sharp Hermann, *The Pursuit of a Dream* (Jackson: University Press of Mississippi, 1999), 3.

26. Keven Dougherty, *The Port Royal Experiment: A Case Study in Development* (Jackson: University Press of Mississippi).

27. Robert Hine, *Community on the American Frontier: Separate but Not Alone* (Norman: University of Oklahoma Press, 1980), 194.

28. Sora Friedman, "Planned Communities of the New Deal," *Communal Societies* 26 (2006): 99–120.

29. The Nation of Islam, with Elijah Mohammed as its leader, was another African American religious group that emerged in the 1930s. This group was not organized communally. See Richard Schaefer and William Zellner, *Extraordinary Groups: An Examination of Unconventional Lifestyles* (Long Grove, IL: Waveland Press, Inc., 2015), 250–53. Readers should also refer to Charles Braden, *These Also Believe: A Study of Modern American Cults and Minority Religious Movements* (New York: Macmillan Company, 1965).

30. Schaefer and Zellner, *Extraordinary Groups*, 239.

31. Francis Shor, "Utopian Aspirations in the Black Freedom Movement: SNCC and the Struggle for Civil Rights, 1960–1965," *Utopian Studies* 15.2 (2004): 173–89.

32. Thomas Kersen, "Communal Living in the Heart of Dixie," *Tributaries: Journal of the Alabama Folklife Association* 11.2 (2009): 22–24.

33. Chris Rice, *Grace Matters: A True Story of Race, Friendship, and Faith in the Heart of the South* (San Francisco: Jossey-Bass, 2002), 62–63.

34. Southern Poverty Law Center, "Hate Map by State." Accessed https://www.splcenter.org/hate-map/by-state on January 13, 2019.

35. Donna Kossy, *Kooks: Guide to the Outer Limits of Human Belief* (Portland, OR: Feral House, 1994), 21.

36. Kossy, 21.

37. Kossy, 21–39.

38. Kossy, 21.

39. Jacqueline Froelich, "The Purple People," *Arkansas Times* 45.20 (April 2019): 23.

40. Nazimoreh, "Who on Earth . . ." Accessed September 17, 2016 from https://nmcnews.org/Who%20on%20Earth.pdf, 52.

41. *San Antonio Register*, "Stephanie King Joins Religious Cult," December 7, 1989, 1.

42. Jacqueline Froelich, "Reclusive Ozarks Commune Operates Under Veil of Violence," Ozarks at Large Program, KUAF 91.3 FM, National Public Radio aired on February 25. Accessed May 14, 2018 from http://www.kuaf.com/post/reclusive-ozarks-commune-operates-under-veil-violence#stream/0.

43. Froelich, "Reclusive Ozarks Commune."

44. Froelich.

45. Nazimoreh, "Who on Earth . . .," 13.

46. Christine Ramos, *A Journey into Being: Knowing and Nurturing Our Children as Spirit* (Huntsville, AR: Ozark Mountain Publishing, 2006), 17.

47. Julia Hanson, *Awakening to Your Creation* (Huntsville, AR: Ozark Mountain Publishing, 2009).

48. Nazimoreh, "Who on Earth . . .," 3.

49. Nazimoreh, "Who on Earth . . .," 3.

50. Nazimoreh, "Who on Earth . . .," 9–10.

51. Benjamin Zablocki, *Alienation and Charisma: A Study of Contemporary American Communes* (New York: Free Press, 1980), 47; Rosabeth Moss Kanter, *Commitment and Community: Communes and Utopias in Sociological Perspective* (Cambridge, MA: Harvard University Press, 1973), 70–73; William Smith, "Intentional Communities 1990–2000: A Portrait," *Michigan Sociological Review* 16 (2002): 116.

52. Kanter, *Commitment and Community*, 70–73.

53. Joseph Washington, Jr., *Black Sects and Cults: The Power Axis in an Ethnic Ethic* (Garden City, NY: Doubleday & Company, 1972), 12.

54. Fred Davis, "Why All of Us May be Hippies Someday," in *Down to Earth Sociology: Introductory Readings*, ed. James Henslin (New York: MacMillan Company, 1972), 118.

55. Washington, *Black Sects and Cults*, 121.

56. Washington, 158.

57. Kanter, *Commitment and Community*, 70–73; Froelich, "Reclusive Ozarks Commune."

58. Kanter, *Commitment and Community*, 110–11; see also Hugh Gardner, *The Children of Prosperity: Thirteen Modern American Communes* (New York: St. Martin's Press, 1978), 24–27.

59. *Arkansas Democrat*, "Odd Community Grows Rapidly," Little Rock, AR, December 18, 1922, 2.

Chapter 7. The Group

1. *Odessa American*, "KBSN Radio," September 13, 1964, 11.

2. *Amarillo Globe Times*, "Folk Choir Hootenanny Saturday," August 5, 1965, 15.

3. *Amarillo Globe Times.*

4. *San Bernardino County Sun*, "Block Singers to Debut," September 17, 1966, 19; *Daily Herald*, "How Block Singers Got Their Name," Provo, UT, July 3, 1967, 25.

5. *Salina Journal*, "'Hoss' Helps Singers by Lending His Name," Salina, KS. April 4, 1967, 12.

6. Jack Smith, "They All Live Together in One Little House . . . ," *Democrat and Chronicle*, Los Angeles Times Service. January 29, 1967, 73.

7. Smith; *Daily Herald*, "How Block Singers Got Their Name," 25.

8. Smith; *Daily Herald*, "How Block Singers Got Their Name," 25.

9. Jean Ater, "In the Spotlight," *Amarillo Globe Times*, September 7, 1966, 26.

10. Dean Gysel, "It's About Time Berle Came Back," *Corpus Christi Caller Times*, July 24, 1966, 14F; *Daily Herald*, "Diller, Not Lucy, to be on Premiere," Provo, UT, August 7, 1966, Weekly TV and Amusements Guide, 3; *Times Record*, "TV Friday," Troy, NY, September 2, 1966, B-14; *Simpson's Leaders-Times*, "Television Program," Kittanning, PA, September 3, 1966, 8; *Salina Journal*, "Fri., Sept. 9," Salina, KS. September 2, 1966, T-7; Jack Gaver, "Television Highlights for Next Week," *Statesville and Record Landmark*, Statesville, NC. September 3, 1966, 22.

11. Rick DuBrow, "Berle Premier Impresses Critic," *Simpson's Leader-Times*, Kittanning, PA. September 10, 1966, 12.

12. *San Bernardino County Sun*, "Block Singers to Debut," 19.

13. Smith, "They All Live Together," 73.

14. *Dayton Daily News*, "Dan Blocker Singers at Nugget," March 25, 1967, entertainment section, 11; *Reno Gazette-Journal*, "Blocker Singers at the Nugget," March 25, 1967, 26.

15. *Reno Gazette-Journal*, "Blocker Singers at the Nugget."

16. *San Bernardino County Sun*, "Block Singers to Debut," September 17, 1966, 19.

17. *Independent*, "Television Log," Long Beach, CA, September 30, 1966, D-7.

18. Jean Ater, "In the Spotlight," *Amarillo Globe Times*, November 11, 1966, 30.

19. *Redlands Daily Facts*, "Annual Hollywood Y-Day Offers Wide Activities," Redlands, CA. October 15, 1966, 3.

20. Ater, "In the Spotlight," September 30.

21. *Bonham Daily Favorite*, "Back-to-Back Tragedies Shatter Commune," Bonham, TX, February 9, 1971, 2.

22. Daly McKinsey, "Commune Seeks Another Answer," *Courier News*, Blytheville, AR. July 15, 1970, 12.

23. Dan Hazel, personal communication with the author, December 19, 2019.

24. Hazel, December 19, 2019.

25. Hazel.

26. Ed Eudy, personal communication with the author, January 26, 2020.

27. Thomas Bevier, "The Group," *Mother Earth News* 10 (July 1971), 41. Reprinted from Mid-South Magazine, *Memphis Commercial Appeal*.

28. Bevier, "The Group," 41–43; Eudy, January 26, 2020.

29. Bevier, 41–43; Eudy, January 26, 2020.

30. Connie Rosenbaum, "The Group, Inc. One Man's Family," *St. Louis Post-Dispatch*, April 7, 1971, 77.

31. Hazel, December 19, 2019; Eudy, January 26, 2020.

32. *Bonham Daily Favorite*, "Back-to-Back Tragedies"; *Lubbock Avalanche Journal*, "Tragedies." February 8, 1971, 1.

33. *Index-Journal*, "Businessman Criticizes Two Funeral Homes," Greenwood, SC. June 30, 1976, 25.

34. Bevier, "The Group," 43.

35. Eudy, January 26, 2020; Rosenbaum, "The Group, Inc.," 77; Connie Rosenbaum, "Commune Runs Afoul of City Regulations," *St. Louis Dispatch*, April 18, 1971, 26.

36. George Benson, "Commune in Trouble," *El Dorado Times*, November 3, 1973, 4.

37. Rosenbaum, "The Group, Inc.," 77; Bevier, "The Group," 41.

38. Randy Brookman, personal communication with the author, November 12, 2014.

39. Bevier, "The Group," 43.

40. Hazel, December 19, 2019; Eudy, January 26, 2020.

41. Brookman.

42. Brookman; Bevier, "The Group," 41.

43. Hazel, December 19, 2019.

44. Hazel.

45. Hazel; McKinsey, "Commune Seeks Another Answer," 12.

46. Bevier, "The Group," 41–42.

47. The Group also founded the town's Chamber of Commerce and Optimist Club. Roy Reed, "Civic Minded Commune May be Forced to Move," *Lakeland Ledger*, Lakeland, FL. October 1, 1973, 2A.

48. Reed.

49. Hazel, December 19, 2019.

50. Hazel.

51. *Hope Star*, "21 Defendants Out on Bond," Hope, AR, August 27, 1973, 2.

52. *Hope Star*, "Theatre Closed," September 21, 1973, 12.

53. *Odessa American*, "Commune Closing Business Ventures," February 14, 1974, 7.

54. Eudy, January 26, 2020.

55. Brookman, November 12, 2014.

56. Eudy, January 26, 2020.

Chapter 8. When Electric Music Came to the Ozarks

1. Brooks Blevins, *Arkansas/Arkansaw: How Bear Hunters, Hillbillies, and Good Ole Boys Defined a State* (Fayetteville: University of Arkansas Press, 2009), 158.

2. Ronald Brownstein, *The Power of Glitter: The Hollywood-Washington Connect* (New York: Pantheon Books, 1992); see also Mark Kemp, *Dixie Lullaby: A Story of Music, Race and New Beginnings in a New South* (New York: Free Press, 2004), 133.

3. Jarl Ahlkvist, "Sound and Vision: Using Progressive Rock to Teach Social Theory," *Teaching Sociology* 29 (2001): 472.

4. Denelle Campbell, *Aquarian Revolution: Back to the Land: 32 Personal Stories* (Create Space Independent Publishing Platform, 2013), kindle location 2639.

5. Pierre Bourdieu, *Distinction: A Social Critique of the Judgment of Taste* (Cambridge, MA: Harvard University Press, 1984).

6. Russell Lynes, "Highbrow, Lowbrow, Middlebrow," *Harper's Magazine*, February 1949, 19.

7. Bill Malone and David Stricklin, *Southern Music/American Music* (Lexington: University Press of Kentucky, 2003), 63–67.

8. Kemp, *Dixie Lullaby*, 183.

9. Malone and Stricken, *Southern Music*, 109.

10. Benjamin Zablocki, *Alienation and Charisma: A Study of Contemporary American Communes* (New York: Free Press, 1980), 51.

11. Paul Radin, *The Trickster: A Study in American Indian Mythology* (New York: Schokken Books, 1972), 167.

12. Malone and Stricklin, *Southern Music*, 98.

13. Dan Peek, *Live at the Ozark Opry* (Charleston, South Carolina: History Press, 2010), chapter 14.

14. Dick Kleiner, "Shed a Tear for Hillbilly Music-It's Rock 'n' Roll for Country Kids, Too," *Courier News* (Blytheville, Arkansas. May 1, 1956), 8.

15. Archie Green, "Hillbilly Music: Source and Symbol," *Journal of American Folklore* 78 (1965): 205.

16. Tom Dearmore, "Ozark Outlook," *Baxter Bulletin*, Mountain Home, February 13, 1958, 4.

17. Art Gates, "Mountain Music," *Hillbilly Comics*, Charlton Publication 1 (1955): 23–28.

18. *Baxter Bulletin*, "Folk Festival at Eureka Springs This Week End," Mountain Home, October 18, 1956, 3.

19. Robert Cochran, *Our Own Sweet Sounds: A Celebration of Popular Music in Arkansas* (Fayetteville: University of Arkansas Press, 1996), 1853*; Jason Heller, "Billy Lee Riley and His Little Green Men, 'Flyin' Saucers Rock 'n' Roll,'" Frequency Rotation. Accessed https://www .tor.com/2010/09/02/frequency-rotation-billy-lee-riley-and-his-little-green-men-qflyin -saucers-rock-n-rollq/ on May 29, 2018.

20. Arnold Kirby, "Black Oak Blends Hard Rock, Easy Living," *Springfield Leader and Press*, September 8, 1975, 5.

21. Kemp, *Dixie Lullaby*, 52–53; Barney Hoskyns, *Across the Great Divide: The Band and America* (New York: Hal Leonard Corporation, 2006), 29–49.

22. Hoskyns, 2006; Robbie Robertson, *Testimony* (New York: Random House, 2016), chapter 9.

23. Robert Cochran, "Long on Nerve: An Interview with Ronnie Hawkins," *Arkansas Historical Quarterly* 65.2 (2006): 99–115.

24. Jim Kelton, "Cate Brothers," In *Encyclopedia of Arkansas Music*, ed. Ali Welky and Mike Keckhaver (Little Rock, AR: Butler Center Books, 2013), 70–71.

25. Cochran, "Long on Nerve."

26. Campbell, *Aquarian Revolution*, Kindle position 1807.

27. Ellis Amburn, *Buddy Holly: A Biography* (New York: St. Martin's Press, 1995), 129.

28. Cochran, *Our Own Sweet Sounds*, 58.

29. Mike Kelly, "Black Oak Shakes the Shrine," *Springfield Leader and Press*, November 18, 1973, 71.

30. Mary Campbell, "Black Oak Arkansas Shows Its Hometown," *Neosho Daily News*, February 14, 1974, 2.

31. Kelly, "Black Oak Shakes," 71.

32. *Northwest Arkansas Times*, "Weekend Rock Festival Set at Washington County Farm," Fayetteville. June 24, 1970, 1; *Northwest Arkansas Times*, "Festival May Draw 10,000," Fayetteville, Arkansas. June 26, 1970, 1; *Northwest Arkansas Times*, "No Favoritism," Fayetteville, Arkansas. July 2, 1970, 4.

33. Gorton D. Hitte, "Wake Up Fayetteville," *Northwest Arkansas Times*, August 5, 1970, 4.

34. *Northwest Arkansas Times*, "Rock Concert to be Held at University," Fayetteville, Arkansas, July 17, 1970, 11.

35. *Northwest Arkansas Times*, "Rock Festival Ends in Arrest," Fayetteville, Arkansas, June 29, 1970, 2.

36. Jeffrey Thomas, "Music and Life," Letters to the Editor, *Northwest Arkansas Times*, July 3, 1970, 4.

37. *Northwest Arkansas Times*, "Folkfair Dates Set at Eureka," Fayetteville, AR. April 7, 1973, 2; According to Michael Granda, all bands stayed at the famous haunted Crescent Hotel. See Michael Supe Granda, *It Shined: The Saga of the Ozark Mountain Daredevils* (Bloomington, Indiana: AuthorHouse, 2008), 107.

38. April Griffith, "Ozark Mountain Folk Fair," *The Encyclopedia of Arkansas History and Culture*, 2015. Accessed http://www.encyclopediaofarkansas.net/encyclopedia/entry-detail .aspx?entryID=7958 on January 11, 2019.

39. Bonnie Burch, "Catholic Musicians Bring Tour to Brentwood," *Tennessean*, Nashville, Tennessee, February 11, 1998, 10W.

40. Mike Kelly, "Folk Hero Triumphs Sans '60s Nostalgia," *Springfield Leader and Press*, February 5, 1974, 12.

41. Dave Thompson, *I Hate the New Music: The Classic Rock Manifesto* (New York: Hal Leonard Corporation, 2008),158.

42. Thompson.

43. Lester Bangs, *Psychotic Reactions and Carburetor Dung: The Work of a Legendary Critic* (New York: Vintage Books, 1988), 98.

44. Because of their antics in Black Oak, the band were classified as 4F and Jim had to wait out an eight-year suspended sentence. Campbell, "Black Oak Arkansas Shows," 2.

45. Mike Kelly, "Black Oak Shakes," 71; Mary Campbell, "The Continuing Saga of Black Oak Arkansas," *Neosho Daily News*, February 21, 1974, 2.

46. Kelly; Campbell.

47. Kelly, 71.

48. Kirk Hutson, "Hot 'n' Nasty: Black Oak Arkansas and Its Effect on Rural Southern Culture," *Arkansas Historical Quarterly* 54 (1995): 196–99.

49. Kelly, "Black Oak Shakes," 71.

50. Hutson, "Hot 'n' Nasty," 193 quoting Michael Gross, "'Ain't Life Grand'—A Dandy Black Oak Kick Up Their Heels in Europe," *Circus*, July 1975, 4–8.

51. Hutson, "Hot 'n' Nasty," 211.

52. Gary Z. McGee, "The Path of the Sacred Clown: Where Trickster and Shaman Converge," Fractal Enlightenment. Accessed at https://fractalenlightenment.com/25726/spirituality/the-path-of-the-sacred-clown-where-trickster-and-shaman-converge, on December 29, 2019; Ernest Hartman, *Boundaries in the Mind: A New Psychology of Personality* (New York: Basic Books, 1991), 143.

53. Carl Jung, "On the Psychology of the Trickster Figure," in *The Trickster: A Study in American Indian Mythology*, ed. Paul Radin (New York: Schocken Books, 1972), 195. Campbell, "Black Oak Arkansas Shows," 2; Arnold, "Black Oak Blends," 5.

54. Campbell, "Black Oak Arkansas Shows," 2.

55. Campbell, 2.

56. Campbell, 2.

57. *Washington Citizen*, "Sigma Deltas Plan to See Shows," Washington, Missouri. March 24, 1973, 3; John Haskins, "Music, Mid-America," *Kansas City Times*, March 26, 1973, 10.

58. Dick Richmond, "Two Rock Groups Perform Before Large Crowd at Kiel," *St. Louis Post-Dispatch*, March 23, 1973, 41.

59. Michael Gilmour, *Gods and Guitars: Seeking the Sacred in Post-1960s Popular Music* (Waco, TX: Baylor University Press, 2009), 97–99.

60. Michael Supe Granda, *It Shined: The Saga of the Ozark Mountain Daredevils* (Bloomington, Indiana: AuthorHouse, 2008), 175.

61. Granda, 175.

62. Mary Campbell, "Ozark Mountain Daredevils Stick to Missouri Roots," *Neosho Daily News*, May 1, 1975, 2.

63. Granda, *It Shined*, 201.

64. Granda, 201.

65. Campbell, "Ozark Mountain Daredevils Stick," 2.

66. Black Oak Arkansas has a long biker history. In 1971, BOA played after Evil Knievel completed a motorcycle jump over 10 trucks in Topeka Kansas. See David Arnold. "Evel Knievel: Gladiator on Motorcycle," *St. Louis Post-Dispatch*, November 7, 1971, 139.

67. Campbell, "Black Oak Arkansas Shows," 2.

68. Hutson, "Hot 'n' Nasty," 96.

69. Willie Morris, *Terrains of the Heart and Other Essays on Home* (Oxford, MS: Yoknapatawpha Press, 1985), 38.

70. Thompson, *I Hate the New Music*, 64.

71. Campbell, *Aquarian Revolution*, Kindle location 897.

72. Duke Ellington's quote was the moto of *Schickele Mix*, a public radio classical music show hosted by Peter Schickele.

Chapter 9. The Hot Mulch Band and the Missouri Back-to-the-Land Experience

1. *The Dr. Demento Show*, "The Dr. Demento Show" #82–07. February 14, 1982. Accessed September 1, 2018 at http://www.drdemento.com/playlists/drd82.0214.html.

2. Victor Turner, *The Ritual Process: Structure and Anti-Structure* (New Brunswick, NJ: Aldine Transaction, 2009), 128.

3. Claire Dunne, *Carl Jung—Wounded Healer of the Soul* (New York: Watkins, 2000), 221.

4. David Haenke, personal communication, January 6, 2019.

5. Turner, *The Ritual Process*, 140, 164.

6. Turner, 140, 164.

7. Joel Davidson, "Living in the Ozarks," *Communities: A Journal of Cooperative Living* 22 (1975): 24.

8. Joel Davidson, 25.

9. Eliot Wigginton, *The Foxfire Book* (Garden City, New Jersey: Anchor Press/Doubleday, 1972), dedication page.

10. Yaacov Oved, *Two Hundred Years of American Communes* (New Brunswick, NJ: Transaction Books, 1988), 485–90.

11. For a more detailed account about these and other 19th Century Missouri intentional communities, please refer to Grant, H. Roger, "Missouri's Utopian Communities," *Missouri Historical Review* 66.1 (1971): 20–48.

12. David Haenke, "Ozark Evolutionary Front, 1971–1976," *Communities: A Journal of Cooperative Living* 22 (1975): 32–35.

13. Lewellyn Hendrix, "Kinship, Social Networks, and Integration among Ozark Residents and Out-Migrants," *Journal of Marriage and Family* 88.1 (1976): 103.

14. Timothy Miller, *The Quest for Utopia in Twentieth Century America: 1900–1960* (New York: Syracuse University Press, 1998), 253–85.

15. Timothy Miller listed Edge City in Missouri Ozarks as having been established in 1974. One community called Satsang Farm (mid-1970s) located in Texas County, MO, never really was an intentional community. Further, some of the dates in Miller's listing are inaccurate. For example, Dragonwagon existed around 1971–1972, not 1974. FIC 1972, 1975; Timothy Miller, *The 60s Communes: Hippies and Beyond* (New York: Syracuse University Press, 1999), 261; John Mercer, *Communes: A Social History and Guide* (Dorset, UK: Prism Press, 1984); *Communities: A Journal of Cooperative Living*, Special Directory Issue, *Communities*, 1 (December 1972); *Communities: A Journal of Cooperative Living*, Commune Directory, *Communities*, 7 (March–April 1974); *Communities: A Journal of Cooperative Living*, Community Directory, *Communities* 12 (January–February 1975); *Communities: A Journal of Cooperative Living*, Directory of Intentional Communities, *Communities* 30 (January–February 1978); *Communities: A Journal of Cooperative Living*, Special 1981 Directory and Resources, *Communities* 46 (December–January 1981); *Communities: A Journal of Cooperative Living*, 10th Anniversary Issue and the Directory of Intentional Communities, *Communities* 56 (December–January 1983); *Communities: A Journal of Cooperative Living*, the 1985 Directory, *Communities* 66 (Spring 1985).

16. Haenke, "Ozark Evolutionary Front," 32–35.

17. David Haenke, personal communication, January 6, 2019.

18. Miller, *The 60s Communes*, 8.

19. *Communities: A Journal of Cooperative Living* 7(1974): 38; 12 (1975): 35.

20. *Communities: A Journal of Cooperative Living* 1 (1972): 36.

21. *Communities: A Journal of Cooperative Living* (1974): 32; cf. (1975): 27.

22. David Haenke, personal communication, January 6, 2019.

23. Nancy Spaeder, personal communication, January 4, 2019.

24. Spaeder.

25. Miller, *The 60s Communes*, 11.

26. Miller, 166.

27. Cat Yronwode, personal communication, January 8, 2020; Cat Yronwode, personal conversation, January 12, 2020. See also *Springfield Leader and Press*, "Cosmic Art Shrine Planned Adjoining Buck's Space Farm." June 30, 1971, 32.

28. The link between the old timers and the back-to-landers was exemplified by Garden of Joy Blues according to Denise Vaughn in an interview she had with me on January 6, 2019. Jared Phillips, Hipbillies: *Deep Revolution in the Arkansas Ozarks* (Fayetteville: University of Arkansas Press, 2019); Catherine Yronwode, Facebook post December 25, 2016, accessed on https://www.facebook.com/catherine.yronwode, January 3, 2020; J. Blake Perkins, Hillbilly Hell-Raisers: Federal Power and Populist Defiance in the Ozarks (Urbana: University of Illinois Press, 2017).

29. Catherine Yronwode, "Catherine Yronwode." Accessed www.yronwode.com/catherine .html on January 2, 2019; cf. Bob Andleman, *Will Eisner: A Spirited Life. Deluxe Edition* (Raleigh, NC: TwoMorrows Publishing, 2015), 120.

30. Miller, *The 60s Communes*, 226.

31. Catherine Yronwode, Facebook post March 7, 2018. Accessed https://www.facebook .com/catherine.yronwode, January 3, 2020.

32. Ron Hughes, personal communication, January 5, 2019, February 20, 2019.

33. Bob Andelman, "Ch. 14. Cat's Tale," in *Will Eisner: A Spirited Life*, 120–28.

34. Kirk Chritton, "My First Night in Fandom," 2008. Accessed January 2, 2019 http:// www.comicscareer.com/?p=21.

35. Ronn Foss, "The Local Scene: *Your Times-X-Press*," *Communities: A Journal of Cooperative Living*, 22 (1975): 28–31; Catherine Yronwode, personal conversation, January 12, 2020.

36. Jared Phillips, "Hipbillies and Guerilla Press." 10th annual Ozark Symposium. West Plains, MO, September 24, 2018; Catherine Yronwode, personal conversation, January 12, 2020.

37. *Communities: A Journal of Cooperative Living* 12 (1975): 26.

38. Ron Hughes. personal communication, February 20, 2019.

39. *Communities: A Journal of Cooperative Living* 12 (1975): 27.

40. *Communities: A Journal of Cooperative Living* 18 (1975): 21.

41. See also Federation of Egalitarian Communities, 78, which also is at Tecumseh. *Communities: A Journal of Cooperative Living* 35 (1978): 78.

42. *Communities: A Journal of Cooperative Living* 46 (1981): 37–38.

43. *Communities: A Journal of Cooperative Living* 56 (1983): 63.

44. Megan Elias, *Food on the Page: Cookbooks and American Culture* (Philadelphia, PA: Simon and Schuster, 2017), 169.

45. Crescent Dragonwagon, *The Common Cookbook* (New York: Simon and Schuster, 1972), 12, 186–87; John Edge, *The Potlikker Papers: A Food History of the Modern South* (New York: Penguin Books, 2017), 96.

46. Ron Hughes, personal communication, January 5, 2019, and February 20, 2019.

47. Arnold van Gennep, *The Rites of Passage* (London: Routledge and Kegan Paul, 1909).

48. William Rice, "A Misfit Who Fits In," *Chicago Tribune*, October 28, 1991. Accessed https://www.chicagotribune.com/news/ct-xpm-1992-10-28-9204070879-story.html on December 29, 2018.

49. Robert Carey, "Children's Book Author Finds Her Name's a Pain to Explain," *Springfield Leader and Press*, December 11, 1976, 16; Sarah Overstreet, "Crescent's Credo: 'I Simply Don't Do Anything I Don't Want to Do,'" *Springfield News-Leader*, February 15, 1987, 9.

50. Barbara Goedde, Interviewed and transcribed by Ayana Arrington, November 5, 2017. Washington University, St. Louis. Accessed http://omeka.wustl.edu/omeka/files/original/5a2c0 9c9d8d436dc64e959a6fe379624.pdf on December 29, 2018 c.f. Miller, *The 60s Communes*, 139.

51. Denise Henderson Vaughn, personal communication. January 6, 2019.

52. *Communities: A Journal of Cooperative Living* 7 (1974): 38.

53. *Communities: A Journal of Cooperative Living* 35 (1978): 53–54.

54. *Communities: A Journal of Cooperative Living* 46 (1981): 53.

55. *Communities: A Journal of Cooperative Living* 56 (1983): 78.

56. Foss, "The Local Scene," 28–31.

57. Joshua Lockyer, "Intentional Communities and Sustainability," *Communal Studies* 30.1 (2010): 19.

58. Margaret Norris, "A Not-So-Counter Culture," *Springfield News Leader*, October 12, 1982, 13.

59. The land was divided into 40-acre lots among the original 15 members. Members shared the land except for the immediate five acres around their individual homesteads. In addition to the land, members paid the group an annual tax of ten dollars. Real estate and other group assets became a problem for Seven Springs and bankers, who did not know the way or want to work with a community's finances.

60. Ron Hughes, "Ozark Mountain Mother Earth News Freak," Hot Mulch Band, Grinola Records. Brixey, Missouri, 1975.

61. Hughes.

62. Norris, "A Not-So-Counter Culture," 13.

63. Norris; Nancy Spaeder, personal communication, January 5, 2019.

64. Thompson, *Angels and Aliens*, 145–54.

65. Jared Phillips, *Hipbillies: Deep Revolution in the Arkansas Ozarks* (Fayetteville: University of Arkansas Press, 2019), 131.

66. Ron Hughes, personal communication with author, February 20, 2019.

67. Hughes.

68. Carter Seaton, *Hippie Homesteaders: Traditional Handcrafts in West Virginia* (Morgantown: West Virginia University Press, 2014); cf, Jared Phillips, "Hipbillies and Hillbillies: Back-to-the-Landers in the Arkansas Ozarks during the 1970s," *Arkansas Historical Quarterly* 75.2 (2016): 89–110.

69. Bill Maurer, "Farms Can Produce Energy Supply, Too," *Springfield News Leader*, February 18, 1976, 54.

70. Hughes, *Ozark Mountain Mother.*

71. Brian Campbell, "Growing an Oak: An Ethnography of Ozark Bioregionalism," in *Environmental Anthropology Engaging Ecotopia: Bioregionalism, Permaculture, and Ecovillages*, ed. Joshua Lockyear and James R. Veteto (Oxford, NY: Berghahn Books, 2013), 68.

72. *Communities: A Journal of Cooperative Living* 45 (1981): 87. The 1983 FIC highlights education and training opportunities for those interested in conservation, self-reliance, bioregionalism, and continuing education; see FIC 45; 56 (1983), 87.

73. Environmental anthropologist Brian Campbell offered an excellent account of OACC and other related Ozark organizations, such as Ozark Organic Growers Association. Campbell, "Growing an Oak," 60.

74. Denise Henderson Vaughn, personal communication with the author. February 10, 2019.

75. Vaughn.

76. *St. Louis Post-Dispatch*, "Energy Dept. Gets "Fleece" for Elevated Outhouse Test," December 13, 1979, 12B.

77. Ron Hughes, personal communication with the author, February 20, 2019.

78. John Hofheimer, "Local Man Spreads Gospel of Solar Energy," *Baxter Bulletin*, Mountain Home, Arkansas, July 22, 1983, 2, 9.

79. Denise Henderson Vaughn, personal communication with the author, February 10, 2019.

80. Mike Penprase, "New Life Farm Not Just Whistling in Brixey," *Springfield News Leader*, March 5, 1986, 15.

81. Denise Henderson Vaughn, personal communication, January 6, 2019.

82. Haenke, "Ozark Evolutionary Front," 34.

83. Haenke, 34–35.

84. Jeff Dunshee, Email correspondence with the author, November 16, 2017.

85. Hughes, *Ozark Mountain Mother*.

86. Haenke.

87. Haenke, personal communication with the author, January 6, 2019.

88. Hughes, *Ozark Mountain Mother*.

89. Eric Bogwalker, personal communication, January 4, 2019.

90. A. Whitney Sanford, "Being the Change: Food, Nonviolence, and Self-Sufficiency in Contemporary Intentional Communities," *Communal Studies* 34.1 (2014): 52.

91. Louise Wienkowski, personal communication with the author, November 18, 2018.

Chapter 10. Back-to-Landers in the Arkansas Ozarks

1. Fred Davis, "Why All of Us May be Hippies Someday," in *Down to Earth Sociology: Introductory Readings*, ed. James Henslin (New York: MacMillan Company, 1972), 121–23.

2. Louise Meijering, Paulus Huigen, and Bettina van Hoven, "Intentional Communities in Rural Spaces," *Journal of Economic and Social Geography* 98 (2007): 48.

3. Jared Phillips, *Hipbillies: Deep Revolution in the Arkansas Ozarks* (Fayetteville: University of Arkansas Press, 2019).

4. Josh Lockyer, "Intentional Communities and Sustainability," *Communal Studies* 30 (2010): 20.

5. Benjamin Zablocki, *Alienation and Charisma: A Study of Contemporary American Communes* (New York: Free Press, 1980), 42, 53; Michael Nolan, R. Paul Lasley, Gary Green, and William Heffernan, "A Note on Ozark Migrants and Nonmigrants," *Growth and Change: A Journal of Urban and Regional Policy* 12 (1981): 51.

6. Thomas O'Neil, "The Ozarks: Jewel of the Heartland," in *America's Hidden Corners: Places off the Beaten Path*, ed. Donald Crump (Washington DC: National Geographic Society, 1983), 165.

7. Timothy Miller, "A Matter of Definition: Just what is an Intentional Community?" *Communal Societies* 30.1 (2010): 7–8.

8. Angela Aidala and Benjamin Zablocki, "The Communes of the 1970s: Who Joined and Why?" *Marriage and Family Review*, 17 (1991): 89.

9. Timothy Miller, "The Roots of the 1960s Communal Revival," *American Studies* 33 (1992): 74.

10. Phillips, *Hipbillies*, xxi.

11. Frank Fellone, "Oh, Pioneers," *Arkansas Democrat Gazette*, December 14, 2010, 3E, 6E.

12. Fellone.

13. Ken Carey, *Flat Rock Journal: A Day in the Ozark Mountains* (San Francisco: Harper, 1994), 24.

14. Denelle Campbell, *Aquarian Revolution: Back to the Land: 32 Personal Stories* (Create Space Independent Publishing Platform, 2013), Kindlebook loc 1886.

15. Joel Davidson, "Living in the Ozarks," *Communities*, Fellowship of Intentional Communities, 22 (1975): 25. For a detailed account of this and other activities occurring in the Ozarks when many of the back-to-landers arrived, refer to Phillips, *Deep Revolution*, chapters 3–4.

16. Ruth McShane, "A Force for Social Change: Back-to-the-Land Settlements, 1970–1995," unpublished manuscript funded in part by the Arkansas Humanities Council and the National Endowment for the Humanities (Marshall, Arkansas, 1996), 110.

17. McShane, "A Force for Social Change," 6; Maurice Tudo, *Pictorial Crackerbarrel*, Marshall, AR (1997), 6.

18. Fellone, "Oh, Pioneers," 3E.

19. McShane, "A Force for Social Change," 6.

20. *Communities Directory*, Fellowship of Intentional Communities, 7 (1974), 33.

21. *Communities Directory*, Fellowship of Intentional Communities, 12 (1975), 30.

22. Communities Directory, Fellowship of Intentional Communities, 22 (1975), 33.

23. Phillips, *Hipbillies*, 124, and more generally about women in the BTL movement read chapter 6.

24. *Communities Directory*, Fellowship of Intentional Communities, 35 (1978), 43.

25. *Communities Directory*, Fellowship of Intentional Communities, 18 (1975), 25.

26. *Communities Directory*, Fellowship of Intentional Communities, 46 (1981), 62; Ron Hughes, personal communication, January 5, 2019.

27. Campbell, *Aquarian Revolution,* chapter 22. the *Agriculturalist;* According to Ron Hughes, leader of the Hot Mulch Band, the Orr Brothers stayed at his residence in the Missouri Ozarks, Elixir Farms, until they located land in Fox, Arkansas, for the Meadow Creek Project. Ron Hughes, personal communication, January 5, 2019. David Haenke, personal communication, January 6, 2019.

28. Miller, "The Roots of the 1960s," 86.

29. Michael Brown, "The Condemnation and Persecution of Hippies" in *Total Institutions,* ed. Samuel Wallace (New York: Aldine Publishing, 1971), 180.

30. Davidson, "Living in the Ozarks," 27.

31. Jared Phillips, "Hipbillies and Hillbillies: Back-to-the-Landers in the Arkansas Ozarks during the 1970s," *Arkansas Historical Quarterly* 75 (2016): 99; Phillips, *Hipbillies*, chapter 2; Joel Davidson, "Living in the Ozarks," *Communities*, Fellowship of Intentional Communities, 22 (1975): 24–27.

32. United States Census Bureau, "Arkansas Population of Counties by Decennial Census: 1900 to 1990," 1995, Compiled and edited by Richard L. Forstall. Accessed https://www.census .gov/population/cencounts/ar190090.txt on August 1, 2017.

33. Thomas Graff and Earl Neel, "Reversal of Southern Population Trends: An Example from Arkansas," *The Mississippi Geographer* 7 (1979): 51; Fred Shelley, "Search Behavior and Place Utility of Recent Migrants to the Arkansas Ozarks," unpublished manuscript, Department of Geography, University of Iowa, 30.

34. Shelley, "Search Behavior," 5.

35. Phillips, "Hipbillies and Hillbillies," 94.

36. Hugh Gardner, *The Children of Prosperity: Thirteen Modern American Communes* (New York: St. Martin's Press, 1978), 4; Benjamin Zablocki, *Alienation and Charisma: A Study*

of Contemporary American Communes (New York: Free Press, 1980); Nolan et al., "A Note on Ozark Migrants," 59; Phillips, *Hipbillies*, 23.

37. Phillips, "Hipbillies and Hillbillies," 94; Gardner, *The Children of Prosperity*, 4.

38. No Author, "Mulberry Farm," *Communitas* 2 (1972): 29–34.

39. Dana Strubel, emailed comments from Cathy Strubel to the author, February 7, 2020.

40. McShane, "A Force for Social Change," 94; Headwaters School. "Our School." Accessed http://headwaters-school.org/school.html on March 3, 2019; Phillips, *Hipbillies*, 24.

41. Nancy and Manny, "We Make a School," *Communities* 22 (1975): 35.

42. O'Neill, "The Ozarks," 166.

43. Zablocki, *Alienation and Charisma*, 55.

44. Alice Driver, "Not Yet Lost," *Oxford American*, May 11, 2016. Accessed https://www.oxfordamerican.org/item/855-not-yet-lost on March 27, 2018.

45. O'Neill, "The Ozarks," 166.

46. McShane, "A Force for Social Change," 111.

47. Phillips, "Hipbillies and Hillbillies"; Carter Seaton, *Hippie Homesteaders: Traditional Handcrafts in West Virginia* (Morgantown: West Virginia University Press, 2014).

48. Michael Woods, *Rural Geography* (Thousand Oaks, CA: Sage Publications, 2005), 296; Louise, Meijering, Paulus, Huigen, and Bettina van Hoven, "Intentional Communities in Rural Spaces," *Journal of Economic and Social Geography* 98 (2007): 41–52.

49. Phillips, Hipbillies, 78.

50. U.S. Census Bureau, 1995; Seaton, *Hippie Homesteaders*, 215.

51. Delores Barclay, "Commune Kids Faring Well, Parents, Scientists Claim," *Courier News, Blytheville News*, September 10, 1976, 6; Timothy Miller, *The 60s Communes: Hippies and Beyond* (New York: Syracuse University Press, 1999), 239; William Smith, "Families in Contemporary Intentional Communities: Diversity and Purpose," *Communal Societies* 21 (2001): 87.

52. Phillips, *Hipbillies*, 130–32.

53. Fellone, "Oh, Pioneers," 6E.

54. O'Neill, "The Ozarks," 166.

55. Seaton, *Hippie Homesteaders*, 1, 6.

Chapter 11. Conclusions

1. Walter Cralle, "Social Change and Isolation in the Ozark Mountain Region of Missouri," *American Journal of Sociology* 41.4 (1936): 436.

2. *Neosho Times*, "The Changing Ozarks," October 22, 1925, 3.

3. Cralle, "Social Change," 446.

4. A. J. Meigs, "The Changing Ozarks," *Monthly Review*, Federal Reserve Bank of St. Louis, 39 (1957), 19–24. Accessed from https://fraser.stlouisfed.org/files/docs/publications/frbslreview/rev_stls_195702.pdf on December 15, 2018; see also *Springfield Leader and Press*, "Bank Magazine Lauds Ozarks," February 10, 1957, 40.

5. Meigs, "The Changing Ozarks," 19.

6. Bob Franson, "The Changing Ozarks," *Springfield Leader and Press*, July 3, 1977, F1.

7. Kim McCully-Mobley, "The Saltiest of the Old Timers Are Dead Now," Ozark Symposium, West Plains, Missouri, September 19, 2015.

8. Otto Rayburn, *The Eureka Springs Story*, Diamond Jubilee edition (Eureka Springs, AR: Wheeler Printing, Inc., 1982).

9. Michael Nolan, Paul Lasley, Gary Green, and William Heffernan, "A Note on Ozark Migrants and Nonmigrants," *Growth and Change: A Journal of Urban and Regional Policy* 12 (1981): 47–52.

10. Didi Tang, "New Neighbors: Hmong," *Springfield News-leader*, November 27, 2005, 1.

11. Tang, 8a.

12. Willie Morris, *Terrains of the Heart and Other Essays on Home* (Oxford, MS: Yoknapatawpha Press, 1985), 53.

13. The most popular of the movies about the Ozarks were *Three Billboards Outside of Ebbing, Missouri* (2017), *Girl of the Ozarks* (1936), *The Shepherd of the Hills* (1919), *Winter's Bone* (2010), *Mountain Music* (1937), *Stark Love* (1927), *The Voice of Bugle Ann* (1936), *Arkansas Judge* (1941), and *Where the Red Fern Grows* (1974). Some of the films rated worst, many of them of horror/thriller genre, were *Its Alive!* (1969), *Good Chemistry* (2008), *Scarce* (2008), *Copperhead* (1985), *Child Bride* (1938), and *Swing Your Bride* (1938).

14. Elijah Anderson, *The Cosmopolitan Canopy: Race and Civility in Everyday Life* (New York: W. W. Norton and Company, 2011), 278–79.

15. Leo Marx, *The Machine in the Garden: Technology and the Pastoral Ideal in America* (New York: Oxford University Press, 1969), 9–10.

16. Denise Henderson-Vaughn, "Idealism Tempered by Tenacity." Presentation given at the Ozarks Symposium, West Plains, MO, 2014.

17. Jared Phillips, "Hipbillies and Hillbillies: Back-to-the-Landers in the Arkansas Ozarks during the 1970s," *Arkansas Historical Quarterly* 75.2 (2016): 94, 96.

18. Carter Taylor Seaton, *Hippie Homesteaders: Arts, Crafts, Music and Living in the Land of West Virginia* (Morgantown: West Virginia University Press, 2014), Kindlebook location page 9.

19. However, I should note that the Missouri back-to-the-landers seemed to network and form groups to a greater extent than did their Arkansas counterparts.

20. Brian C. Campbell, "Growing an Oak: An Ethnography of Ozark Bioregionalism," in *Environmental Anthropology Engaging Ecotopia: Bioregionalism, Permaculture, and Ecovillages*, ed. Joshua Lockyer, James Veteto, and E. N. Anderson (New York: Berghahn Books, 2013), 58–75.

21. Hugh Gardner, *The Children of Prosperity: Thirteen Modern American Communes* (New York: St. Martin's Press, 1978), 17.

22. Erik Tumminia, personal communication with the author, January 4, 2019.

23. George Ritzer, *The McDonaldization of Society* (New Century Edition. Thousand Oaks, CA: Sage Publications, 2000), 12–15.

24. Ken Carey, *Flat Rock Journal: A Day in the Ozark Mountains* (San Francisco: Harper, 1994), 131.

Bibliography

Abe, Janet. "Sacred Place: An Interdisciplinary Approach for Social Science." In *Communities, Neighborhoods, and Health*, edited by Linda M. Burton, 145–62. New York: Springer, 2001.

Ahlkvist, Jarl. "Sound and Vision: Using Progressive Rock to Teach Social Theory." *Teaching Sociology* 29 (2001): 471–82.

Aidala, Angela, and Benjamin Zablocki. "The Communes of the 1970s: Who Joined and Why?" *Marriage and Family Review* 17 (1991): 89.

Alderman, Derek, and Robert Beavers. "Heart of Dixie Revisited: An Update on the Geography of Naming in the American South." *Southeastern Geographer* 36 (1999): 190–205.

Alonzo, Linda. "Eight Arlington Groups to Hoot." *Indianapolis News*. February 20, 1964, 16.

Amarillo Globe Times. "Folk Choir Hootenanny Saturday." August 5, 1965, 15.

Amburn, Ellis. *Buddy Holly: A Biography*. New York: St. Martin's Press, 2014.

Andelman, Bob. *Will Eisner: A Spirited Life*. Raleigh, NC: TwoMorrows Publishing, 2015.

Anderson, Benedict. *Imagined Communities: Reflections on the Origin and Spread of Nationalism*. New York: Verso, 1991.

Anderson, Elijah. *The Cosmopolitan Canopy: Race and Civility in Everyday Life*. New York: W. W. Norton and Company, 2011.

Anderson, Sylvia. "Little Switzerland: Discover the Magic of Eureka Springs." *St. Joseph News Press*. March 7, 2010.

Andelman, Bob. 2015. *Will Eisner: A Spirited Life. Deluxe Edition*. Raleigh, NC: TwoMorrows Publishing.

Arkansas Democrat. "Basin Park Hotel Advertisement." Little Rock, AR. June 23, 1913, 10.

Arkansas Democrat. "Cult Declares Strikes Are the Beginning of the End." July 17, 1922, 3.

Arkansas Democrat. "Odd Community Grows Rapidly." Little Rock, AR. December 18, 1922, 2.

Arkansas Democrat. "A Trip to Eureka." Little Rock, AR. June 19, 1900, 4.

Arkansas Democrat. "Twelve Spinning Wheels Are Ordered by Members of Cult." February 6, 1922, 2.

Arkansas Secretary of State. "Search Incorporations, Cooperatives, Banks and Insurance Companies." Accessed at https://www.sos.arkansas.gov/corps/search_all.php on June 24, 2014.

Arnold, David. "Evel Knievel: Gladiator on Motorcycle." *St. Louis Post-Dispatch*. November 7, 1971, 139.

225

Arnold, Kirby. "Black Oak Blends Hard Rock, Easy Living." *Springfield Leader and Press.* September 8, 1975, 5.

Asheville Citizen-Times. "Spacecraft Meeting Draws Few Members." June 28, 1964, 11(57).

Ater, Jean. "In the Spotlight." *Amarillo Globe Times.* September 7, 1966, 26.

Ater, Jean. "In the Spotlight." *Amarillo Globe Times.* November 11, 1966, 30.

Bad Cat Records. "Mason Proffit." Bad Cat Records. Accessed http://badcatrecords.com /BadCat/MASONproffit.htm on November 13, 2018.

Bader, Christopher, J. Gordon Melton, and Joseph Baker. *Paranormal America: Ghost Encounters, UFO Sightings, Big Foot Hunts, and Other Curiosities in Religion and Culture.* New York: New York University Press, 2010.

Bader, Christopher, F. Carson Mencken, and Joseph Baker. "Survey of Attenders: Texas Bigfoot Research Conservancy Annual Meeting 2009." Waco, TX: Baylor University Department of Sociology [producer], 2009.

Bader, Christopher, J. Gordon Melton, and Joseph Baker. "Survey of Attenders: International UFO Congress Convention and Film Festival, 2010." Waco, TX: Baylor University Department of Sociology [producer], 2010.

Bangs, Lester. *Psychotic Reactions and Carburetor Dung: The Work of a Legendary Critic.* New York: Alfred A. Knopf, Inc., 2013.

Barclay, Delores. "Commune Kids Faring Well, Parents, Scientists Claim." *Courier News. Blytheville News.* September 10, 1976, 6.

Batesville Daily Guard. Advertisement for Eureka Springs. Batesville, AR. August 4, 1914, 2.

Baudrillard, Jean. *Simulations.* New York: Semiotext, 1983.

Baxter Bulletin. "Folk Festival at Eureka Springs This Week End." Mountain Home. October 18, 1956, 3.

Baxter Bulletin. "New Religious Cult." January 28, 1921, 1.

Baylor University. The Baylor Religion Survey, Wave II. Waco, TX: Baylor Institute for Studies of Religion [producer], 2007.

Bearden, Michelle. "Born Again Musicians Uses Talents to Spread God's Words." *Tampa Tribune.* October 28, 2000, Faith and Values Section, 8.

Bearden, Michelle. "The Troubadour Offers Peace in Crazy World." *Tampa Tribune.* April 17, 2004, Faith and Values Section, 4.

Becker, Howard. *Sociological Work: Method and Substance.* Chicago, IL: Aldine Publishing Company, 1970.

Becker, Howard. *What about Mozart? What about Murder?: Reasoning from Cases.* Chicago: University of Chicago Press, 2014.

Bender, Thomas *Community and Social Change in America.* Baltimore, MD: Johns Hopkins University Press, 1991.

Benson, George. "Commune in Trouble." *El Dorado Times.* November 3, 1973, 4.

Berger, Arthur. *Li'l Abner: A Study in American Satire.* Jackson: University Press of Mississippi, 1994.

Berger, Peter. *The Sacred Canopy: Elements of a Sociological Theory of Religion.* Garden City, NY: Anchor Books Doubleday, 1990.

Bertrand, Alvin. "Regional Sociology as a Special Discipline." *Social Forces* 31 (1952): 132–36.

Bevier, Thomas. 1971. "The Group." *Mother Earth News.* July, 1971. Issue 10. Reprinted from Mid-South Magazine, *Memphis Commercial Appeal.*

Black, James. "'Amoozin' but 'Confoozin': Comic Strips as a Voice of Dissent in the 1950s." *ETC: A Review of General Semantics* 66.4 (2009): 460–77.

Blair, Walter. "Laughter in Wartime America." *English Journal* 34.4 (1945): 179–85.

Blevins, Brooks. *Arkansas/Arkansaw: How Bear Hunters, Hillbillies, and Good Ol' Boys Defined a State*. Fayetteville: University of Arkansas Press, 2009.

Blevins, Brooks. *Hill Folks: A History of Arkansas Ozarkers and Their Image*. Chapel Hill: University of North Carolina Press, 2002.

Blevins, Brooks. "Life on the Margins: The Diaries of Minnie Atteberry." *Arkansas Historical Quarterly* 64.4 (Winter 2016).

Blevins, Brooks. "Retreating to the Hill: Population Replacement in the Arkansas Ozarks." *Agricultural History* 74.2 (2000): 475–88.

Blevins, Brooks. "When an Ozark Boyhood Isn't: Reconsidering Wayman Hogue's *Back Yonder*." Ozark Symposium. West Plains, Missouri. September 18, 2015.

Blevins, Brooks. "Wretched and Innocent: Two Mountain Regions in the National Consciousness." *Journal of Appalachian Studies* 7.2 (2001): 257–71.

Blythville Courier News. "Farmer Near Fayetteville Reports Saucers Flying Low on 2 Different Days." July 7, 1947, 1.

Bogart, Leo. "Adult Talk about Newspaper Cartoons." *American Journal of Sociology* 61.1 (1955): 26–30.

Bonham Daily Favorite. "Back-to-Back Tragedies Shatter Commune." Bonham, TX. February 9, 1971, 2.

Boston Globe. "Latest Books." November 28, 1936, 15.

Bourdieu, Pierre. *Distinction: A Social Critique of the Judgment of Taste*. Cambridge, MA: Harvard University Press, 1984.

Braden, Charles. *These Also Believe: A Study of Modern American Cults and Minority Religious Movements*. New York: Macmillan Company, 1965.

Brearly, H. C. "Homicides in South Carolina: A Regional Study." *Social Forces* 8 (1929): 218–21.

Bridgeport Post. "Arkansas to Get 'Dogpatch' as New Tourist Attraction." Bridgeport, CT. January 6, 1967, 44.

Brookman, Randy. Personal communication. Jackson State University, November 12, 2014.

Brown, Michael. "The Condemnation and Persecution of Hippies," In *Total Institutions*, edited by Samuel Wallace. New York: Aldine Publishing, 1971.

Brownstein, Ronald. *The Power of Glitter: The Hollywood-Washington Connect*. New York: Pantheon Books, 1992.

Buel, James William. *Legends of the Ozarks*. St. Louis: W. S. Bryan, Publisher, 1880.

Bullard, Thomas. "Folklore Scholarship and UFO Reality." *International UFO Report*. July/August (1988): 9–13.

Burch, Bonnie. "Catholic Musicians Bring Tour to Brentwood." *The Tennessean*. Nashville, Tennessee. February 11, 1998, 10W.

Burton-Christie, Douglas. "Place-making as Contemplative Practice." *Anglican Theological Review* 91.3 (2009): 347–71.

Camden News. "Artists Named to University." Camden, AR. April 14, 1948, 2.

Campbell, Brian C. "Growing an Oak: An Ethnography of Ozark Bioregionalism." In *Environmental Anthropology Engaging Ecotopia: Bioregionalism, Permaculture, and Ecovillages*, edited by Joshua Lockyer, James Veteto, and E. N. Anderson, 58–75. New York: Berghahn Books, 2013.

Campbell, Denelle. *Aquarian Revolution: Back to the Land: 32 Personal Stories*. Create Space Independent Publishing Platform, 2013, Kindle location 2639.

Campbell, Howard. "Escaping Identity: Border Zones as Places of Evasion and Cultural Reinvention." *Journal of the Royal Anthropological Institute* 21 (2105): 296–312.

Campbell, Mary. "Black Oak Arkansas Shows Its Hometown." *Neosho Daily News*. February 14, 1974, 2.

Campbell, Mary. "The Continuing Saga of Black Oak Arkansas." *Neosho Daily News*. February 21, 1974, 2.

Campbell, Mary. "Ozark Mountain Daredevils Stick to Missouri Roots." *Neosho Daily News*. May 1, 1975, 2.

Caplin, Elliott. *Al Capp Remembered*. Bowling Green, OH: Bowling Green State University Popular Press, 1994.

Carey, Ken. *Flat Rock Journal: A Day in the Ozark Mountains*. San Francisco: Harper, 1994.

Carey, Robert. "Children's Book Author Finds Her Name's a Pain to Explain." *Springfield Leader and Press*. December 11, 16, 1976.

Carroll, Michael. "The Trickster as Selfish-Buffoon and Cultural Hero." *Ethos* 12.2 (1984): 105–31.

Casey, Edward. "Between Geography and Philosophy: What Does It Mean to Be in the Place-World?" *Annals of the Association of American Geographers* 91.4 (2001): 683–93.

Cash, W. J. *The Mind of the South*. New York: Vintage Books, 1969.

Catholic Advance. "John Michael Talbot to Make Stop in Hutchinson, January 30." Wichita, Kansas, October 25, 1996, 11.

Center for the Study of the American South. Odum Institute for Research in Social Science, University of North Carolina at Chapel Hills, 2007, "Southern Focus Poll, Fall 1992." Accessed https://hdl.handle.net/1902.29/D-20174, UNC Dataverse, V1.

Center for the Study of the American South. "Southern Focus Poll, Spring 2001." Accessed at https://hdl.handle.net/1902.29/D-31552 UNC Dataverse, V1.

Chase, Richard. *The Jack Tales*. Cambridge, MA: Houghton Mifflin Company, 1943.

Chetopa Advance. "Eureka Springs." Chetopa, KS. January 18, 1883, 1.

Childress, David. *Antigravity and the World Grid*. Kempton, IL: Adventures Unlimited Press, 2013.

Chritton, Kirk. "My First Night in Fandom," 2008. Accessed January 2, 2019 http://www.comicscareer.com/?p=21.

Cobb, James C. *Away down South: A History of Southern Identity*. Oxford; New York: Oxford University Press, 2005.

Cobb, James C. *Redefining Southern Culture: Mind and Identity in the Modern South*. Athens: University of Georgia Press, 1999.

Cochran, Robert. "Long on Nerve: An Interview with Ronnie Hawkins." *Arkansas Historical Quarterly* 65.2 (2006): 99–115.

Cochran, Robert. *Our Own Sweet Sounds: A Celebration of Popular Music in Arkansas*. Fayetteville: University Press of Arkansas, 1996.

Communities: A Journal of Cooperative Living. Commune Directory. *Communities* 1 (July 1972).

Communities: A Journal of Cooperative Living. Commune Directory. *Communities* 7 (March–April 1974).

Communities: A Journal of Cooperative Living. Community Directory. *Communities* 12 (January–February 1975).

Communities Directory. Fellowship of Intentional Communities 18 (1975).

Communities Directory. Fellowship of Intentional Communities 35 (1978).

Communities: A Journal of Cooperative Living. Directory of Intentional Communities. *Communities* 30 (January–February 1978).

Communities: A Journal of Cooperative Living. Special 1981 Directory and Resources. *Communities* 46 (December–January 1981).

Communities: A Journal of Cooperative Living. 10th Anniversary Issue and the Directory of Intentional Communities. *Communities* 56 (December–January 1983).

Communities: A Journal of Cooperative Living. The 1985 Directory. *Communities* 66 (Spring 1985).

Cooper, Christopher, and H. Gibbs Knotts. "Declining Dixie: Regional Identification in the Modern American South." *Social Forces* 88 (2010): 1083–1101.

Copsy, Diane. "'Knight Train' Show Scheduled." *Indianapolis Star.* October 5, 1963, 8.

"Counties." *Rural Sociology* 76.1 (2011): 74–100.

Cox, Karen. "Branding Dixie: The Selling of the American South, 1890–1910." In *Dixie Emporium: Tourism, Foodways, and Consumer Culture in the American South,* edited by Anthony J. Stanonis, 50–68. Athens: University of Georgia Press, 2008.

Cox, Karen. "The South and Mass Culture." *Journal of Southern History* 75.3 (2009): 677–90, 681.

Cralle, Walter. "Social Change and Isolation in the Ozark Mountain Region of Missouri." *American Journal of Sociology* 41.4 (1936): 435–46.

Creswell, John. *Qualitative Inquiry and Research Design: Choosing among Five Traditions.* Thousand Oaks, CA: Sage Publications, 1998.

Cumberland Evening Times. "Air Outfit Creates Li'l Abner Settlement in Fighting Area." Cumberland, MD. January 18, 1951, 15.

Daily Arkansas Gazette. "The Airships Are Coming." Little Rock, Arkansas. May 14, 1897, 4.

Daily Arkansas Gazette. "Local Paragraphs." Little Rock, Arkansas. May 19, 1880, 8.

Daily Arkansas Gazette. Untitled piece. Little Rock, Arkansas. May 9, 1897, 4.

Daily Arkansas Gazette. "Versicles." Little Rock, Arkansas. May 14, 1897, 4.

Daily Herald. "Better Practice on Your Runnin' Fellers, It's Sadie Hawkins Day." Provo, Utah. October 29, 1939, 5.

Daily Herald. "Diller, Not Lucy, to Be on Premiere." Provo, UT. August 7, 1966, Weekly TV and Amusements Guide, 3.

Daily Herald. "How Block Singers Got Their Name." Provo, UT. July 3, 1967.

Daily Intelligencer. "Li'l Abner: Goodbye, Dogpatch . . . Farewell Mammy Yokum." Doylestown, PA. October 8, 1977, 13.

Daily Reporter. "Miss Dogpatch Pageant at Phila. July 25, 26." July 16, 1975, 13.

Davidson, Joel. "Living in the Ozarks." *Communities.* Fellowship of Intentional Communities 22 (1975): 24–27.

Davis, Fred. "Why All of Us May Be Hippies Someday." In *Down to Earth Sociology: Introductory Readings,* edited by James Henslin, 118. New York: MacMillan Company, 1972.

Davis, Randall. *Arcadia Tribune* "Musical Notes." Arcadia, CA. November 19, 1972, 6.

Davis, Randall. "Quinchords—1965." Vinylfool. *60's Indiana Band Szene,* 2009. Accessed http://indiana-bands-60s.blogspot.com/2009/11/quinchords-1965.html on November 13, 2018.

Dayton Daily News. "Dan Blocker Singers at Nugget." March 25, 1967, entertainment section, 11.

Dearmore, Tom. 1958. "Ozark Outlook." *Baxter Bulletin.* Mountain Home. February 13, 1958, 4.

DeCurtis, Anthony. "The Eighties." In *Present Tense: Rock & Roll and Culture*, edited by Anthony DeCurtis, 1–12. Durham, NC: Duke University Press, 1992.

Degh, Linda. "UFOs and How Folklorists Should Look at Them." *Fabula* 18 (1977): 242–48.

Deming, David. "The Hum: An Anomalous Sound Heard Around the World." *Journal of Scientific Exploration* 18.4 (2004): 571–95.

Denzin, Norman. *Interpretive Interactionism*. Thousand Oaks, CA: Sage Publications, 1989.

Dewan, William. "A Saucerful of Secrets: An Interdisciplinary Analysis of UFO Experiences." *Journal of American Folklore* 119.472 (2006): 184–202.

Dickson, Terry. "Space Ships Welcome." *St. Louis Post-Dispatch*. July 10, 1966, 1, 7.

Dickson, Terry. "With Flying Saucers, Can Spring Be Far Behind?" *St. Louis Post-Dispatch*. March 17, 1974, 10G.

Dodds, Paisley. "Cultists Just 'Too Weird' for UFO Enthusiasts." *Calgary Herald*, April 13, 1997, A8.

Donald, Leroy. 1969. "Speaks Out against Town Benefactor." *Kansas City Times*. November 29, 1969, 44.

The Dr. Demento Show. "The Dr. Demento Show" #82–07. February 14, 1982. Accessed September 1, 2018 at http://www.drdemento.com/playlists/drd82.0214.html.

Dougherty, Keven. *The Port Royal Experiment: A Case Study in Development*. Jackson: University Press of Mississippi.

Dragonwagon, Crescent. *The Commune Cookbook*. New York: Simon and Schuster, 1972.

Driver, Alice. "Not Yet Lost." *Oxford American*. Accessed https://www.oxfordamerican.org/item/855-not-yet-lost on March 27, 2018 on May 11, 2016.

DuBrow, Rick. "Berle Premier Impresses Critic." *Simpson's Leader-Times*. Kittanning, PA. September 10, 1966, 12.

Dundes, Alan. "Folklore as a Mirror of Culture." In *Meaning of Folklore*, edited by Simon Bronner, 53–66. University Press of Colorado, Utah State University, 2007.

Dundes, Alan. *International Folkloristics: Classic Contributions by the Founders of Folklore*. New York: Rowman and Littlefield Publishers, Inc., 1999.

Dunne, Claire. *Carl Jung-Wounded Healer of the Soul*. New York: Watkins, 2000.

Dunshee, Jeff. Personal correspondence with the author, November 16, 2017.

Edge, John. *The Potlikker Papers: A Food History of the Modern South*. New York: Penguin Books, 2017.

Edwards, Sharon. "Quinchords—5 Teens on Their Way." *The Indianapolis Star*. March 27, 1965, 5A.

Egerton, John. *The Americanization of Dixie*. New York: Harper's Magazine Press, 1974.

El Dorado Times. "Vacation Trip to Harrison an Answer to Fuel Savers." El Dorado, AR. March 25, 1974, 7.

Eliade, Mircea. *The Quest: History and Meaning in Religion*. Chicago: University of Chicago Press, 1971.

Elias, Megan. 2017. *Food on the Page: Cookbooks and American Culture*. Philadelphia, PA: Simon and Schuster, 2017.

Ellwood, Robert. "UFO Religious Movements." In *America's Alternative Religions*, edited by Timothy Miller, 393–99. New York: State University of New York Press, 1995.

Emmons, Charles, and Jeff Sobal. "Paranormal Beliefs: Testing the Marginality Hypothesis." *Sociological Focus* 14.1 (1981): 49–56.

Eudy, Ed. Personal communication. January 26, 2020.

Evans, Sara, and Harry Boyte. *Free Spaces: The Sources of Democratic Change in America.* New York: Harper and Row Publishers, 1986.

Faddoul, John. "'Li'l Abner' Comes to an End." *Daily Leader.* Pontiac, IL. November 5, 1977, 8.

Fausset, Richard. 2015. "Two Faces of Tourism Are Clashing in Arkansas." *New York Times.* April 20, 2015, 10.

Fayettville Weekly Democrat. "Eureka Springs: A Pen Picture of the Place." May 15, 1880, 2.

Fayettville Weekly Democrat. "Eureka Springs Items." April 3, 1880, 1.

Fazio, Michael. "Architectural Preservation in Natchez, Mississippi: A Conception of Time and Place." In *Order and Image in the American Small Town,* edited by Michael Fazio and Peggy Prenshaw, 136–49. Jackson: University Press of Mississippi, 1981.

Feather River Bulletin. "Rehearsals in Full Swing for 'Li'l Abner." Quincy, CA. October 7, 1992, 22.

Federal Elections Commission. "Campaign finance data, Advanced data, Filings." Accessed https://www.fec.gov/data/filings/?data_type=processed on October 30, 2018.

Fellone, Frank. "Oh, Pioneers." *Arkansas Democrat Gazette.* December 14, 2010, 3E, 6E.

Festinger, Leon, Riecken, Henry, and Schacter, Stanley. *When Prophecy Fails: A Social and Psychological Study of a Modern Group that Predicted the Destruction of the World.* New York: Harper Torchbooks, 1956.

Flammonde, Paris. *The Age of Flying Saucers: Notes on a Projected History of Unidentified Flying Objects.* New York: Hawthorne Books, Inc., 1971.

Florida, Richard. *The Rise of the Creative Class and How It's Transforming Work, Leisure, Community and Everyday Life.* New York: Basic Books, 2002.

Foss, Ronn. 1975. "The Local Scene: Your Times-X-Press." *Communities: A Journal of Cooperative Living* 22 (1975): 28–31.

Francaviglia, Damien. "Branson, Missouri: Regional Identity and the Emergence of a Popular Culture Community." *Journal of American Culture* 18 (1995): 57–73.

Frankel, Todd. "Ozark City a Haven Divided." *St. Louis Post-Dispatch.* July 2, 2007, A1.

Franson, Bob. "The Changing Ozarks." *Springfield Leader and Press.* July 3, 1977, F1.

Frantova, Elena, Elizaveta Solomonova, and Timothy Sutton. "Extra-Personal Awareness through the Media-Rich Environment." *AI and Society* 26 (2011): 179–86.

Fredericks, S. C. "Roger Zelazney and the Trickster Myth: An Analysis of Jack of Shadows." *Journal of American Culture* 2.1 (1979): 271–78.

Friedman, Sora. "Planned Communities of the New Deal." *Communal Societies* 26 (2006): 99–120.

Froelich, Jacqueline. "The Purple People." *Arkansas Times* 45.20 (April 2019): 22–27.

Froelich, Jacqueline. "Reclusive Ozarks Commune Operates Under Veil of Violence." Ozarks at Large Program. KUAF 91.3 FM. National Public Radio aired on February 25. Accessed http://www.kuaf.com/post/reclusive-ozarks-commune-operates-under-veil-violence#stream/0. Accessed May 14, 2018.

Frosch, Franz. "Hum and Otoacoustic Emissions May Arise out of the Same Mechanism." *Journal of Scientific Exploration* 27.4 (2013): 603–24.

Gardner, Hugh. 1978. *The Children of Prosperity: Thirteen Modern American Communes.* New York: St. Martin's Press, 1978.

Garreau, Joel. *The Nine Nations of North America.* New York: Avon Books, 1981.

Gates, Art. "Mountain Music." *Hillbilly Comics,* Charlton Publication, 1 (1955): 23–28.

Gates, Gary, and Abigail Cooke. "Arkansas Census Snapshot: 2010." The Williams Institute. University of California, Los Angeles School of Law. Accessed https://williamsinstitute .law.ucla.edu/wpcontent/uploads/Census2010Snapshot_Arkansas_v2.pdf on August 8, 2018.

Gaver, Jack. "Television Highlights for Next Week." *Statesville and Record Landmark*. Statesville, NC. September 3, 1966, 22.

Genius lyrics search engine. Accessed https://genius.com/ on January 11, 2019.

Gennup, Arnold Van. *The Rites of Passage*. London: Routledge and Kegan Paul, 1909.

Gieryn, Thomas. "A Space for Place in Sociology." *Annual Review of Sociology* 26 (2000): 463–96.

Gilbert, Allan, Jr. "Dogpatch U.S.A." *Northwest Arkansas Times*. Fayetteville, AR. October 10, 1967, 7.

Gilmour, Michael. *Gods and Guitars: Seeking the Sacred in Post-1960s Popular Music*. Waco, Texas. Baylor University Press, 2009.

Glasgow, Nina, and David L. Brown. "Social Integration among Older In-migrants in Non-metropolitan Retirement Destination Counties." In *Population Change and Rural Society*, edited by William A. Kandel and David L. Brown, 177–96. Netherlands: Springer, 2006.

Gleick, Elizabeth "The Strangers among Us." In *Religious Cults in America*, edited by Robert Long, 99–104. New York: H. W. Wilson Company, 1994.

Goedde, Barbara. Interviewed and transcribed by Ayana Arrington. November 5, 2017. Washington University, St. Louis. Accessed http://omeka.wustl.edu/omeka/files/original /5a2c09c9d8d436dc64e959a6fe379624.pdf on December 29, 2018.

Gordon, Ronald. "The Alamo Christian Foundation." *Arkansas Historical Quarterly* 76.3 (2017): 218–47.

Graff, Thomas, and Earl Neel. 1979. "Reversal of Southern Population Trends: An Example from Arkansas." *Mississippi Geographer* 7 (1979): 48–57.

Granda, Michael Supe. *It Shined: The Saga of the Ozark Mountain Daredevils*. Bloomington, IN: Author House, 2008.

Grant, H. Roger. "Missouri's Utopian Communities." *Missouri Historical Review* 66.1 (1971): 20–48.

Grantham, Dewey. "The Regional Imagination: Social Scientists and the American South." *Journal of Southern History* 34 (1968): 3–32.

Graves, John Williams. *Town and Country: Race Relations in an Urban-Rural Context, Arkansas, 1865–1965*. Fayetteville: University of Arkansas Press, 1990.

Green, Archie. "Hillbilly Music: Source and Symbol." *Journal of American Folklore* 78 (1965): 204–28, 205.

Griffin, Larry. "The Promise of a Sociology of the South." *Southern Cultures* 7.1 (2001): 50–71.

Griffith, April. "Ozark Mountain Folk Fair." *The Encyclopedia of Arkansas History and Culture*, 2015. Accessed http://www.encyclopediaofarkansas.net/encyclopedia/entry-detail .aspx?entryID=7958 on January 11, 2019.

Grinstead-Schneider, Mary, and Bernal Green. "Adjustment Stresses on Rural Laborers in the Mississippi Delta and the Ozarks." *Growth & Change* 9.3 (1978): 37–43.

Gross, Michael. "'Ain't Life Grand'—A Dandy Black Oak Kick Up Their Heels in Europe." *Circus*, July 1975, 4–8.

Grossman, Ron. "Civil War." *Chicago Tribune*. March 31, 1988, 63.

Guenther, Jack. "Sport Parade." *Tucson Daily Citizen*. April 30, 1942, 10.

Gysel, Dean. "It's About Time Berle Came Back." *Corpus Christi Caller Times*. July 24, 1966, 14F.

Haenke, David. "Ozark Evolutionary Front, 1971–1976." *Communities: A Journal of Cooperative Living* 22 (1975): 32–35.

Haenke, David. Personal communication. January 6, 2019.

Haenke, David. Personal communication. November 18, 2018.

Hall, Baxter C., and Cecil T. Wood. *The South*. New York: Scribner, 1995.

Hand, Eric. "In a Town Full of B and Bs, the Candlestick Has Its Own Allure." *St. Louis Post-Dispatch*. October 23, 2005, 5.

Hannibal Journal. "Phrenological Democracy—A Lecture on Heads." Hannibal, MO. October 7, 1852, 2.

Hansen, George. *The Trickster and the Paranormal*. Xlibris Corp.: Kindle Edition, 2001.

Hanson, Julia. *Awakening to Your Creation*. Huntsville, AR: Ozark Mountain Publishing, 2009.

Harbison, Robert. *Eccentric Spaces*. New York: Avon Books, 1977.

Hardeman, W. O. "Eureka Springs: A Grand Description." *Arkansas Democrat*. Little Rock. March 10, 1880, 1.

Harper, Edward, and Mary Townsend. "Eccentricity at an Old Spa in the Ozarks." *New York Times*. May 28, 1989, 5.8.

Hartman, Ernest. *Boundaries in the Mind: A New Psychology of Personality*. New York: Basic Books, 1991.

Haskins, John. "Music, Mid-America." *Kansas City Times*. March 26, 1973, 10.

"Haunted Places." Accessed http://www.hauntedplaces.org/state/Arkansas on April 29, 2016.

Hazel, Dan. Personal communication. December 19, 2019.

Headwaters School. "Our School." Accessed http://headwaters-school.org/school.html on March 3, 2019.

Heller, Jason. "Billy Lee Riley and His Little Green Men, 'Flyin' Saucers Rock 'n' Roll.'" Frequency Rotation. Accessed https://www.tor.com/2010/09/02/frequency-rotation-billy-lee-riley-and-his-little-green-men-qflyin-saucers-rock-n-rollq/ on May 29, 2018.

Henderson, Jack. "Arkansas Mystery Lights." *Fate Magazine* 8.8 (1955): 68–72.

Hendrix, Lewellyn. "Kinship, Social Networks, and Integration among Ozark Residents and Out-Migrants." *Journal of Marriage and Family* 88.1 (1976): 97–104.

Herberle, Rudolf. "Regionalism: Some Critical Observations." *Social Forces* 21.3 (1943): 280–86.

Hermann, Janet Sharp. *The Pursuit of a Dream*. Jackson: University Press of Mississippi, 1999.

Hesseltine, William, and David Smiley. *The South in American History*. New York: Prentice-Hall, 1943.

Hiller, Herb. 1992. "Only a Day Away." *St. Petersburg Times*. May 3, 1992, 1-E.

Hine, Robert. *Community on the American Frontier: Separate but Not Alone*. Norman: University of Oklahoma Press, 1980.

Hitte, Gorton D. "Wake Up Fayetteville." *Northwest Arkansas Times*. August 5, 1970, 4.

Hofheimer, John. "Local Man Spreads Gospel of Solar Energy." *Baxter Bulletin*. Mountain Home, Arkansas. July 22, 1983, 2, 9.

Hope Star. "Charlene Gilbert Is Miss Dogpatch." Hope, Arkansas. May 25, 1975, 1.

Hope Star. "Dogpatch Opens 7th Season Today." May 3, 1975, 1.

Hope Star. "Theatre Closed." September 21, 1973, 12.

Hope Star. "21 Defendents Out on Bond." Hope, Arkansas. August 27, 1973, 2.

Hoskyns, Barney. *Across the Great Divide: The Band and America.* New York: Hal Leonard Corporation, 2006.

House, Jeff. "Sweeny among the Archetypes: The Literary Hero in American Culture." *Journal of American Culture* 16.4 (1993): 65–71.

Howerton, Phillip. *The History of Tree Roots: Poems.* Kirksville, MO: Golden Antelope Press, 2015.

Hubbell, Sue. "Buck Nelson and the Little Men." *St. Louis Post-Dispatch.* June 29, 1977, 2F (58).

Huber, Patrick. "The Riddle of the Horny Hillbilly." In *Dixie Emporium: Tourism, Foodways, and Consumer Culture in the American South,* edited by Anthony J. Stanonis, 69–86. Athens: University of Georgia Press, 2008.

Huber, Patrick, and Kathleen Drowne. "Hill Billy: The Earliest Known African American Usuages." *American Speech* 83.2 (2008): 214–21.

Hughes, Ron. "Ozark Mountain Mother Earth News Freak." Hot Mulch Band. Grinola Records. Brixey, Missouri, 1975.

Hughes, Ron. Personal communication. January 5, 2019.

Hughes, Ron. Personal communication. February 20, 2019.

Hutson, Kirk. "Hot 'n' Nasty: Black Oak Arkansas and Its Effect on Rural Southern Culture." *Arkansas Historical Quarterly* 54 (1995): 185–211.

Immen, Wallace. "Beauty and the Bizarre: Red Cliffs and Rocky Spires Have Become Magnets for Mystics, Healers and Flying-Saucer Buffs." *Globe and Mail.* Canada. January 22, 1992.

Independent. "Television Log." Long Beach, California. September 30, 1966, D-7.

Index-Journal. "Businessman Criticizes Two Funeral Homes." Greenwood, SC. June 30, 1976, 25.

Indianapolis News. "Music for Mods." August 18, 1967, 16.

Industrial and Labor Relations Review 23.3 (1970): 406–13.

Inge, M. Thomas. 2011. "Li'l Abner, Snuffy, Pogo, and Friends: The South in the American Comic Strip." *Southern Quarterly* 48.2 (2011): 6–74, 13.

Internal Revenue Service. "Exempt Organizations Select Check." Accessed at https://apps .irs.gov/app/eos/ on May 24, 2014.

Irby, Brian. Personal communication. December 23, 2019.

Jacobs, David. *The UFO Controversy in America.* Bloomington: Indiana University Press, 1975.

Jacobs, Jane. *The Death and Life of Great American Cities.* New York: Vintage Books, 1961.

Jenkins, Phillip "Sideways into Sociology." *American Sociologist* 29.3 (1998): 5–8.

Johnson, Kenneth. "The Continuing Incidence of Natural Decrease in American Counties." *Rural Sociology* 76.1: 74–100.

Jones, Nathan. Correspondence with the author. Arkansas Cosplay Network. Facebook Group page. Accessed November 1, 2018.

Jones, Steve. "Arlington Quintet Gets 'Big Break.'" *Indianapolis News.* March 31, 1965, 29.

Jung, Carl. *Flying Saucers: A Modern Myth of Things Seen in the Skies.* Princeton: Princeton University Press, 1978.

Jung, Carl. "On the Psychology of the Trickster Figure." In *The Trickster,* edited by Paul Radin, 1972.

Kansas City Times. "Can't Tell the Whole Story." September 22, 1959, J4(54).

Kanter, Rosabeth Moss. *Commitment and Community: Communes and Utopias in Sociological Perspective*. Cambridge: Harvard University Press, 1973.

Karell, Docia. 1930. "Ozarks 'Culture Preserve' Is Suggested by Teacher." *Springfield Leader and Press*. October 29, 1–2.

Keaggy, Dianne. "Artistic Arkansas Sprawling Museum in Bentonville, Built with Wal-Mart Fortune, Has Emerged as a Must-See Destination for Art Lovers." *St. Louis Post-Dispatch*. April 29, 2012, H1.

Kelly, Mike. "Black Oak Shakes the Shrine." *Springfield Leader and Press*. November 18, 1973, 71.

Kelly, Mike. "Folk Hero Triumphs Sans '60s Nostalgia." *Springfield Leader and Press*. February 5, 1974, 12.

Kelton, Jim. "Cate Brothers." In *Encyclopedia of Arkansas Music*, edited by Ali Welky and Mike Keckhaver, 70–71. Little Rock, Arkansas: Butler Center Books, 2013.

Kemp, Mark. *Dixie Lullaby: A Story of Music, Race and New Beginnings in a New South*. New York: Free Press, 2004.

Kerenyi, Karl. "The Trickster in Relation to Greek Mythology." In *The Trickster: A Study in American Mythology*, edited by Paul Radin, 173–91. New York: Schocken Books, 1972.

Kersen, Thomas. "Communal Living in the Heart of Dixie." *Tributaries: Journal of the Alabama Folklife Association* 11 (2009): 20–32.

Kersen, Thomas. "The Power of the Quest Narrative: Metaphors, Modernity, and Transformation." In *The Power of the Word: The Sacred and the Profane*, edited by Patsy J. Daniels, 185–97. Newcastle, UK: Cambridge Scholars Publishing, 2015.

Kersen, Thomas, and Candis Pizzetta. "Exploring Regional Identity in Arkansas: The Salience of the Ozark Term." *Elder Mountain: A Journal of Ozark Studies* 7 (2017): 66–83.

Keys, Laurinda. "Singer Extolls Virtues of St. Francis." *Santa Cruz Sentinel*. October 8, 1982, B-5.

Kinsella, Michael. *Legend-Tripping Online: Supernatural Folklore and the Search for Ong's Hat*. Jackson: University Press of Mississippi, 2011.

Kleiner, Dick. "Shed a Tear for Hillbilly Music—It's Rock 'n' Roll for Country Kids, Too." *Courier News*. Blytheville, Arkansas. May 1, 1956, 8.

Knippenberg, Jim. "One of Rock's Most Unusual Sounds Will Be Heard at UC." *Cincinnati Enquirer*. July 25, 1970, 5.

Kokomo Tribune. "The Young America Fair: 'Where the Action Is.'" July 31, 1967, 14.

Kononenko, Natalie, and Svitlana Kukharenko. "Borat the Trickster: Folklore and the Media, Folklore in the Media." *Slavic Review* 67.1 (2008): 8–18.

Koonce, Bob. "The Strange World of an Ozarks 'Saucerman.'" *Kansas City Times*, April 8, 1961.

Kossy, Donna. 1994. *Kooks: Guide to the Outer Limits of Human Belief*. Portland, Oregon: Feral House, 1994.

Kuehn, John, and Lloyd Bender. "A Dissent: Migration, Growth Centers, and the Ozarks." *Growth & Change* 6.2 (1975): 43–48.

La Crosse Tribune. "Community Spirit Dwells in Arkansas Monastery: Inhabitants Called Monks, Monk-ettes, and Monk-eyes." October 17, 1992, B-5.

Lambiek Comiclopedia. "Ron Foss." Accessed on February 5, 2019. https://www.lambiek.net/artists/f/foss_ronn.htm

Lane, Beldon. *Landscapes of the Sacred*. Baltimore, MD: Johns Hopkins University Press, 2008.

Leonard Corporation, 2008, 158.

Leadabrand, Russ. "As I See It." *Pasadena Independent*. September 19, 1958, 10.

Lewis, James. *Legitimating New Religions*. New Brunswick, NJ: Rutgers University Press, 2003.

Library of Congress. "Conversations with 16-year-old white female, Arkansas (Transcription)." 1986a. Accessed at http://www.loc.gov/resource/afc/986022.afc1986022_ms4402.

Library of Congress. "Conversations with 23-year-old White Male, Arkansas (Transcription)." 1986b. Accessed http://www.loc.gov/resource/afc/986022.afc1986022_ms4403.

Library of Congress. "Conversations with 59-year-old White Male, (Transcription)." 1986c. Accessed http://www.loc.gov/resource/afc/986022.afc1986022_ms4501.

Library of Congress. "Conversations with 77-year-old White Male, Pettigrew, Arkansas (Transcription)." 1986d. Accessed http://www.loc.gov/resource/afc/986022.afc1986022_ms4505.

Lindsay, Rob, and Wendy Lindsay. "A Warm Welcome to Sunny Sedona: New Age Mystics Claim the Arizona Town is Situated on one of Earth's Energy Vortexes Which Energizes Visitors and Draws Them Back." *Vancouver Sun*. British Columbia. November 7, 2000, D19.

Lockyer, Joshua. "Intentional Communities and Sustainability." *Communal Studies* 30.1 (2010): 17–30.

Loewen, James. *Sundown Towns: A Hidden Dimension of American Racism*. New York: Simon & Schuster, 2006.

Lofland, Lyn. *A World of Strangers: Order and Action in Urban Public Space*. Prospect Heights, IL: Waveland Press, Inc., 1985.

Los Angeles Times. Entertainment notices. August 29, 1968, 9.

Lubbock Avalanche Journal. "Tragedies." February 8, 1971, 1.

Lynes, Russell. "Highbrow, Lowbrow, Middlebrow." *Harper's Magazine*. February 1949, 19.

MacDonald, William. "The Popularity of Paranormal Experience in the United States." *Journal of American Culture* 17.3 (1994): 35–42.

MacPherson, Glen. "Who is behind this project?" Accessed https://hummap.wordpress.com/about/ on April 29, 2016.

Malone, Bill C., and David Stricklin. *Southern Music/American Music*. Lexington, Kentucky: University Press of Kentucky, 2003.

Manning, Anita. "Fast Getaways: Ozark Retreat Is Balm for the South." *USA Today*. May 24, 1990, 5.

Marx, Leo. *The Machine in the Garde: Technology and the Pastoral Ideal in America*. New York: Oxford University Press, 1969.

Maurer, Bill. "Farms Can Produce Energy Supply, Too." *Springfield News Leader*. February 18, 1976, 54.

Maxwell, Angie. "The Duality of the Southern Thing." *Southern Cultures* 20.4 (1982): 89–105.

Maxwell, Angie. "Southern Political Attitudes: Geography versus Identity, Results from the 2012 Blair Center of Southern Politics and Society." Accessed at https://blaircenter.uark.edu/polling-data-reports/2012-poll/geography-versus-identity on December 13, 2019.

McCanse, Keith. 1923. "Seeing the Ozarks First: A Weekend Trip to Eureka Springs." *Joplin Globe*. August 19, 1923, 7.

McCully-Mobley, Kim. "The Saltiest of the Old Timers Are Dead Now." Ozark Symposium. West Plains, Missouri. September 19, 2015.

McGarry, James, and Benjamin Newberry. "Beliefs in Paranormal Phenomena and Locus of Control: A Field Study." *Journal of Personality and Social Psychology* 41.4 (1981): 725–36.

McGee, Gary Z. "The Path of the Sacred Clown: Where Trickster and Shaman Converge." Fractal Enlightenment. Accessed at https://fractalenlightenment.com/25726/spirituality/the-path-of-the-sacred-clown-where-trickster-and-shaman-converge on December 29, 2019.

McGuire, John M. "Just Say Cheese: How to Photograph an Extraterrestrial." *St. Louis Post-Dispatch.* August 12, 1997, 38.

McGuire, John M. "Well, Come Down!" *St. Louis Post-Dispatch.* July 20, 1997, C-1.

McKinsey, Daly. 1970. "Commune Seeks Another Answer." *Courier News.* Blytheville, AR. July 15, 1970, 12.

McShane, Ruth. "A Force for Social Change: Back-to-the-Land Settlements, 1970–1995." Unpublished manuscript funded in part by the Arkansas Humanities Council and the National Endowment for the Humanities. Marshall, Arkansas, 1996, 73.

Meheust, Bertrand. 1987. "UFO Abductions as Religious Folklore." In *UFOs, 1947–1987: The 40-year Search for an Explanation,* edited by Hilary Evans and John Spencer, 352–58. London, Forten Press, 1987.

Mehta, Diane. "In the Ozarks, Mountain Greenery and Gingerbread." *New York Times.* July 6, 2007, 8.

Meigs, A. J. "The Changing Ozarks." *Monthly Review.* Federal Reserve Bank of St. Louis. 39 (1957): 19–24. Accessed https://fraser.stlouisfed.org/files/docs/publications/frbslreview/rev_stls_195702.pdf on December 15, 2018.

Meijering, Louise, Paulus Huigen, and Bettina van Hoven. "Intentional Communities in Rural Spaces." *Journal of Economic and Social Geography* 98 (2007): 41–52.

Menand, Louis. "Thinking Sideways: The One-Dot Theory of History." *New Yorker.* Accessed http://www.newyorker.com/magazine/2015/03/30/thinking-sideways March 2015.

Mercer, John. *Communes: A Social History and Guide.* Dorset, UK: Prism Press, 1984.

Miller, E. Joan. "The Ozark Culture Region as Revealed by Traditional Materials." *Annals of the Association of American Geographers* 58.1 (1968): 51–77.

Miller, E. Joan. "The Naming of the Land in the Ozarks: A Study in Cultural Arkansas." *Annals of the Association of American Geographers* 59.2 (1969): 240–51.

Miller, Timothy. "A Matter of Definition: Just What Is an Intentional Community?" *Communal Societies* 30.1 (2010):1–15.

Miller, Timothy. *The Quest for Utopia in Twentieth Century America: 1900–1960.* New York: Syracuse University Press, 1998.

Miller, Timothy. "The Roots of the 1960s Communal Revival." *American Studies* 33 (1992): 73–93.

Miller, Timothy. *The 60s Communes: Hippies and Beyond.* New York: Syracuse Press, 1999.

Moberly Monitor Index. 1947. "Spiderwebs-New Theory in Mystery of Flying Saucers." Moberly, Missouri. July 8, 1947, 2.

Moore, E. B., and W. B. Moore. "Eureka Springs." *Fayetteville Weekly Democrat.* April 17, 1880, 4.

Morris, Robert. "The Arkansan in American Folklore." *Arkansas Historical Quarterly* 9.2 (1950): 99–107. 104.

Morris, Willie. *Terrains of the Heart and Other Essays on Home.* Oxford, Mississippi: Yoknapatawpha Press, 1985.

Morrison, Kathleen. "The Ties that Bind: The Impact of Isolation on Income in Rural America." *Journal of Public Affairs* 7.1 (2004): 17–38.

Mount Pleasant News. "Major Accomplishments and Activities of 1953." Mount Pleasant, IA. December 30, 1953, 3.

Mountain Echo. Yellville, AR. April 23, 1909, 2.

Mountain Echo. Advertisement for "Primary Lessons in the Science of Prophecy." Yellville, AR. March 19, 1921, 3.

Mullaney, Dean, and Bruce Canwell, eds. *Al Capp's: Li'l Abner: Complete Daily and Sunday Comics, 1949–1950.* San Diego, CA: IDW Publishers, 2016.

Murrell, T. E. "Letter to Dr. P. O. Hooper." *Arkansas Democrat.* Little Rock. August 17, 1880, 3–4.

Nancy and Manny. 1975. "We Make a School." *Communities* 22 (1975): 35.

National Oceanic and Atmospheric Administration. "Earthquake Intensity Database 1638—1985." Accessed https://www.ngdc.noaa.gov/nndc/struts/form?t=101650&s=35&d=35 on April 29, 2016.

National UFO Reporting Center. "State Report Index for AR." Accessed http://www.nuforc.org/webreports/ndxlAR.html on April 29, 2016.

National UFO Reporting Center. "State Report Index for MO." Accessed http://www.nuforc.org/webreports/ndxlMO.html on August 21, 2016.

Nazimoreh. "Who on Earth . . ." Accessed https://nmcnews.org/Who%20on%20Earth.pdf on September 17, 2016, 52.

Nelson, Lindsey. "Grammay Winner John Michael Talbot Coming to Sioux City." *Sioux City Journal.* May 26, 2017, D1.

Nelson, Melissa. "Ozarks Town Welcomes Eccentrics." *Toronto Star.* October 28, 2000.

Neosho Daily News. "Incoming Kingdom-Missionary Unit." Neosho, Missouri. August 7, 1925, 4.

Neosho Times. "The Changing Ozarks." October 22, 1925, 3.

Newman, Joshua I., and Michael D. Giardina. "NASCAR and the 'Southernization' of America: Spectatorship, Subjectivity, and the Confederation of Identity." *Cultural Studies Critical Methodologies* 8.4 (2008.): 479–506.

No Author. "Mulberry Farm." *Communitas* 2 (1972): 29–34.

Nolan, Michael, Paul Lasley, Gary Green, and William Heffernan. "A Note on Ozark Migrants and Nonmigrants." *Growth and Change: A Journal of Urban and Regional Policy* 12 (1981): 47–52.

Norris, Margaret. "A Not-So-Counter Culture." *Springfield News Leader.* October 12, 1982, 13.

Northwest Arkansas Times. "Art School to Open at Eureka Springs June 7." Fayetteville, Arkansas. June 7, 1948, 3.

Northwest Arkansas Times. "As They Might Appear over Fayetteville." Fayetteville, Arkansas. July 7, 1947, 1.

Northwest Arkansas Times. "Festival May Draw 10,000." Fayetteville, Arkansas. June 26, 1970, 1.

Northwest Arkansas Times. "Folkfair Dates Set at Eureka." Fayetteville, AR. April 7, 1973, 2.

Northwest Arkansas Times. "Near Walnut Ridge: Body of Boy, 6, Found Buried at Missing Cult Leader's Home." Fayetteville, Arkansas. September 21, 1964, 3.

Northwest Arkansas Times. "No Favoritism." Fayetteville, Arkansas. July 2, 1970, 4.

Northwest Arkansas Times. "Rock Concert to Be Held at University." Fayetteville, Arkansas. July 17, 1970, 11.

Northwest Arkansas Times. "Rock Festival Ends in Arrest." Fayetteville, Arkansas. June 29, 1970, 2.

Northwest Arkansas Times. "Weekend Rock Festival Set at Washington County Farm." Fayetteville, Arkansas. June 24, 1970, 1.

Northwest Arkansas Times. "Writers and Artists Guild Convention June 20–22 at Eureka." Fayetteville, Arkansas. June 15, 1940, 1.

O' Connor, Flannery. *Mystery and Manners: Occasional Prose.* Edited by Sally and Robert Fitzgerald, 192. New York: Farrar, Straus, and Giroux, 1969.

O'Neil, Thomas. "The Ozarks: Jewel of the Heartland." In *America's Hidden Corners: Places off the Beaten Path,* edited by Donald Crum Washington, 144–69. Washington DC: National Geographic Society, 1983.

Odessa American. "Commune Closing Business Ventures." February 14, 1974, 7.

Odessa American. "KBSN Radio." September 13, 1964, 11.

Odum, Howard. "From Community Studies to Regionalism." *Social Forces* 23.3 (1945): 245–58.

Odum, Howard. "A Sociological Approach to the Study and Practice of American Regionalism: A Factorial Syllabus." *Social Forces* 20 (1942): 425–36.

The Oneonta Star. "Psychic Artist for Lecture in Area Town." September 12, 1951, 9.

Osceola Times. "Eureka Springs." Reprint from St. Louis. Osceola, AR. May 7, 1881, 1.

Oved, Yaacov. *Two Hundred Years of American Communes.* New Brunswick, NJ: Transaction Books, 1988.

Overstreet, Sarah. "Crescent's Credo: 'I Simply Don't Do Anything I Don't Want to Do.'" *The Springfield News-Leader.* February 15, 1987, 9.

Pampa Daily News. "Nominations for H. J. [Hairless Joe] Wanted." Pampa, TX. October 19, 1939, 1.

The Pantagraph. "Eureka Springs, Arkansas: A Born-Again Ozarks Town." Bloomington, IL. September 22, 1985, 12.

The Pantagraph. "Hunted Chief Held in Arkansas." Bloomington, IL. September 20, 1964, 1.

Park, Robert. "Human Migration and the Marginal Man." In *Classic Essays on the Culture of Cities,* edited by Richard Sennett, 131–42. New York: Appleton-Century-Crofts, 1969.

Parker, Holt. "Toward a Definition of Popular Culture." *History and Theory* 50 (2011): 147–70.

Peckham, Howard. "Flying Saucers as Folklore." *Hoosier Folklore* 9.4 (1950): 103–7.

Peek, Dan. *Live at the Ozark Opry.* Charleston, South Carolina: History Press, 2010.

Pennington, Gail. "Eureka! Found: A Spot in Northern Arkansas Where Whole Grains Reign Supreme." *St. Louis Post-Dispatch.* February 27, 1989, 1F.

Penprase, Mike. "New Life Farm Not Just Whistling in Brixey." *Springfield News Leader.* March 5, 1986, 15.

Perkins, J. Blake. *Hillbilly Hell-Raisers: Federal Power and Populist Defiance in the Ozarks.* Urbana: University of Illinois Press, 2017.

Persig, Robert. *Zen and the Art of Motorcycle Maintenance.* New York: Bantam Books, Inc., 1985.

Peters, Ted. *UFOs-God's Chariots? Flying Saucers in Politics, Science, and Religion.* Atlanta: John Knox Press, 1977.

Petto, Anthony, and Lloyd Bender. "Responsiveness to Local Economic Conditions in the Ozarks." *Growth & Change* 5.2 (1974): 8–12.

Phillips, Jared. "Hipbillies and Guerilla Press." 10th annual Ozark Symposium. West Plains, MO, September 24, 2018.

Phillips, Jared. "Hipbillies and Hillbillies: Back-to-the-Landers in the Arkansas Ozarks during the 1970s." *Arkansas Historical Quarterly* 75.2 (2016): 89–110.

Phillips, Jared. *Hipbillies: Deep Revolution in the Arkansas Ozarks*. Fayetteville: University of Arkansas Press, 2019.

Pinkley-Call, Cora. *Stair-Step-Town*. Eureka Springs, Arkansas: Times-Echo Press, 1952.

Plummer, Ken. *Documents of Life: An Introduction to the Problems and Literature of a Humanistic Method*. Boston, MA: George Allen and Unwin, 1983.

Polidata. "Region Maps: County-Based Regions and Markets for Arkansas." Accessed http://www.polidata.us/pub/maps/rg2000/ar_reg.pdf on October 9, 2018.

Polletta, Francesca. "Free Spaces in Collective Action." *Theory and Society* 28 (1999): 1–38.

Powell, Douglas. *Critical Regionalism: Connecting Politics and Culture in the American Landscape*. Chapel Hill: University of North Carolina Press, 2007.

Prosser, Lee. *UFOs in Missouri: True Tales of Extraterrestrial and Related Phenomena*. Arglen, PA: Schiffer Publishing Ltd., 2011.

Radin, Paul. *The Trickster: A Study in American Mythology*, 173–91. New York: Schocken Books, 1972.

Rafferty, Milton. *The Ozarks: Land and Life*. Fayetteville: University of Arkansas Press, 2001.

Ramos, Christine. *A Journey into Being: Knowing and Nurturing Our Children as Spirit*. Huntsville, AR: Ozark Mountain Publishing, 2006.

Randolph, Vance. *Ozark Magic and Folklore*. New York: Dover Publications, Inc., 2016.

Rayburn, Otto. *The Eureka Springs Story*. Diamond Jubilee edition. Eureka Springs, AR: Wheeler Printing, Inc., 1982.

Redlands Daily Facts. "Annual Hollywood Y-Day Offers Wide Activities." Redlands, CA. October 15, 1966, 3.

Reed, John. "The Dissolution of Dixie and the Changing Shape of the South." *Social Forces* 69 (1990): 221–33.

Reed, John. "The Heart of Dixie: An Essay in Folk Geography." *Social Forces* 69 (1976): 221–33.

Reed, John. *One South: An Ethnic Approach to Regional Culture*. Baton Rouge: Louisiana State University Press, 1982.

Reed, Roy. "Civic Minded Commune May be Forced to Move." *Lakeland Ledger*. Lakeland, FL. October 1, 1973, 2A.

Reno Gazette-Journal. "Blocker Singers at the Nugget." March 25, 1967, 26.

Rice, Tom. "Believe It or Not: Religious and Other Paranormal Beliefs in the United States." *Journal of Scientific Study of Religion* 42.1 (2003): 95–106.

Rice, William. "A Misfit Who Fits In." *Chicago Tribune*. October 28, 1991. Accessed https://www.chicagotribune.com/news/ct-xpm-1992-10-28-9204070879-story.html on December 29, 2018.

Richmond, Dick. "Two Rock Groups Perform before Large Crowd at Kiel." *St. Louis Post-Dispatch*. March 23, 1973, 41.

Ritzer, George. *Enchanting a Disenchanting World: Revolutionizing the Means of Consumption*. Thousand Oaks, CA: Pine Forge Press, 1999.

Ritzer, George. *The McDonaldization of Society*. New Century Edition. Thousand Oaks, CA: Sage Publications, 2000.

Robbins, William. "Where a Good Squabble Mellows the Ozark Chill." *New York Times*. November 1, 1987, 42.

Robertson, David. *UFOs, Conspiracy Theories, and the New Age: Millennial Conspiracism.* New York: Bloomsbury Academic, 2015.

Robertson, Robbie. *Testimony.* New York: Random House, 2016.

Rolla Herald. "The Ozarks." Rolla, MO. September 9, 1897, 7. Originally published in the *Fayetteville Sentinel.*

Romero, Adam, Amanda Baumle, M.V. Lee Badgett, Gary Gates,. "Arkansas-Census Snapshot: 2000." The Williams Institute. University of California, Los Angeles School of Law, 2007. Acccessed https://williamsinstitute.law.ucla.edu/demographics/arkansas/arkansas-census-snapshot-2000/ on August 7, 2018.

Rose, John. *Barney Google and Snuffy Smith. Baxter Bulletin.* Mountain Home. May 3, 2005.

Rose, John. *Barney Google and Snuffy Smith. Baxter Bulletin.* Mountain Home. February 20, 2010.

Rosenbaum, Connie. "Commune Runs Afoul of City Regulations." *St. Louis Dispatch.* April 18, 1971, 26.

Rosenbaum, Connie. "The Group, Inc. One Man's Family." *St. Louis Post-Dispatch.* April 7, 1971, 77.

Saenger, Gerhart. "Male and Female Relations in the American Comic Strip." *Public Opinion Quarterly* 19.2 (1955): 195–205.

Saliba, John. "UFO Contactee Phenomena from a Sociopsychological Perspective: A Review." In *The Gods Have Landed: New Religions from Other Worlds,* edited by James R. Lewis, 207–50. New York: State University of New York Press, 1995.

Salina Journal. "Fri., Sept. 9." Salina, KS. September 2 1966, T-7.

Salina Journal. "'Hoss' Helps Singers by Lending His Name." Salina, KS. April 4, 1967, 12.

San Antonio Register. "Stephanie King Joins Religious Cult." December 7, 1989, 1.

San Bernardino County Sun. "Block Singers to Debut." September 17, 1966, 19.

San Bernardino County Sun. "Royal Tahitian Concludes Outdoor Summer Concerts." September 11, 1966, D-9.

Sanarov, Valerii, "On the Nature and Origins of Flying Saucers and Little Green Men." *Current Anthropology* 22 (1981): 163–67.

Sandmeyer, Robert, and Larkin Warner. "A Note on the Discouragement Effect." *Industrial and Labor Relations Review* 23.2 (1970): 406–13.

Sanford, A. Whitney. "Being the Change: Food, Nonviolence, and Self-Sufficiency in Contemporary Intentional Communities." *Communal Studies.* 34.1 (2014): 52.

Santa Cruz Sentinel. "Curry Favors Arkansas as a 'jolly-good' Spot." April 10, 1988, 103.

Santa Cruz Sentinel. "Things Are 'Hummin' Down in Dogpatch." Santa Cruz, CA. August 1, 1965, 24.

Schaefer, Richard, and William Zellner. *Extraordinary Groups: An Examination of Unconventional Lifestyles.* Long Grove, Illinois: Waveland Press, Inc., 2015.

Schmidt, Barbara. "Hillbilly Characters a Hit in 'Li'l Abner' Production." *Chilliwack Progress.* Chilliwack, British Columbia, Canada. February 16, 1977, 6.

Schroeder, Fred. "Types of American Small Towns and How to Read Them." In *Order and Image in the American Small Town,* edited by Michael Fazio and Peggy Prenshaw, 104–35. Jackson, Mississippi: University Press of Mississippi, 1981.

Seaton, Carter Taylor. *Hippie Homesteaders: Arts, Crafts, Music and Living in the Land of West Virginia.* Morgantown: West Virginia University Press, 2014.

Segal, Al. "Plain Talk: Smart Mammy Yokum." *Wisconsin Jewish Chronicle.* October 12, 1956, 8.

The Shadowlands. "Haunted Places in Arkansas." Accessed http://www.theshadowlands.net
   /places/Arkansas on April 29, 2016.

Shelley, Fred. "Search Behavior and Place Utility of Recent Migrants to the Arkansas Ozarks."
   Unpublished manuscript. Department of Geography, University of Iowa. No date.

Shiras, Peter. "County Beat." *Baxter Bulletin*, Mountain Home, Arkansas. July 11, 1947, 2.

Shor, Francis. "Utopian Aspirations in the Black Freedom Movement: SNCC and the Struggle for Civil Rights, 1960–1965." *Utopian Studies* 15.2 (2004): 173–89.

Shumway, David. "Rock & Roll as Cultural Practice." In *Present Tense: Rock & Roll and Culture*, edited by Anthony DeCurtis, 117–33. Durham, NC: Duke University Press, 1992.

Simmel, Georg. *On Individuality and Social Forms*. Edited by Donald Levine. Chicago, IL:
   University of Chicago Press, 1971.

Simp-Li-Me. "An Open Letter to The Hill-Billies of Arkansas" The *Madison County Record*.
   Letter to the editor. April 27, 1950, 1.

Simpson's Leaders-Times. "Television Program." Kittanning, PA. September 3, 1966, 8.

Smith, Jack. "They All Live Together in One Little House . . ." *Democrat and Chronicle*. Los
   Angeles Times Service. January 29, 1967, 73.

Smith, Prior. "See Stunning Sedona" *Toronto Star*. November 25, 2000, T-1.

Smith, Tom W., Michael Hout, and Peter V. Marsden. General Social Survey, 1972–2012
   [Cumulative File]. ICPSR34802-v1. Storrs, CT: Roper Center for Public Opinion
   Research, University of Connecticut/Ann Arbor, MI: Inter-university Consortium for
   Political and Social Research [distributors], 2013–09–11. http://doi.org/10.3886
   / ICPSR34802.v1.

Smith, William. "Families in Contemporary Intentional Communities: Diversity and Purpose." *Communal Societies* 21 (2001): 79–93.

Smith, William. "Intentional Communities 1990–2000: A Portrait." *Michigan Sociological
   Review* 16 (2002): 107–31.

Solomonova, Elizaveta, Elena Frantova, Tore Nielsen,. "Felt Presence: The Uncanny
   Encounters with the Numinous Other." *AI and Society* 26 (2011): 171–78.

Sorokin, Pitirim. *Contemporary Sociological Theories: Through the First Quarter of the
   Twentieth Century*. New York: Harper Torchbooks, 1956.

Southern Poverty Law Center. "Hate Map by State." Accessed https://www.splcenter.org
   /hate-map/by-state on January 13, 2019.

Southern Standard. "Swear They Saw It: Two Reputable Citizens of Hot Springs Maintain
   that They Saw an Airship." Arkadelphia, Arkansas. May 14, 1897, 2.

Spaeder, Nancy. Personal communication, January 5, 2019.

Speer, Jean. "Hillbilly Sold Here." In *Parkways: Past, Present, and Future*, by International
   Linear Parks Conference. Appalachian State University, 1987. JSTOR/stable/jctt1xp3kv8.

Spengler, Oswald. "The Soul of the City." In *Classic Essays on the Culture of Cities*, edited by
   Richard Sennett, 61–88. New York: Meredith Corporation, 1969.

Spindler, George, and Louise Spindler. "Anthropologist View America Culture." *Annual
   Review of Anthropology* 12 (1983): 49–78.

Spokesman-Review. "Trip to Venus Talk Packs Sunday School." Spokane, Washington.
   March 23, 1956, 5.

Springfield Leader and Press. "A Colony Breaks Up." Springfield, MO. September 6, 1927, 2.

Springfield Leader and Press. "Bank Magazine Lauds Ozarks." February 10, 1957, 40.

Springfield Leader and Press. "Cosmic Art Shrine Planned Adjoining Buck's Space Farm."
   June 30, 1971, 32.

Springfield Leader and Press. "Eureka Springs: A Beautiful Health Resort in North Arkansas." October 9, 1897, 16.

Springfield Leader and Press. "Fire Information Reward by Nelson." February 21, 1966, 46.

Springfield Leader and Press. "Split in Cult of the Kingdom: Views on Bobbed Hair and Whiskers Drive Out Barber." Springfield, MO. April 12, 1928, 5.

Springfield Leader and Press. "The Wastebasket." April 19, 1929, 20.

St. Louis Post-Dispatch. "Energy Dept. Gets "Fleece" for Elevated Outhouse Test." December 13, 1979, 12B.

St. Louis Post-Dispatch. "St. Louisan Reports Seeing 'Flying Saucers'; Silver Discs 'Sighted' at Many Points." July 5, 1947, 1.

St. Louis Star and Times. "More 'Flying Saucers' (Or Beer Discs) Seen." June 30, 1947, 6.

Stark, Rodney, and William Banbridge. "Of Churches, Sects, and Cults: Preliminary Concepts for a Theory of Religious Movements." *Journal for the Scientific Study of Religion* 18.2 (1979): 125.

Starr, Fred. "Hillside Adventures." *Northwest Arkansas Times.* Fayetteville, AR. July 12, 1952, 2.

Stearn, Jess. "Blonde Venus in a Saucer: Some Dish." *Daily News.* New York, July 14, 1959, 24.

Steward, Gary, Thomas Shrivers, and Amy Chasteen. "Participant Narratives and Collective Identity in a Metaphysical Movement." *Sociological Spectrum* 22 (2002): 107–35.

Suedfeld, Peter, and John Geiger. "The Sensed Presence as a Coping Resource in Extreme Environments." In *Miracles: God, Science, and Psychology in the Paranormal, Volume 3: Parapsychological Perspectives,* edited by J. Harold Ellers, 1–15. Westport, CT: Praeger, 2008.

Sutphen, Dick. *Sedona: Psychic Energy Vortexes.* New York: Crown Publishers, 1994.

Sverdlik, Alan. "In Arkansas, a Passion for Drama." *Washington Post.* September 6, 1998, E02.

Swami, Viren, Adrian Furnham, Janja Haubner, Stefan Stieger, and Martin Voracek. "The Truth Is Out There: The Structure of Beliefs about Extraterrestrial Life among Austrian and British Respondents." *Journal of Social Psychology* 149.1 (2009): 29–43.

Talbott, Oakley. "Out and About: Epiphanies in Eureka Springs, Ark." *Santa Fe New Mexican.* June 3, 2007, RE-75.

Tang, Didi. "New Neighbors: Hmong." *Springfield News-Leader.* November 27, 2005, 1-8a.

Thomas, Jeffrey. "Music and Life." Letters to the Editor. *Northwest Arkansas Times.* July 3, 1970, 4.

Thompson, Craig, and Kelly Tian. "Reconstructing the South: How Commercial Myths Compete for Identity Value through the Ideological Shaping of Popular Memories and Countermemories." *Journal of Consumer Research* 34.5 (2008): 5 95–613.

Thompson, Dave. *I Hate the New Music: The Classic Rock Manifesto.* New York: Backbeat Books, 2008.

Thompson, Edgar. "Sociology and Sociological Research in the South." *Social Forces* 23.3 (1945): 356–65.

Thompson, Keith. *Angels and Aliens.* New York: Fawcett Columbine, 1991.

Thompson, Stith. *Motif-Index of Folk Literature.* Volume Two D-E. Bloomington: Indiana University Press, 1966.

Tillich, Paul. "The Metropolis: Centralizing and Inclusive." In *The Metropolis in Modern Life,* edited by Robert Fisher, 346–48. New York: Russell and Russell, 1955.

Tillman, J. C. "Nobody Seems to Know Just Where 'The Ozarks' Lie." *Northwest Arkansas Times.* Fayetteville, AR. June 13, 1964, 2.

Times and Transcript. "Town's Divisions Clear in Vote to Ban Discrimination of Gays." May 11, 2015, B6.

Times Record. "TV Friday." Troy, NY. September 2, 1966, B-14.

Tiryakian, Edward. "Toward the Sociology of Esoteric Culture." *American Journal of Sociology* 78.3 (1972): 491–512.

Troy Record. "Siena Slates Rock Concert for Feb. 20." Troy, NY. February 3, 1972, 7.

Tudo, Maurice. 1977. *Pictorial Crackerbarrel.* Marshall, AR, 1997, 6.

Tumminia, Diana. "In the Dreamtime of the Saucer People: Sense-making and Interpretive Boundaries in a Contactee Group." *Journal of Contemporary Ethnography* 3.6 (2002): 675–705.

Tumminia, Eric. Personal communication, January 4, 2019.

Turner, Frederick Jackson. *The Frontier in American History.* New York: Henry Holt and Company, 1920.

Turner, Victor. *The Ritual Process: Structure and Anti-Structure.* New Brunswick, NJ: Aldine Transaction 2009.

Uhlenbrock, Tom. "Eureka Springs' Serene Setting Has a Healing Touch." *St. Louis Post Dispatch.* October 26, 2008, T1.

Uhlenbrock, Tom. "Saving Grace." *St. Louis Post Dispatch.* February 4, 2001, T1.

Uhlenbrock, Tom. "Tour Reveals Town's Quirks and History." *St. Louis Post Dispatch.* February 4, 2001, T5.

Underwood, Edward, and Karen Underwood. *Forgotten Tales of Arkansas.* Charleston: History Press, 2012.

United States Census Bureau. "Arkansas Population of Counties by Decennial Census: 1900 to 1990." Compiled and edited by Richard L. Forstall 1995. Accessed https://www.census.gov/population/cencounts/ar190090.txt on August 1, 2017.

United States Department of Agriculture data. "County Level Data Sets." Accessed http://www.ers.usda.gov/data-products/county-level-data-sets.aspx on February 23, 2015.

Vallee, Jacques. *Passport to Magonia.* Chicago: Henry Regnery Co., 1969.

Vance, Rupert. "The Concept of the Region." *Social Forces* 8 (1929): 208–18.

Vance, Rupert. "The Sociological Implications of Southern Regionalism." *Journal of Southern History* 26.1(1960): 44–56.

Vaughn, Bill. "The Nicest People See Strange Things." *St. Louis Post-Dispatch.* April 4, 1966, 3D.

Vaughn, Denise Henderson. "Idealism Tempered by Tenacity." Presentation given at the Ozarks Symposium. West Plains, Missouri, 2014.

Vaughn, Denise Henderson. Personal communication. January 6, 2019.

Vaughn, Denise Henderson. Personal Communication. February 10, 2019.

Vinylfool. "Quinchords—1965." *60's Indiana Band Szene,* 2009. Accessed http://indiana-bands-60s.blogspot.com/2009/11/quinchords-1965.html on November 13, 2018.

Vitali, Marc. "Janis Joplin's Ravinia Jam, Part 1." Accessed https:news.wttv.com/2013/20/03/Janis-joplins-ravinia-jam-part-1 on November 13, 2018.

Wallace, Samuel. "Regional Sociology: The South." *Sociological Spectrum* 1(1981): 429–42.

Wallerstein, Immanuel. "The West, Capitalism, and the Modern World-System." *Review* 15.4 (1992): 561–619.

Washburn, Alex. "Eureka Springs Ozark Resort Stages Comeback." *Hope Star.* Hope, AR. November 19, 1946, 6.

Washburn, Alex. "Jones Returns: APA Delegation Scatters to Dog Patch, Hot Springs." *Hope Star.* Hope, AR. June 14, 1971, 1.

Washington, Joseph, Jr. *Black Sects and Cults: The Power Axis in an Ethnic Ethic.* Garden City, NY: Doubleday & Company, 1972.

Washington Citizen. "Sigma Deltas Plan to See Shows." Washington, MO. March 24, 1973.

Weber, Max. *From Max Weber: Essays in Sociology.* Edited and translated by H. H. Gerth and C. Wright Mills. New York: Oxford University Press, 1980.

Weber, Max. *The Sociology of Religion.* Translated by Ephraim Fischoff. Boston: Beacon Press, 1969.

The Week. "Hearing the Hum." June 3, 2016, 15:36–37.

Weiner, Eric. *The Geography of Genius.* New York: Simon & Schuster, 2016.

Wheaton Journal. "Sadie Hawkins Day November 4." Wheaton, MO. October 26, 1939, 1.

Whitmore, John. "Religious Dimensions of the UFO Abductee Experience." In *The Gods Have Landed: New Religions from Other Worlds,* edited by James Lewis, 65–84. Albany: State University of New York Press, 1995.

Wichita Star. "As a Kansan Sees It: How Eureka Springs, Ark., Looks to a Wichita Man with a Glass Eye." August 31, 1900, 4.

Wiegenstein, Steve. "The Lure of the Ozarks: What's the Bait and Who's the Fish?" Ozark Symposium. West Plains, MO. September 19, 2015.

Wienkowski, Louise. Personal communication. January 4, 2019.

Wigginton, Eliot. *The Foxfire Book.* Garden City, NJ: Anchor Press/Doubleday, dedication page, 1972.

Williams, Martha. "Dogpatch Drag Brings Out the Hillbillies." *The Bridgeport Post.* Bridgeport, CT: May 22, 1960, 50.

Wilsey, Sean. *More Curious.* San Francisco: McSweeney's, 2014.

Wilson, Charles. *Backwoods America.* Chapel Hill: University of North Carolina Press, 1935.

Wilson, Charles. *The Bodacious Ozarks: True Tales of the Backhills.* Gretna, LA: Pelican Publishing Company, 2002.

Woodward, C. Vann. "The Southern Ethic in a Puritan World." *William and Mary Quarterly* 25 (1968): 363-370.

Woodward, C. Vann. *The Burden of Southern History.* Baton Rouge: Louisiana State University Press, 1970.

Woods, Michael. Rural Geography. Thousand Oaks, CA: Sage Publications, 2005.

Yenckel, James. "Arkansas Sampler: Footstompin Fun with an Old-World Twist." *Washington Post.* June 10, 1990, E1.

Yronwode, Catherine. "Catherine Yronwode." Accessed www.yronwode.com/catherine .html on January 2, 2019.

Yronwode, Catherine. Facebook post December 25, 2016. Accessed at https://www.facebook .com/catherine.yronwode on January 3, 2020.

Yronwode, Catherine. Facebook post for March 7, 2018. Accessed at https://www.facebook .com/catherine.yronwode. On January 3, 2020.

Yronwode, Catherine. Personal communication. January 8, 2020.

Yronwode, Catherine. Personal communication. January 12, 2020.

Zablocki, Benjamin. *Alienation and Charisma: A Study of Contemporary American Communes.* New York: Free Press, 1980.

Zelinsky, Wilbur. *The Cultural Geography of the United States.* Revised edition. Englewood Cliffs, NJ: Prentice Hall, 1992.

Zinn, Howard. *The Southern Mystique.* New York: Knopf, 1964.

Zukin, Sharon. *Landscapes of Power: From Detroit to Disney World.* Berkeley and Los Angeles: University of California Press, 1993.

Index

About the Author

Photo by Charles A. Smith, JSU University Communications photographer

Thomas Kersen is associate professor of sociology at Jackson State University. He received his PhD from Mississippi State University. He has a number of articles and book chapters on religion and spirituality, population studies, and the military. Another facet of his teaching and research centers on community and communal living. He lives in Clinton, Mississippi, with his wife Lisa, McKenzie, and four furry babies.

CPSIA information can be obtained
at www.ICGtesting.com
Printed in the USA
BVHW030035300821
615262BV00004B/11